The USA 1917–45

Doug and Susan Willoughby

Series Editors
Martin Collier
Erica Lewis
Rosemary Rees

Heinemann

HEINEMANN ADVANCED HISTORY

HEINEMANN ADVANCED HISTORY

Heinemann Educational Publishers
Halley Court, Jordan Hill, Oxford, OX2 8EJ
Part of Harcourt Education

Heinemann is the registered trademark of
Harcourt Education Limited

First published 2000

10-digit ISBN: 0 435 32723 2
13-digit ISBN: 978 0 435 32723 1

05
10 9 8 7

Designed and typeset by Wyvern 21 Ltd

Printed and bound in Great Britain by CPI Bath

Photographic acknowledgements
The authors and publisher would like to thank the following for permission to reproduce photographs: Bettmann/Corbis: pp. 31, 42, 48, 117, 181, 195; Corbis: pp. 60, 91, 112, 114, 118, 119, 127, 140, 157, 178, 205, 221, 228; Ford Motors: p. 32; Hulton Getty: pp. 6, 19, 20, 49, 65, 86, 101, 108; Popperfoto: p. 16; Scenectady Museum, Hall of Electrical History Foundation/Corbis: p. 186

Cover photograph: Hulton Getty

Written sources acknowledgements
The authors and publishers gratefully acknowledge the following publications from which written sources in the book are drawn. In some sentences the wording or sentence has been simplified. P. Boyer et al, *The Enduring Vision: A History of the American People* (D.C. Heath and Company 1995): pp. 117-8, 163, 205, 227; H. Brogan, *Penguin History of the United States of America* (Penguin 1990): pp. 121 (bottom), 170; J. Brooman, *The New Deal* (Longman 1986): pp. 112, 146, 147, 149; E. Caldwell, *You Have Seen Their Faces* (University of Georgia Press 1994): p. 162 (bottom); D. M. Chalmers, *Hooded Americanism: The History of the Ku Klux Klan* (Duke University Press 1981): p. 162 (middle); A. Cooke, *America* (Pavilion 1973): p. 240; A. Haley, *Autobiography of Malcolm X* (Penguin 1965): p. 162 (top); P. Johnson, *History of the American People* (Phoenix Press 1998): pp. 27, 30, 38, 43, 77, 206-7, 223; *The People's Century* (BBC publication): pp. 33, 34, 50-1, 53; S. Rowbotham, *A Century of Women* (Penguin 1999): pp. 117, 191, 208; N. Smith, *The USA 1917-1980* (Oxford University Press 1996): pp. 9, 35; Spartacus Encyclopaedia website (www.spartacus.schoolnet.co.uk): pp. 66, 102, 111, 121 (top), 125, 133, 137, 161, 163, 165-6, 166, 167, 229, 230, 231, 233, 234, 240, 241 (top), 242 (top); J. Steinbeck, *The Grapes of Wrath* (Warner/Chapell Plays 1991): p. 126

CONTENTS

HOW TO USE THIS BOOK

This book is divided into three parts. The first two AS sections, **Boom and Bust: The USA 1917–32** and **The United States of America: 1933–45** are similar in style and contain detailed accounts of the events of the period. Although they are written in a largely descriptive style, they also introduce some analysis of the changes that took place in America during this time and pose some of the questions that students of the period should be asking. The questions at the end of each chapter are intended to stimulate students to think analytically and to encourage a deeper understanding of the issues. They require them to sort, classify and deploy information, to arrive at an informed conclusion and to produce a supported argument in response to the question.

The A2 part of the book is more analytical in style and highlights some of the issues which have been the subject of varied interpretations and considerable historical debate. It is important, however, that the relevant chapters of the AS book are read in conjunction with the topics in the A2 section so that students are familiar with the details. The purpose of the A2 section is not only to enable a deeper understanding of American political, social and economic developments in the inter-war period, but also to stimulate further research and enquiry. There are significant parts of this book that are, after all, the interpretations of the authors.

At the end of the AS and A2 sections there are Assessment sections. These have been based on the requirements of the new AS and A2 specifications provided by the three Awarding Bodies, Edexcel, AQA and OCR, as appropriate. There are exam-style source and essay questions for each relevant specification, together with advice on how to construct and express the answers.

The book is a text which covers the main features set out in the History specifications. The period 1941–5 is covered only in relation to the New Deal. It is hoped that this important period of American History will be dealt with in a further volume in this series that looks at the years of the Second World War.

AS SECTION: BOOM AND BUST: THE USA 1917–32

INTRODUCTION

In 1917 the USA, under the leadership of President Woodrow Wilson, joined the war against Germany and Austria–Hungary. Although the war benefited American businessmen and bankers, it created unrest and social disturbance at home. The huge loss of life in a foreign cause that seemed to have little to do with the USA profoundly affected the American people. They emerged from the First World War wary of further involvement in European affairs. Unfortunately, this was at odds with the policies of their President who, during the closing months of the war, had arrived at a plan for lasting peace. His vision included a key role for the USA but the majority of the representatives in Congress did not share it. Woodrow Wilson died in 1921 still struggling to persuade the politicians and people of America to accept his Fourteen Points and the principle of **collective security** that would protect the world from another catastrophic war.

KEY TERM

Collective security is when states promise to act together to protect any one of them attacked by an aggressor.

Throughout the 1920s, Republican candidates were repeatedly successful in presidential elections. The 1920s proved to be a remarkable period in American history. It was also a period of contradictions. On the one hand, America's manufacturing industry boomed, and the USA enjoyed the kind of prosperity that made it the envy of the rest of Europe. Cars, radios, refrigerators and vacuum cleaners that were luxuries only for the rich in Britain, were everyday items in many working-class American homes. On the other hand, the affluence of a significant number of Americans was in stark contrast to the poverty of millions of others. Moreover, the razzamatazz that fascinated the rest of the world hid a deeply divided society. America's history of immigration had created a country full of prejudice, discrimination, racism and an almost fanatical fear of political extremism that was thinly disguised by the glamorous façade.

In 1929 the bubble burst when the Wall Street Crash sent the US economy spiralling into depression. As billions of dollars were lost in the stock market collapse, fortunes were destroyed overnight and subsequently the numbers of unemployed soared. The Republican administration under Herbert Hoover did little, believing that the recession would be only temporary. As millions were thrown into poverty, disillusionment with the ability of the Republicans set in. Americans searched desperately for a saviour. He appeared in the person of Franklin Delano Roosevelt, a Democrat, who won a landslide victory in the elections of 1932.

The key areas for study in this section of the book are:

- **Why the USA entered the First World War.** The reasons are, to some extent, controversial, but here the events leading up the point where US troops were sent to the Western Front and the reasons for the subsequent rejection of the Treaty of Versailles are described and explained as foundation for future analysis.
- **The Republican ascendancy.** An understanding of the approach of the Republican presidents to government is important. It helps to explain, for example, why the USA maintained its isolationist approach in foreign affairs and created the climate for the economic boom of the 1920s. It compares and contrasts the presidents of the period in order to identify their common elements and to illustrate the nature of Republicanism throughout the period. It is also interesting to consider the extent to which America really was isolated from the rest of the world during the twenties.
- **The American boom.** The economic prosperity of the 1920s is one of its most important characteristics. The development of credit facilities and their availability to a wide range of the social spectrum, the expansion of investment and the development of methods of mass production all combined to create an advanced capitalist economy and a large-scale consumer society. The speed of the development is also striking.

- **The 'roaring twenties'.** This period is one of the most fascinating in US history. The very public affluence of a few, the jazz, the flamboyant females and the cinema are seen in sharp contrast to the moral crusade against alcoholic drink and the passing of the Prohibition laws. These led to an increase in organised crime. At the same time the re-appearance of the Ku Klux Klan and the increasing vehemence of racist clashes emphasised the deep divisions in society at all levels.
- **The Wall Street Crash and the Great Depression.** The end of the decade is marked by both the Wall Street Crash and the onset of the Great Depression. It is important to understand the following points:
  - why the Great Depression happened;
  - the impact of the Great Depression in America;
  - why the Republicans failed to respond to the Depression with a recovery programme.

CHAPTER 1

Woodrow Wilson and the First World War

Woodrow Wilson.

SOCIETY, ECONOMICS AND POLITICS BY 1917

Introduction. On the eve of its entry into the First World War, America had become the world's leading industrial nation. It produced and consumed 70 per cent of the world's oil and was its leading producer of coal and steel. On the Great Plains of the Midwest, large, efficient farms supplied the rest of the world with 30 per cent of its wheat and 75 per cent of its corn and flooded European markets with vast amounts of cheap food.

America was, without doubt, a wealthy country. The standard of living for many American families was much higher than that of their European counterparts. However, wealth in America was unequally distributed and millions of Americans still did not have a share in the nation's prosperity in this 'land of the free'. Many industrial workers found themselves at the mercy of the large **business corporations** who employed them and refused them any negotiating rights over working hours or rates of pay. Low wages forced them to live in slum areas of towns. Small farmers were also facing financial difficulties as they struggled to compete with larger agricultural enterprises and competition from Argentina, Canada, Australia and New Zealand. Their efforts to remain viable were further hampered by the high cost of borrowing money from banks.

KEY TERM

Business corporations These were huge, powerful organisations many of which had grown in the late nineteenth century. The most powerful monopolised the commodity they produced or the service they provided, Ford, General Motors, John D. Rockefeller, the railway companies and Standard Oil being prime examples. This, together with the lack of government control, increased their power. They had almost total control over prices, wages and working conditions.

American society was diverse and multi-cultural. At its core were the ancestors of the original white, English Protestant settlers, but they were joined in America by Germans, Poles, Italians, Irish, Chinese, Russian Jews and other immigrants who had come in search of the 'American dream'. The first two decades of the twentieth century saw further waves of immigrants, though the

The American system of government

The United States of America is a **federal** union of states, united by their national government. Each state is given a degree of independence to govern itself. All are bound by the terms of the US Constitution.

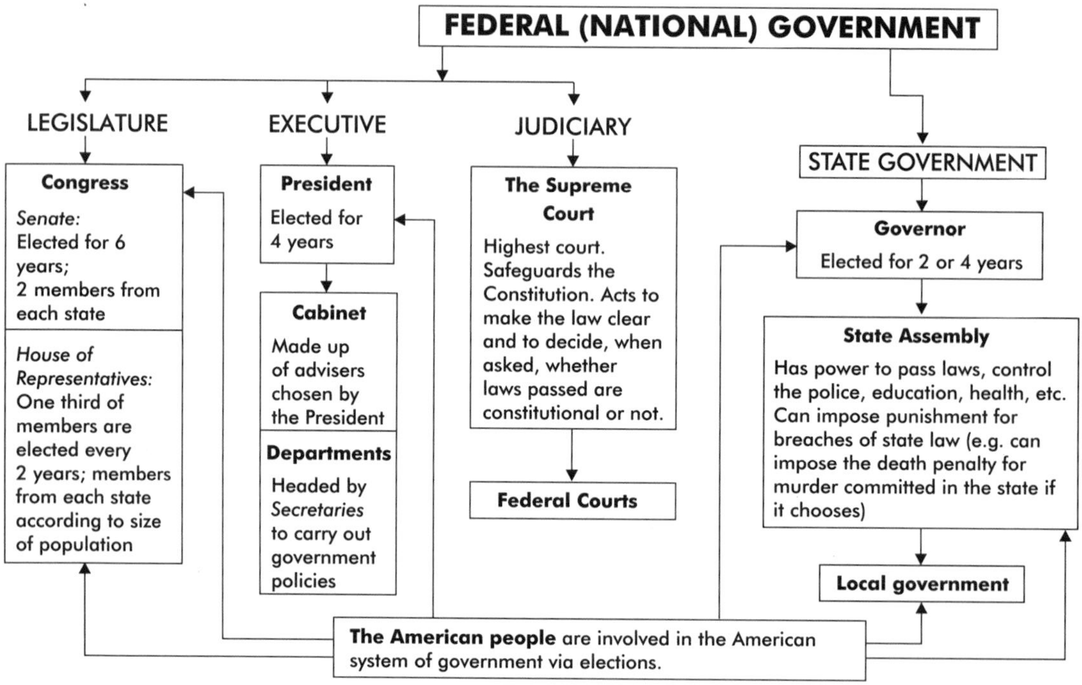

reality they experienced was often poverty and exploitation. By adding their own cultural dimensions to the American scene, they created a society unlike any other in the world. It aggravated the racial tension that existed in America despite the end of slavery. This remained a serious problem for the USA everywhere, not only in the southern states.

Until the presidential inauguration of **Woodrow Wilson** in 1913, the US government had played little part in the creation of wealth and prosperity. It had created a ***laissez-faire*** society with minimal government control, upholding the principle of individual liberty embodied in the US Constitution. Wilson's presidency, however, marked a turning point in American political life as he embarked on a series of measures to make his vision of government a reality. His New Freedom Program consisted

KEY TERM

Federalism The American Constitution of 1789 created the United States of America as a federal state. This meant that power was to be shared between the central federal government and the state governments. This was a central feature of the constitution which was to have a considerable impact on how the nation developed. In the federal state there were parallel systems of government (federal and state). The issue of federalism became central in the debate about the New Deal.

KEY PERSON

Woodrow Wilson was a Democrat. Unlike earlier presidents, he was an academic. His beliefs about the role of government developed from his studies at John Hopkins University. His own Scots-Irish Calvinist background also influenced him. He believed that government should have the power to intervene to defend ordinary men and women against large corporations and unscrupulous employers. He admired the nineteenth-century English, reforming prime minister, William Gladstone.

His success as governor of New Jersey, where he led a generally honest administration, made him the surprise front runner for the **Democratic** presidential nomination in 1912. As president, he was determined to act in the public interest. This meant an end to *laissez-faire* politics and the beginning of what came to be known as **progressivism**.

KEY CONCEPT

'Laissez-faire' was the idea adopted by some politicians, mainly in the Republican Party, that it was not the responsibility of government to be involved in social and economic issues. This allowed businesses to develop and expand almost without restriction.

of a series of legislative measures by which the government intervened, for example, to investigate and regulate matters such as the finances of the large business corporations. He passed laws to limit the extent of the working day, to make available low cost finance for the smaller farmers and to create a progressive system for the levying of income tax.

However, when the First World War broke out, Wilson's New Freedom Program still had some way to go. It had done nothing, for example, to stop racial segregation or to set up in America any welfare provisions for the needy, such as those that were in their infancy in Britain at this time. Nevertheless, Wilson did display strong leadership in attempting to solve social and economic problems and gained the support of a wide spectrum of America's diverse population.

The origins of America's neutrality. On 4 August 1914, following the outbreak of the First World War, Wilson proclaimed US neutrality. This policy had the support of the vast majority of American people in spite of the fact that many Americans held strong anti-British or pro-German views. Indeed, to have supported one side or the other would have been divisive in a society that still did not have a distinctively 'American' identity. The USA had kept out of all the negotiations between the European powers in the years preceding 1914 that had led to the creation of the two major alliance systems. Wilson's offer to mediate in 1914 was rejected. Many Americans, whatever their origins, must have realised the economic advantages of neutrality for, whilst staying out of the fighting, America lent money to the Allies and sold Britain and France munitions and foodstuffs. As the German chemical and plastics industries were disrupted by war, those in America boomed and the average wage rose by 25 per cent. US exports to areas of the world controlled by Europe's colonial powers also significantly increased. Given, then, the apparent advantages of neutrality, how did America become involved in the war?

Why did America enter the conflict? No single factor explains America's declaration of war on Germany. It is perhaps best understood as a gradual drift into the conflict.

- Public opinion in the USA increasingly turned against Germany as U-boat attacks on Atlantic shipping increased, whereas American trade with Britain and France had more than trebled since the war began. The sinking of the British North Atlantic passenger liner, *Lusitania*, without warning, on 7 May 1915 was an international crime without precedent or reason. Nearly 1,200 passengers drowned, 128 of them American. The incident provided sufficient reason for the USA to enter the conflict but, with the election approaching, Wilson was content with German assurances that such a crime would not be repeated. In the 1916 presidential elections, Wilson was re-elected on the slogan, 'He kept us out of the war'. However, his re-election was with a substantially reduced vote suggesting that the tide of opinion was turning.
- **Wilson's sympathies.** Wilson's personal sympathies lay with Britain. The two countries had strong economic links and a German victory would have been very damaging financially. By early 1917, the Allies had borrowed $2 billion from the USA and many American factories were dependent upon Allied purchases of war equipment. The German declaration in January 1917 of unrestricted submarine warfare was followed, on 3 February, by the severing of relations with the German government.
- **Zimmermann telegram.** Wilson and his government had been further infuriated by a proposal from the German Foreign Minister, Alfred Zimmermann, in January 1917 that Mexico should support Germany against the USA. In return, the Mexicans were offered the possibility of gaining US territory. This proposal, contained in a note from Zimmermann to the German Ambassador in Mexico (see page 9), was published in March 1917 by British intelligence. This came at a sensitive time for the USA as there had been military clashes with the Mexicans in 1916 as a result of raids on the Texan border. Consequently, Americans were outraged by these latest revelations. The note, together with the German refusal to stop their attacks on neutral shipping, was clear

KEY CONCEPTS

Democrats were members of the Democratic Party, one of the two main political parties in the USA. They were generally in favour of reform.

Progressivism was a political response to industrialisation and its social consequences. Progressives were reformers. They wanted to put right the negative effects of the *laissez-faire* policy that allowed capitalists to expand freely. They were not opposed to capitalism, but they believed that there should be some form of control, for example, to protect workers. Some progressives concentrated on reforming aspects of government or on social problems. Progressivism was a feature of the policies of the Democrats in the early part of the twentieth century.

KEY THEME

Mexican incidents 1916
After a revolution in 1911, Mexico fell into a state of political chaos and confusion. Numerous leaders held power in different regions. In 1915 the USA recognised Carranza as President of Mexico. One of Carranza's opponents, Francisco Villa, invaded new Mexico in 1916 in response. Wilson ordered US troops into Mexico. US and Mexican forces met at Carrizal in June 1916. The affair was settled by diplomacy and the Americans left Mexico in February 1917.

> **The Zimmermann Telegram**
>
> The telegram sent by Zimmermann was most provocative. It read:
>
> Berlin, January 19, 1917
>
> On the first of February we intend to begin submarine warfare unrestricted. In spite of this it is our intention to keep neutral the United States of America. If this attempt is not successful, we propose an alliance on the following basis with Mexico: That we shall make war together and together make peace . . . it is understood that Mexico is to reconquer their lost territory in New Mexico, Texas and Arizona . . . the employment of ruthless submarine warfare now promises to compel England to make peace in a few months.
>
> Zimmermann

> 'Property can be paid for but the lives of peaceful and innocent people cannot be. The present German submarine warfare against commerce is warfare against mankind.'
>
> President Wilson in a message to Congress in January 1917

evidence of aggression and removed any doubt in the minds of Wilson and most Americans that war was now inevitable. Consequently, on 2 April 1917, Wilson went to Congress demanding a declaration of war against Germany (see left, below). His request was granted by a large majority both in the Senate and in the House of Representatives.

America prepares for war. Wilson insisted from the beginning that America had declared war on the German government and not on the German people. Congress moved quickly to approve budgets that allowed for the rapid mobilisation and equipping of over 3 million men. For the first time, America's industries were brought under tight government control as part of the special powers given to the government to deal with the wartime emergency.

The American people, however, showed little enthusiasm for war. The main reasons were these:

- The horrors of trench warfare on the Western Front were well known. Equally important was that the memories of the experiences of trench warfare from the American Civil War (1861–5) were still clear in the American psyche.
- Many Americans still felt that the war was Europe's war, not theirs.

When only 75,000 volunteers responded to the call to arms, Congress passed a Selective Service Act requiring 30 million young Americans to register for military service. George Creel, an experienced newsman, was made Director of the Committee on Public Information. His job was to whip up enthusiasm for war. Thousands of speakers were sent across America to organise rallies and deliver five-minute pep talks.

Espionage Act. To create and maintain support for the war, Congress passed, at Wilson's request, an Espionage Act in June 1917 (this became the Sedition Act in 1918). This made it a punishable crime to criticise the government for its conduct of the war. Shortly after the passing of this Act, the government ordered the suppression of a magazine, *The Masses*, which described itself as 'a monthly revolutionary journal'. This was on the grounds that some of the articles and cartoons in the issue of August 1917 attacking the war, violated the Act. The judgement of the courts went against the government on the grounds that it infringed the freedom of the press. However, this decision was reversed on appeal. This clearly shows that Wilson had taken the USA into the war and was not prepared to tolerate any criticism of his actions even if it left him open to accusations of undermining the principles of liberty embodied in the Constitution.

America at war. The Selective Service Act raised the numbers of America's standing army from 200,000 to a potential 4 million, of whom 2 million made up the American Expeditionary Force posted to France throughout the remaining period of the war. About 75 per cent of these saw action. In August 1917, units of the American army found themselves on the Western Front near Verdun. By the beginning of 1918, following the surrender of Russia, Germany was busily transferring divisions to the Western Front. On 21 March, a strong German offensive broke through the British and French lines and reached the Marne once again. The American Expeditionary Force, under the command of General John Pershing, joined forces with the Allied armies to stop the German advance.

In August 1918, the Allies took the offensive. This time, Pershing was able to deploy his forces as a separate command both at St Mihiel (12–16 September) and in the Meuse–Argonne offensive (28 September) where 1,200,000 American troops were sent into battle.

The presence on the Western Front of large numbers of fresh and well-equipped American troops proved to be a major turning point in the war, contributing significantly to the German surrender in November 1918. However, this contribution had cost 112,432 American lives – and this was considered by the people back home far too high a price to pay. The fact that Wilson had taken America into such a destructive war would not be forgotten either.

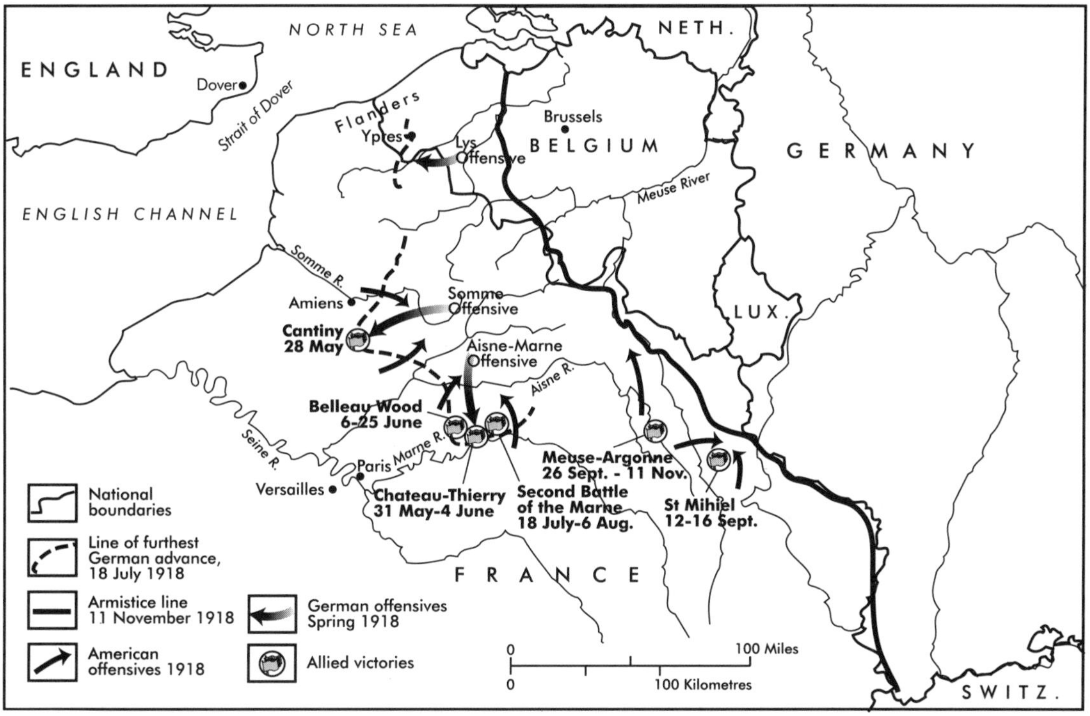

American offensives on the Western Front, 1918.

WHAT WAS WILSON'S PEACE PROGRAMME?

For all the nations engaged in the horror and destruction of the First World War, this had to be the war to end all wars. Yet the paths to peace were diverse and conflicting. Each nation's representatives came to the peace-making process with different aspirations. For the French, led by Clemenceau, the major issue was to 'make Germany pay', to weaken it so much that the peace of the world could never be broken again. This was a very short-sighted view.

Wilson had begun his preparations for the peace-making eleven months before the war ended. His proposals were issued on 8 January 1918 in the form of **Fourteen Points** put together after consultation with US foreign policy experts. These points reflected the aspirations of other nations which fought on the side of the Americans during the war. In particular, many of the points had been agreed by members of the British cabinet. In November 1918 the Germans requested a peace on the basis of the Fourteen Points.

Wilson's Fourteen Points

1 There should be no more secret treaties.
2 Absolute freedom of the seas at all times.
3 Free trade between nations.
4 All armaments to be reduced.
5 The rights and opinions of people living in colonies to be considered when settling colonial claims.
6 The Germans must withdraw from Russian territory.
7 Belgium must be free and independent.
8 France will regain the territory of Alsace-Lorraine (lost in 1871).
9 The border between Austria and Italy to be readjusted (in Italy's favour).
10 The peoples of Eastern Europe must have self-determination in their own independent nations.
11 Romania, Serbia and Montenegro must be liberated and their territory guaranteed by international agreement.
12 The people in the Turkish Empire must decide upon their own future (Turkey had fought on the side of Germany and Austria–Hungary).
13 Poland should be an independent nation with access to the Baltic Sea.
14 An association of nations – the League of Nations – to be set up to settle all disputes between countries.

The first five points dealt with general principles of international conduct between nations. Points 6 to 13 were concerned with specific problems including claims made by Russia, France and Italy. The fourteenth point recommended the creation of a **League of Nations**. This was very much the brainchild of Wilson himself. His aim was to create an international organisation, which, by settling disputes between nations peacefully, would prevent any further wars. In the event of acts of aggression by one country against another, the member nations would respond collectively to stop the aggressor. Wilson's concept of collective security could take the form of **economic sanctions** or, if all else failed, military assistance.

Wilson at Versailles. All the major countries involved in the First World War disliked some aspects of Wilson's Peace Programme. The British and French accused him of

KEY TERM

League of Nations was an international peace-keeping organisation set up at the Treaty of Versailles. Its aim was to avoid future conflict by settling disputes between member states. Wilson's original idea was that all world powers would be members.

KEY CONCEPT

Economic sanctions are either the cutting off from a country of essential commodities such as oil, or the boycotting of goods from that country in order to damage its economy. They are actions taken against one country by others in order to control its actions.

'going soft' on Germany. However, when the peace negotiations began in the last days of the war, Wilson insisted that his Fourteen Points should be the basis for the Armistice signed with the Germans in November 1918.

Wilson attended the Paris Peace Conference and supported the Treaty of Versailles even though some of its terms conflicted with his own views. Reparations, for example, and the harsh territorial and military restrictions that stemmed from the French desire for revenge conflicted with his far-sighted, idealistic vision of perpetual peace. Nevertheless, his proposal for a League of Nations was accepted.

Why were Wilson's ideas rejected? Wilson returned to the USA feeling satisfied with his diplomatic achievements in Paris. But the impact of the war had had its effect and the mood at home was generally hostile to any plan for further international involvement. The public at large did not want to see the blood of Americans spilt again on foreign soil in conflicts which were, in reality, not of their concern. Many Americans had fled from Europe as emigrants and they felt that the United States should not be involved in Europe's affairs. There was a view that America should concentrate instead on its own internal affairs. This belief was strongly held amongst many members of the **Republican Party**. Unfortunately for Wilson, they now controlled the Senate. They refused to ratify the Versailles Treaty disliking, in particular, his proposals for a League of Nations. Opposition to the Treaty and to the League was led by Henry Cabot Lodge, chairman of the Senate Foreign Relations Committee. Contrary to the popular view, he was not **isolationist** nor was he totally opposed to the concept of the League of Nations. He opposed it because he thought many of Wilson's idea were woolly and ill-considered.

Cabot Lodge produced fourteen 'reservations' of Wilson's proposals for the League of Nations. He claimed that they represented a threat to America's **sovereignty** and to its freedom of action. Wilson, however, refused to compromise. In spite of the fact that he had already suffered a stroke during the Peace Conference at Versailles,

KEY TERM

The **Republican Party** is one of the two main political parties in the USA. It has traditionally tended to be right-wing, believing in low taxes and minimal government intervention.

KEY CONCEPTS

Isolationism was the idea held by many Americans, particularly after the First World War, that the USA should turn its back on specifically European affairs. Isolationism did not prevent America protecting its interests, especially in the Americas!

Sovereignty is the independence and freedom of action for a state to govern and control its own affairs without interference from outside. The fear for many in Congress was that collective security would draw the USA into a war situation which would undermine Congress's constitutional role in declarations of war.

KEY THEME

Republicans and isolationism Not all leading Republicans were isolationist. Herbert Hoover as Secretary of Commerce in 1920 promoted a highly activist international commercial policy.

he embarked on a gruelling tour of the USA to gather support for his plans. Whilst on this tour, he collapsed on 26 September 1919 after suffering a second stroke. This was followed by a third in October from which he never recovered. He remained an invalid for the last three and a half years of his life, dying on 3 February 1924.

The Treaty is rejected. On 19 March 1920, the Senate decided that the United States would not sign the Treaty of Versailles or join the League of Nations. A Democratic defeat in the presidential election of 1920 set the seal on the demise of Wilson and his ideals for post-war world peace. Whether this refusal of the US Senate represents a return to the policy of isolationism is a question to which we will return later in this book. America's membership of the League was crucial to its success as a peace-keeping organisation as Wilson must have realised. Certainly, when it came into being, it was much weakened by America's absence and this contributed significantly to its ultimate failure to meet the challenges and threats that lay ahead.

SUMMARY QUESTIONS

1 In what ways did the presidency of Woodrow Wilson represent a change in policies and attitudes from that of previous presidents?

2 Why did the USA remain neutral when war broke out in Europe in 1914?

3 What was Wilson's vision for world peace after the First World War?

4 Why did Wilson's peace plan fail to win support in the USA?

CHAPTER 2

The Republican ascendancy 1921–33

Between 1921 and 1933, American political life was dominated by the Republican Party. Three Republican presidents governed the USA with massive popular support, backed invariably by Republican control of Congress. The first two of these presidents – **Warren Harding (1921–3)** and **Calvin Coolidge (1923–9)** – presided over a period of unrivalled economic prosperity. The third and most able, **Herbert Hoover (1929–33)**, found himself in the White House in the year of the **Wall Street Crash** and the years of economic depression that followed. The purpose of this chapter is to examine these presidencies in detail in order to highlight and consider their common themes.

WARREN HARDING (1921–3)

Early career. Harding was born into a poor family in Corsica, Ohio in 1865 and studied law at Ohio Central College. He achieved his first success as the creator, editor and publisher of *The Marion Star*, a country newspaper in the small town of Marion, Ohio. Very much a self-made man, Harding went on to become a bank director and the owner of a building society as well as telephone and timber companies. His early successes are a good example of how the *laissez-faire* economic system that operated in the USA at this time benefited enterprising individuals. By hard work and good business dealing, they could prosper.

In 1891, he married Florence Kling De Wolfe. She has since been seen as a major force in his political life. (He once commented, 'Mrs Harding wants to be the drum major in every band that passes'.) He subsequently served in the Ohio State Senate (1900–4) and as lieutenant-governor of the state. His election to the US Senate in 1914, where he served until 1921, projected him onto the national political stage. However, when the Republican Party Convention met in June 1920 to decide their

Warren Harding with his wife at his presidential inauguration.

presidential nomination, Harding was not considered a front runner.

Harding's nomination for the presidency. In the end, the Convention was hopelessly split and Harding was accepted as a compromise candidate. As one prominent delegate succinctly put it, 'Harding is no world beater but he's the best of the 2nd raters'. His running mate was Calvin Coolidge, the governor of Massachusetts. Perhaps this view of Harding's nomination in 1920 ignores the appeal of his policies to those Republicans who supported him, since they both represented a rejection of Woodrow Wilson's liberalism. He favoured:

- higher **tariffs**
- lower taxes on business and private income
- fewer immigrants
- more farm aid
- rejection of the League of Nations.

These policies appeared to reflect exactly the mood of the American people at this time, so much so that even those Convention delegates who supported American membership of the League found no difficulty in backing Harding despite his opposition to American participation in the new international body.

KEY TERM

Tariffs are taxes placed on imported goods. The main purpose of these was to **protect** home industry from foreign competition by making imported goods more expensive. This had a negative effect as it resulted in other countries raising import taxes on American goods in retaliation. The net effect in the 1930s was to exacerbate the Depression by hampering world trade. During the Second World War America developed plans to reduce tariffs and to remove other barriers to international trade.

Success in the 1920 presidential elections. The result of the election entirely vindicated the Republican choice of Harding. Harding secured 16,152,000 votes (60.3 per cent) compared to the 9,147,000 votes cast for the Democratic candidate, James Cox. Harding clearly appealed to the American electorate. What was the source of this popular appeal?

Undoubtedly, his campaign slogan, 'Let us return to normalcy', was overwhelmingly attractive to a nation still recovering from the effects of involvement in the First World War. To them, 'normalcy' implied the removal of wartime restrictions and a rejection of Wilson's policy of continued involvement in international affairs. He represented the thinking of 'decent small-town America' that had flourished throughout the USA before Wilson's presidency. The swing to the Republicans was also reflected in elections to Congress. With a majority of 22 in the Senate and of 172 seats in the House of Representatives, the Republicans were now in a strong position to reverse the **progressivism** of the Wilson years with a return to *laissez-faire* politics and a reduction in government intervention.

KEY TERM

Progressivism Not only were the Democrats under Wilson progressive, there were also Republicans who were termed progressive. These included Theodore Roosevelt and Herbert Hoover. As Secretary of Commerce, Hoover took measures to help US companies expand exports and their presence overseas.

Harding's presidency. To ensure the effective implementation of his policies, Harding delegated much of his presidential authority to the leaders of his government departments. In certain areas, their work was new for them, for example, hiring workers during an employment slump for public works and introducing farm credits to help small farmers. In 1922, at the Washington Conference on Naval Disarmament, **Charles Evans Hughes** managed to get the Great Powers to agree to limit their warship tonnage in fixed ratios (see Chapter 6). Harding himself became involved in the movement to limit the long working hours in the American steel industry.

KEY PEOPLE

Herbert Hoover, Secretary at the Department of Commerce

Charles Evans Hughes, Secretary of State (Foreign Affairs)

Two other pieces of legislation are more typical of Republican thinking at this time:

- In May 1921, Harding approved a bill limiting immigration to 3 per cent of the population of the respective ethnic groups resident in 1910.

- In September 1922, Congress approved the Fordney–McCumber tariff. This raised import duties on farm products, chemicals, textiles, chinaware, cutlery, guns and other industrial goods. A Tariff Commission was set up to recommend to the President changes in these tariffs, up or down, by as much as 50 per cent. This movement towards **protectionism** represented a distinct break with the Wilson years and, in the Republican view, was the essential basis of US economic prosperity in the 1920s.

Corruption in high places? The final months of Harding's presidency were clouded with rumours about corruption in his administration. There were allegations of 'croneyism' – that Harding was using his presidential office to further the interests of his friends, cynically known as 'The Ohio Gang'. Harding died whilst still in office on 2 August 1923 as these allegations were growing and before they had been fully investigated.

Charles Forbes. As a result of the inquiry that took place in the spring and early summer of 1924, Charles Forbes, formerly Director of the Veterans' Bureau, was indicted for defrauding the government by corrupt contracts. He was convicted on 4 February 1925 and jailed for two years for the misuse of $250 million from the accounts of the Veterans' Bureau. It was alleged that this had been done with Harding's knowledge.

Teapot Dome. In 1923, a Senate investigation took place into the activities of Albert Fall, Secretary of the Interior, and oil executives Harry Sinclair and Edward Doheny. The outcome was an indictment for conspiracy to lease federal oil reserves at Teapot Dome, Wyoming and Elk Hills, California. Fall had received from Doheny a loan of $100,000 and from Sinclair, $223,000 in government bonds, $85,000 in cash and a herd of cattle. Fall and Sinclair, both former associates of Harding, were convicted. In March 1924, US Attorney General, Harry Daugherty was forced to resign when it was proved that he, too, had taken bribes to cover up the current scandals.

KEY TERM

Protectionism is the policy of protecting domestic industries against foreign competition by imposing tariffs (as described on page 16), or quotas, or by discriminatory use of currencies.

Calvin Coolidge.

Recent historical research suggests that Harding was not as closely involved in these scandals as was suggested at the time. Neverthless, the revelations of bribery, influence peddling and outright theft perpetrated by his associates and made public after his death have done much to overshadow his presidency both at the time and since.

CALVIN COOLIDGE (1923–9)

On 3 August 1923 Calvin Coolidge heard the news of the death of Warren Harding. He was quickly sworn in as President and remained in office until he handed over to his successor, Herbert Hoover in 1929.

Early life and career. Coolidge was born in Plymouth, Vermont in 1872 into a strong farming family. He studied law at Amherst College and subsequently was admitted to the bar. In 1905, he married Grace Goodhue whose social graces made up for her husband's straight and often curt manner. After practising law in Northampton, Massachusetts, he served as lieutenant-governor of the state (1916–18) and governor (1919–20). His suppression of a police strike in Boston with the assertion that 'there is no right to strike against the public safety by anybody, anytime, anywhere', brought him national attention especially within the Republican Party.

He managed to remain undamaged by the various scandals surrounding the end of Harding's presidency. Consequently, his succession to the presidency on the death of Harding was uncontroversial. In November 1924, after a low turn-out at the polls (52 per cent), Coolidge was re-elected President, polling 15.7 million popular votes compared with the 8.4 million votes gained by John Davis, his Democratic opponent.

Coolidge as President. Coolidge believed in and practised the idea of minimal government – that the main, possibly the only, role for government was to balance the budget, reduce debt, cut taxes and make easy credit available. His slogan, 'the business of America is business', was based on the conviction that, by allowing big business a free rein within a wall of economic protection, prosperity would be created. Perhaps the best illustration of his thinking came on 12 February 1925, when Congress adopted the Revenue Act. This reduced the tax burden by cutting the maximum surtax payable from 40 per cent to 20 per cent, abolished the gift tax and halved the estate tax. Such action not only increased potential consumer spending power but also created an economic climate that encouraged business investment.

In his foreign policy, it is suggested that Coolidge was isolationist. Whether or not this is true requires further consideration and will be discussed in greater detail in Chapter 6. Certainly, he did endorse America's entry into the International Court of Justice even though this was finally rejected by the Senate because of its links with the League of Nations. Moreover, he was always prepared to become involved in Latin America and to intervene if America's interests were threatened, as they were, for example, in Mexico where US oil interests were in danger from nationalisation.

Popularly known as 'Silent Cal' because of his refusal to engage in small talk, Coolidge, with his belief in minimal government, was in many ways the archetypal Republican politician of the period. Within the limits imposed by these views, he was successful and popular.

HERBERT CLARK HOOVER (1929–33)

Herbert Clark Hoover.

Early life. Herbert Hoover was born in West Branch, Iowa in 1874 into a family of rural Quakers whose influence on him was strong and long lasting. He studied geology and mining at Stanford University where he met Lon Henry, the only female geology student at the university. They married in 1897. Aged 25, Hoover, accompanied by his wife, left America to work in the gold mines of Australia. For the next fifteen years, they travelled to different countries where he worked as a mining engineer. By the age of 40 he had become a multi-millionaire and was able to retire from engineering. He decided to enter politics.

Hoover's political career. His early experiences and great success convinced Hoover that it was not the role of government to interfere automatically in people's lives. Government intervention generally should be restricted to supporting private initiative. The American system of '**rugged individualism**' was to underpin much of his later work. When war broke out in 1914, Hoover organised the return of thousands of Americans stranded in Europe. He then headed a Commission for the Relief of Belgium which aimed to aid that war-torn country. During the next five years, the Commission spent $1 billion in government loans and private donations, operated its own fleet of 200 ships and transported 5 million metric tonnes of food. Returning home in 1917, when the USA entered the war, Hoover headed the Ford Administration that aimed, by voluntary methods, to curb profiteering in food supplies. After the war, he was in charge of an American Relief Administration that distributed food, clothing and medical supplies to refugees in Eastern Europe and the Soviet Union.

KEY TERM

'Rugged individualism' is the term used to describe the American view that people achieved success by their own hard work and effort. It originates from the pioneering days of the nineteenth century when Americans trekked westwards and endured all kinds of hardships in their efforts to make a new life for themselves. This was something of which to be proud in American eyes. In many respects the concept of 'rugged individualism' was used to justify the lack of government intervention in the lives of ordinary Americans. It was their right to be responsible for their own welfare.

Hoover's ideas on government intervention. By the time the war had ended, Hoover had established a considerable reputation as an administrator and was even being mentioned, as early as 1920, as a presidential possibility. His period as Secretary of Commerce (1921–8) illustrates his thinking about the role of government. Hoover believed neither in a traditional *laissez-faire* approach nor in economic planning and state direction. He favoured the idea of voluntary co-operation by private Americans with the support of government. His management of flood relief on the Mississippi in 1927 illustrates his ideas in action when he used voluntary agencies supported by the government. On the other hand, in developing areas of radio broadcasting and commercial aviation, he did increase the extent of government regulation. During his tenure of office as Secretary, the Department of Commerce became an important support of American business overseas – supporting, rather than controlling – in keeping with Hoover's thinking.

Hoover as President. In the presidential election of 1928, Hoover polled over 21 million votes, easily defeating Alf

Smith, the Democratic candidate with his 15 million votes. He was inaugurated in March 1929, but his presidency was doomed to failure. The Wall Street Crash of October 1929 plunged the USA into an economic depression unprecedented in its depth and severity. Faced with the total collapse of banking and investment and rapidly rising unemployment, the major challenge to Hoover's presidency was to lead America through the crisis.

Wall Street Crash. Following his own convictions, Hoover encouraged voluntary measures to deal with the crisis, urging business leaders to maintain production levels and not to cut wages. In November 1929, he managed to persuade both railroad company directors to continue planned railway construction, and city mayors and state governors to increase spending on public works. But this was not sufficient and, as the Depression deepened, this voluntary approach proved inadequate to deal with the scale of the problem. He was forced to:

- increase federal intervention
- increase government expenditure on public works
- provide government loans to business firms through a specially established Reconstruction Finance Corporation.

These initiatives, coupled with direct federal spending on welfare provision, came too late to save Hoover. His political opponents were easily able to brand him a Republican reactionary, doing nothing to help the growing millions of unemployed, hungry and homeless Americans suffering from the effects of what very soon became a world depression. In the 1930 midterm elections the Democrats won control of the House of Representatives. Hoover's defeat by Franklin D. Roosevelt in the presidential election of 1932 effectively ended his political career. His reputation was tarnished by his failure to counter the effects of the Depression. His efforts to find a middle way between a *laissez-faire* approach and direct state intervention were dismissed as being ineffective and inadequate. The defeat of Hoover marked the end of the Republican ascendancy.

IN CONCLUSION: WHAT WERE THE MAIN FEATURES OF THE REPUBLICAN ASCENDANCY?

From an examination of the presidencies of Harding, Coolidge and Hoover, a number of common approaches and themes can be identified:

- Between 1921 and 1933, the United States was generally a *laissez-faire* society. Harding and Coolidge certainly believed that it was not the function of their governments to interfere in people's lives by enacting legislation unless America's vital interests were threatened. So, for example, businesses were left alone to organise their own affairs and workers were free to bargain for their wages at the workplace. This had the effect of making it virtually impossible for workers to improve their conditions without the necessary employment laws to support them. In 1921, 5.1 million Americans were members of trade unions but, by 1929, this number had fallen to 3.6 million, suggesting a growing feeling of helplessness amongst workers trying to improve their working lives. As Hoover's presidency covered the extraordinary events of the Wall Street Crash and the Great Depression, it is difficult to assess his attempts to modify Republican *laissez-faire* thinking by incorporating a voluntary approach.
- Because of the strong Republican belief that it was not the function of government to intervene in people's lives, there were virtually no attempts at social reform during these years. Issues such as welfare provision and women's rights were largely ignored, women in America having been given the vote in 1920, one of the last acts of the Wilson presidency.
- There were limits to *laissez faire* politics. Whilst it was generally applied to the domestic economy, the government did intervene in the economic aspects of foreign policy to protect American industry. The Fordney–McCumber Tariff (1922) and the **Smoot-Hawley Act (1930)** imposed high tariffs on imported foreign goods to protect American industry from foreign competition.
- The government also intervened in certain social and moral issues. Of these, the imposition of **Prohibition** is

KEY TERMS

Smoot–Hawley Act, 1930 This imposed a tariff to protect American goods from foreign competition. It was the highest tariff imposed up to that time. It was opposed by contemporary economists who clearly anticipated what did ultimately happen – retaliatory tariffs against American goods that effectively closed European markets to American goods.

Prohibition In 1919 the US Congress passed the 18th Amendment to the American Constitution. Sometimes known as the 'Volstead Act', this measure prohibited the production, sale and transportation of alcoholic beverages throughout the USA. This was controversial and had dramatic consequences.

the most outstanding example. Others include **censorship** in the Hollywood film industry and the **Scopes 'Monkey Trial'** which resulted in the banning of the teaching of evolution in schools.

- The desire to limit immigration was a feature of these Republican years. The boom in the American economy at this time attracted a new flood of immigrants which the government decided to stop. An Immigration Act in 1921 limited the number of immigrants allowed each year from Europe, Australia, Japan, the Near East and Asia to 3 per cent of the numbers already resident in 1910. By 1929, the total number of immigrants allowed into the United States each year had been reduced to 150,000. Such attempts to limit immigration were approved by those WASP (White, Anglo-Saxon, Protestant) Americans who were natural Republican voters.
- During these years, Republican governments followed their belief in low taxation. The Revenue Act of 1925 reduced some taxes and abolished others in line with the Republican belief that people would thereby be able to make their own decisions about providing for their own needs, for example, medical care, thus reducing the need for government involvement. Between 1924 and 1928, taxes on incomes over $1 million a year were reduced from $600,000 to $200,000.
- Throughout these years, Republican governments were consistent in their demands for repayment of war loans to the European Allies, chiefly Britain and France. At the same time, by a policy of low interest rates, they enabled foreign governments and businesses to borrow money cheaply in New York.
- Whilst the Republican foreign policy was apparently *isolationist*, intervention and involvement were never questioned if America's vital interests were threatened – for example, Harding's support for the Washington Treaty in 1922, or Coolidge's intervention in Latin America to protect American oil interests.

KEY TERMS

Censorship During the 1920s and 1930s, the Hollywood film industry boomed. However, the influential puritanical element in the US felt that the new films posed a threat to the morality of American people. The film makers were keen to avoid direct government intervention and so commissioned the politician Will H. Hays to draw up a voluntary code of practice. The 'Hays Code' prohibited anything on screen that may offend. Lengthy kissing, nudity, tolerance of infidelity or illicit sex were all banned as was mockery of the clergy, 'low, disgusting, unpleasant, though not necessarily evil subjects', and films which sympathised with murder, arson, safe-cracking and smuggling.

Scopes 'Monkey Trial' Again, this case reflected the influence of religious bigotry. It arose from the insistence by some Protestant groups on the acceptance of a literal interpretation of the Creation as it is described in the Old Testament of the Bible. A young teacher, John T. Scopes, read a description of Darwin's theory of evolution to his biology class. The school was in Dayton, Tennessee, a state that had already banned this, so Scopes found himself in court as a result.

SUMMARY QUESTIONS

1 Why were the Republicans popular with the American electorate?

2 Why was Hoover called a 'Republican reactionary'? Did he deserve this title?

3 What did all the Republican administrations have in common?

CHAPTER 3

The American boom 1921–9

Between 1921 and 1929, Americans enjoyed a level of economic prosperity which had previously been unknown, either in the United States or anywhere in the world. This widespread prosperity, however, eluded some sections of society. During these years, average wage levels steadily rose and, for the first time, Americans were able to purchase an unprecedented range of consumer goods manufactured by new techniques of mass production.

The level of prosperity was such that, in 1928, Herbert Hoover declared:

> 'We in America are nearer to the financial triumph over poverty than ever before in the history of our land. The poor house is vanishing from among us.'

This widely held view, that American economic progress was unstoppable, was shattered in 1929 with the collapse of the American stock market and the onset of the Great Depression. This chapter examines the causes of this economic prosperity and considers issues relating to its nature and extent. Chapter 7 explains how it all went wrong.

WHY WAS THERE ECONOMIC PROSPERITY IN THE USA IN THE 1920S?

Developments in the early twentieth century. By the beginning of the twentieth century, economic development and technological innovation had brought American industry to the point of making America the world's leading industrial nation. Henry Ford, for example, had introduced the assembly line in 1913. This both speeded up manufacturing and cut its costs, offering American industrialists the chance to make large profits. The First World War presented a golden opportunity for some businesses to maximise their profits by supplying the Allies with food and munitions and in particular, by taking over markets previously supplied by Britain and Germany whose own industries were disrupted by war. So the main effects of war were:

- to accelerate the growth of the United States
- to change the United States from being a debtor nation to being the world's main creditor
- to open up export markets previously serviced particularly by Britain and Germany.

Government and the growth of industry in the twenties. To a large extent, American economic prosperity in the 1920s was underpinned by the thinking of the Republicans who, as we have seen in Chapter 2, governed the US throughout this period (although the Democrats took control of the House of Representatives in 1930). Whilst firmly upholding the idea of minimal government, Republican politicians also believed that it was their role to create the economic climate in which businesses, industry and, thereby, the whole nation could prosper. Their policies of low taxation allowed business and industry to invest some of their profits in future development. This also gave the middle and upper classes the spending power to buy the goods they wanted.

At the same time, high tariffs on foreign imported goods (protectionism) made these goods expensive. The absence of foreign competition guaranteed high sales of home-produced goods which, in turn, stimulated the continued growth of manufacturing industry. This protectionist policy often produced retaliation from other nations who imposed similar high tariffs on US goods entering their countries. In the longer term, this was damaging to the US export industry but, in the short term, pressure from some groups within America to lower tariffs and move towards free trade was ignored. As *The Wall Street Journal* reported:

> 'Never before, here or anywhere else, has the government been so completely fused with business.'

KEY THEME

US export industry The United States relied far less on international trade as a percentage of GNP than did any other industrial country right down to the 1960s.

The development of capital and credit. During the First World War, American banks had profited from lending money to the Allies which, in the 1920s, was in the process of being repaid with interest. The banks were eager to lend money again not only to foreign governments but also, within the USA itself, to businesses and individuals. They also lent abroad, for example, and in particular, to help Germany. This extension of credit was generally at low interest rates. Cheap credit allowed the American people to increase significantly their spending power. It also enabled them to purchase goods by **hire-purchase** schemes. This, in turn, boosted demand and, therefore, production.

KEY TERM

Hire purchase is a means of buying a product by paying for it in instalments. Ownership is achieved when all instalments have been paid.

In 1921, the credit extended by the US Federal Reserve Bank was $45.3 billion; by 1929, it had risen to $73 billion. This cheap money enabled Americans to begin and to develop businesses with relative ease. It also provided them with the means to purchase the goods they wanted. Together, these contributed to a major economic boom.

Summary of reasons for economic growth

- Industrial development and methods of mass production
- Government policies of low taxation and protectionism
- Development of banking – cheap capital and credit
- Increased spending power, hire purchase and demand for consumer goods stimulated further industrial growth

WHAT WERE THE MAIN FEATURES OF ECONOMIC PROSPERITY?

Supply and demand. Between 1921 and 1929, average wages in the USA rose from $1,308 to $1,716 a year. This rise, together with low levels of taxation, resulted in increased spending power for the American people. They spent a sizeable proportion of their increased wealth on a range of new consumer goods, many of which had been manufactured using methods of mass production. These goods included cars, typewriters and, for the home, vacuum cleaners, washing machines, cookers and refrigerators.

KEY TERM

Supply and demand is an economic term referring to the balance that needs to be struck to ensure a healthy economy. This balance is between the supply of goods from the manufacturing industries and the demands of consumers. The economy is adversely affected if there are more goods than buyers, i.e. if supply exceeds demand. This creates a surplus, and if industry cannot sell the goods it produces, then, eventually, it will be difficult for it to survive.

Marketing and the media. Consumer interest in mass-produced goods was aroused by lively advertising on commercial radio. New techniques of advertising and sales gave a significant boost to the creation of a mass consumption economy. Americans owned 60,000 radios in 1920, but 10 million by 1929. This created a mass audience now open to new forms of communication, including the telephone.

Consumer spending. Increasingly, Americans shopped in a growing number of department stores; there were 312 in 1920, but by 1929 there were 1,395. They had little need to worry about paying outright for the goods they bought since they could take advantage of hire-purchase schemes. All that was needed at the time of purchase was an initial deposit. The remaining cost could subsequently be paid off in manageable instalments, either weekly or monthly. Although people paid a higher price for the goods they bought, hire-purchase schemes did mean that they could buy cars, radios, telephones, vacuum cleaners or washing machines immediately rather than saving for them. Provided their income was regular, as it generally was in the boom years, the system worked well. The result was the emergence of the first mass consumer society.

KEY TERMS

Share dividends are the share of the profits made by a company that is paid out to those who have invested in it by buying its shares.

Speculating and accumulating This means investing (and possibly risking) money in shares on the stock market in order to gain even more. Shares bought in companies manufacturing consumer goods were likely to rise greatly in value and so accumulate money for the owner. Although many individuals did invest it was generally not the man in the street who bought shares but banks and other institutions.

The effects of consumer spending. This consumer boom had wide-reaching and often beneficial effects on the American economy (see the tables on page 30). During the 1920s, business profits rose by 80 per cent. The **share dividends** paid out to investors rose by 65 per cent. Industrial firms realised that their profits would increase with greater efficiency. Moreover, the government taxed business profits at a relatively low level. These factors encouraged them to plough back some of their profits into further investment to improve and modernise. In 1914, for instance, only 30 per cent of US factories were powered by electricity but, by 1929, this had reached 70 per cent. As a result of such innovation and increasing mechanisation, output increased by 43 per cent between 1919 and 1929.

Speculating and accumulating. As American companies continued to enjoy large profits, particularly those producing new consumer goods, many Americans took the opportunity to invest in the **stock market**. They bought shares in companies in the expectation, usually firmly grounded, that their value would rapidly rise (see table below, left) giving them the chance to 'get rich quick'. The stock markets looked like short cuts to happiness and it could hardly have been easier to join the game.

Shares could easily be bought 'on the margin'. This meant that the buyer paid a small percentage of the cost of the shares in cash, usually 10 per cent, with the remainder covered by loans. These loans were provided by 'brokers' men' who bought and sold shares on behalf of their clients, borrowing money from the banks on their behalf to do so. The hope was that, by selling the shares at a profit as they were rising, the debts could easily be repaid. The banks seemed happy to play their part and, between 1926 and 1929, brokers' loans jumped from $3.5 billion to $8.5 billion. As long as the markets remained buoyant and prices steadily rose, profits were assured. Many Americans who previously had shown no interest in this sort of economic activity, were tempted to speculate on the stock market in order to accumulate wealth. Some played their part in creating the 'American Dream' by going from rags to riches in no time at all.

Whilst, during these years, Americans were able to buy more consumer goods and acquire more possessions than ever before, the US was not a wholly materialistic society. As early as 1924, some 11 million families owned their own homes and many were also paying for life and home insurance. Between 1910 and 1930, but especially in the

Selected share prices from 'The Wall Street Journal' (1928)

	3/3/28	3/9/28
Montgomery Ward	132	466
New York Central	160	256
Union Carbide & Carbon	145	413
American Telephone & Telegraph	77	181
Anaconda Copper	54	162
Westinghouse	91	313
Electric Bond & Share	89	203

KEY TERM

Stock market In the USA this is on Wall Street in New York. It is the centre for buying and selling shares in national and international businesses. It also monitors the rise and fall in the value of shares.

Gross national product, USA

	$ (billions)
1921	74
1926	97
1929	104

Rising national income, USA

	$ (billions)
1921	59.4 ($522 per head)
1929	87.2 ($716 per head)

Total world production (1929)

	%
USA	34.4
Britain	10.4
Germany	10.3
Russia	9.9
France	5.0
Japan	4.0
Italy	2.5
Canada	2.1
Poland	1.7

second half of the period, total expenditure on education rose five-fold from $426.25 million to $2.3 billion, spending on higher education rising four-fold. Whilst Americans were enjoying the material benefits of increased prosperity, they were also investing for their futures and enjoying a wide range of activities in this increasingly diverse, multi-racial society.

HENRY FORD AND THE FORD MOTOR COMPANY OF DETROIT

Henry Ford.

Early developments. Of all those associated with the American boom years, Henry Ford is perhaps the best known. He was born into a farming family in Dearborn, Michigan in 1863 and, after education in local schools, became a machinist's apprentice in Detroit at the age of 16. From 1888 to 1899, he was a mechanical engineer, rising to become chief engineer with the Edison Illuminating Company. But his main interest was in developing the automobile and, as early as 1893, after many experiments, he completed the construction of his first car.

The beginnings of mass production. In 1903, he founded the Ford Motor Company in Detroit, which, by 1908, was producing a hundred cars a day at its Highland Park factory. This output was achieved by simple mass production methods. These were already established in some industries, for example, in the manufacture of firearms, sewing machines and railway engines. They were later extended to the production of clocks, typewriters and bicycles.

Invariably, this form of production was achieved by the trolley system in which interchangeable parts were moved around the factory to the place where the product was actually being made. Such methods demanded less skill of the workers involved and tended to produce a semi-skilled workforce who were not eligible for membership of craft trade unions.

Part of the Ford assembly line.

Assembly-line production. By 1913, the Ford Motor Company was producing 500 cars a day although it still took 12½ hours to produce each car. For about six years, Ford had been planning a light, cheap car for the mass market but was searching for a far more efficient method of production. The answer was the assembly line. He had got the idea from methods used in slaughterhouses in Chicago and adapted them to speed up the mass production methods already in use in his factory. This was the real breakthrough to cheaper mass production. As the chassis of the car moved through the factory on a conveyor belt, the workers had to perform set tasks, adding parts to the chassis before it passed on to another stage of assembly. The most important skill was speed, as the tasks themselves became simple and repetitive. The result was the cheap Model T Ford or 'Tin Lizzie' as it came to be known.

When the assembly line was introduced, it reduced the production time of a car from 12½ hours to 1½ hours. All Ford cars were now standard, basic models that could be produced quickly and cheaply. Consequently, higher production targets could be set. By developing the principle of the division of labour and by making machinery and equipment more specialised, assembly-line systems could be further developed. As skilled workers were now being replaced by machines, stronger and faster

KEY COMMENTS

Jim Sullivan, one of the workers at Highland Park, spoke of the dull monotony of the work:

'If you were on that line and you had a certain job to do and the cars came by as fast as they did, and you didn't get your part in there, you were in trouble.'

Whilst another employee, Warren Park, spoke of the tighter discipline exerted over the workers as competition increased:

'You had a set figure to produce and if you didn't do that, then you were criticised or maybe moved to another location.'

'In the wake of the $5 day – which overnight more than doubled Ford workers' pay – scores of newspaper and magazine writers swarmed to Highland Park . . . Gaping at the smooth-flowing assembly lines, the writers used such adjectives as "miraculous", "phenomenal", "revolutionary" and "world-shaking" in attempting to describe the process. Syndicated stories on how Ford cars grew up by magic methods appeared in hundreds of newspapers throughout the nation.'

David Lewis, *The Public Image of Henry Ford* (1976)

machine tools were developed with sub-assembly lines feeding the main assembly lines. These developments led to the birth of large new industrial complexes.

As a result of these revolutionary techniques, the Ford Company was able to produce 1 million Model Ts each year in the 1920s and at a much lower cost to the consumer. In 1914, a Model T cost $850; by 1926, the price had dropped to $295. This, together with the availability of cheap credit, explains why the number of cars on the road in America rose from 8 million in 1920 to 23 million by 1930. By 1925, half the world's cars were Model Ts. In the late 1920s, Ford plants had been established in Asia, Australia, Canada, South Africa and South America. So effective were his new techniques that they were adopted by Citroën and Renault in France, by Agnellini (Fiat) in Italy and by Morris and Austin in Britain. Techniques of mass production were also sufficiently adaptable to be transferred to the production of radios, refrigerators and vacuum cleaners. This was the basis for the consumer boom of the 1920s.

The experience of Ford's employees. Whilst Ford, his shareholders and associates were delighted with the progress made and the profits that followed, his workers were less happy. As early as 1914, the unpleasant monotony of assembly-line work and repeated increases in production quotas led to a monthly labour turnover at Highland Park of between 40 and 60 per cent.

In 1914, Ford introduced a number of changes to counteract the discontent of his workers and the rapid labour turnover.

- He reduced the length of the working day to 8 hours and introduced a third shift. This increased the demand for workers who often came from immigrant communities.
- He doubled the daily wage to $5 and introduced a scheme of profit-sharing.
- These changes resulted in the increased stability of his workforce.

These factors, together with the enormous growth in output, led to an increase in company profits from $30 million in 1914 to $60 million in 1916.

In 1927, work was completed on a new Ford factory on the River Rouge at Ford's birthplace, Dearborn, Michigan. The River Rouge plant was the biggest factory complex in the world, employing around 80,000 workers. It contained all that was needed for car production: a foundry to make steel for car bodies, an electricity generating plant, a glass works, a railway and a port. Most significantly of all, it was to be the site for the manufacture of a new Ford car, the Model A. This was intended to replace the Model T, which had achieved sales figures of 15 million but was now to be discontinued.

KEY COMMENT

In this factory, supervision of workers was even closer, as one of the workers, Archie Accicea, commented:

'Once you start the production going . . . you have just got to think, I have got to keep up with this line, because if you don't keep up with the line, you're in trouble.'

Whilst Ford paid his workers relatively well, they were tightly disciplined and their work was closely supervised. Within his factories, Ford's Protection Department employed strong-armed security men who watched over union organisers, intimidating and assaulting them. It was not until 1941 that any labour union was recognised by the Ford Company to represent employees in bargaining for wages. Clearly, Henry Ford took a paternalistic approach – he was a 'father figure' who knew what was best for his workers. Consequently, in his view, there was no need for unions in any of his plants.

WHAT WAS THE IMPACT OF THE MOTOR CAR INDUSTRY ON THE US ECONOMY IN THE 1920S?

The table clearly shows how the production of motor vehicles rose during this period.

KEY STATISTICS

The output of motor vehicles, USA, 1921–9

1921	1,682,000
1922	2,646,000
1923	4,180,000
1924	3,738,000
1925	4,428,000
1926	4,506,000
1927	3,580,000
1928	4,601,000
1929	5,622,000

By 1930, the car industry was contributing 13 per cent of US manufacturing production and employed 4 million workers. But the industry had a much wider economic impact as it stimulated the growth of other industries that served it. By the mid 1920s, the car industry was using:

- 96 per cent of the nation's oil
- 75 per cent of the nation's plate glass

- 65 per cent of the nation's leather
- 80 per cent of the nation's rubber
- 20 per cent of the nation's steel.

It also led to increased road construction, more fuel stations, hotels and restaurants as the nation became more mobile. Thus, with 23 million cars on America's roads by 1929, the motor industry had had an enormous impact on the US economy as a whole.

The end of poverty? Whilst the American economy was undoubtedly booming in the 1920s, not everyone shared in the affluence.

- Those who benefited most were businessmen and those who could afford to buy shares whose value trebled between 1923 and 1929.
- Although average wages did increase throughout the decade, there remained about 6 million families whose income was less than $1,000 a year. Even though the Model T cost only $300 or $400 dollars and could be bought on hire-purchase, the automobile was well beyond the means of these people, as was the radio and mass-produced household gadgets.

So, whilst the number of millionaires increased from 7,000 in 1914, to 35,000 in 1928, this increase represented a widening gap between the rich and the poor. The result was a situation where the total income of one tenth of 1 per cent of families at the top of the economic scale was equivalent to the 42 per cent at the bottom.

KEY COMMENT

In 1928, Fiorella La Guardia, a congressman for East Haarlem, New York City, wrote:

'I confess I was not prepared for what I actually saw. It seemed almost incredible that such conditions of poverty could really exist.'

For those at the bottom, life could be grim. Two million people in New York City lived in tenements condemned as fire traps. Whilst at work, lax safety regulations resulted in accidents that killed 25,000 workers each year and permanently disabled 100,000. The policy of 'rugged individualism', in which all Republican presidents believed, meant little or no welfare support for the poor and a *laissez-faire* approach to such issues as safety at work.

In a number of industries, low pay and dangerous working conditions led to strikes.

- Between April and September 1922, approximately 500,000 miners went on strike against wage reductions.
- Coal miners' strikes in West Virginia in 1919 and 1920 were smashed by state troops. Harding set up an enquiry into mining conditions but took no action to improve them.
- Force was again used in 1927 to suppress a strike of textile workers in Elizabethtown, Tennessee, who were receiving 18 cents an hour for a 56-hour week.

In almost all industrial disputes at this time, the government backed the employers against the workers. The Supreme Court declared unconstitutional two state laws banning child labour, as well as laws establishing a minimum wage for women workers. This was because the majority of Supreme Court judges believed that economic regulation infringed the right of freedom of contracts. In 1920, 5.1 million workers were members of trade unions. By 1929, this number had fallen to 3.6 million.

Poverty in farming. In contrast to many industrial workers, the small farmers of America also did not share in the economic prosperity of the 1920s. During the First World War, farming in America had prospered. Increasing mechanisation, perhaps best illustrated by the introduction of the tractor in Illinois in 1889, led to a reduction in labour costs. With the outbreak of war in 1914, American farmers were well placed to take advantage of the opportunity of supplying relatively cheap food to European markets increasingly disrupted by war. They did this very effectively and enjoyed good profits as a result.

As Europe recovered after the war, American farming slumped. The worsening situation was not helped by increasing competition in world markets from Argentina and Canada. The main problem was overproduction. During the war, to maximise profits, more and more land had been brought into production. As demand fell after the war, wartime production levels were maintained, resulting in falling prices for the food produced. Many farmers reached the point where it was unprofitable to harvest their crops. Between 1919 and 1921, total farm income fell from $10 billion to $4 billion. As prices fell,

KEY TERM

The McNary–Haugen Bill was a plan under which the government would purchase the surplus of six commodities – cotton, corn, rice, hogs, tobacco and wheat – at a guaranteed high price, and sell it on the world market.

farmers were unable to pay off their loans. The **McNary–Haugen Bill** passed Congress in 1927 but was vetoed by Coolidge, an action which increased the likelihood of bankruptcy among many small farmers and resulted in around 6 million Americans leaving the countryside for the cities in the 1920s.

By the time Hoover became President in 1929, it was too late to save many farms. In April of that year, he called Congress into special session to deal with falling prices and farm relief, whilst his Federal Farm Board, set up in June, was furnished with $500 million to offer loans to farm co-operatives. However worthy these attempts may have been, they were insufficient to tackle the problem, for by this time the United States was about to enter the Great Depression. An increasing number of Americans were about to face the same sort of problems which the farmers had already experienced.

SUMMARY QUESTIONS

1 What factors contributed to prosperity in the USA in the 1920s?

2 Were government policies the most important factor in the prosperity of the boom period?

3 What evidence is there that the USA was prosperous in the 1920s?

4 How important was Henry Ford to the prosperity of the period?

5 Did all Americans benefit from the prosperity of the 1920s?

CHAPTER 4

The 'roaring twenties'

> 'By the 1920s, . . . America had much to shock, enthral and fascinate – mass motoring, screaming advertising, endless movies, records sold by millions, twenty-four hour radio . . . But, above all, it had jazz.'
>
> Paul Johnson, *History of the American People*

This was the 'roaring twenties' – the 'Jazz Age' – bold, brash, sometimes bawdy, often shocking and outrageous. It was a wild, violent time, a 'fun' time, a time of protest and rebellion when some accepted norms of behaviour were challenged. For a decade, it set America even further apart from the rest of the world. For those able to travel to the USA in the post-war years, it provided a novel experience. To those suffering economic depression in war-scarred Europe, its apparent affluence made it a fantasy land! In 1920, when the surrealist artist Salvador Dali arrived in America, he remarked, 'In America, surrealism is invisible for all is larger than life'.

What created this incredible phenomenon? It is fair to say that many of the features that characterise this short, but remarkable, period of American history were already underway by 1920. Some of them were a response to the financial boom of the period described in Chapter 3. However, as a starting point, a significant and decisive influence in the creation of the rebellious spirit of the twenties must be the imposition of Prohibition.

KEY THEME

18th Amendment to the Constitution Article 5 of the Constitution lays down that either two-thirds of both Houses of Congress or two-thirds of the member states can propose an amendment. Then three-quarters of the states have to ratify the proposal before it can come into effect. Over Prohibition, the sequence of events was:

December 1917 Congress passed the amendment

January 1919 Three-quarters of states had ratified

January 1920 It came into effect.

The Volstead Act of 1919 provided for enforcement of the 18th Amendment in respect of Prohibition.

PROHIBITION

Why was Prohibition introduced? The power to ban (prohibit) the production, export, import, transportation or sale of alcoholic beverages was given by the **18th Amendment to the Constitution**, which was passed in 1917. It was gradually adopted by state governments across America and was followed up in 1919 by the National

Prohibition or Volstead Act that defined liquor as drink containing 0.5 per cent of alcohol and prescribed penalties for breaking the law. By 1919, three-quarters of the states of America had approved Prohibition. It finally applied to the whole of the USA in 1920. It was an amazing law partly because the legal liquor industry was the seventh largest industry in a country where, even in the latter part of the nineteenth century, 'big business' was established and respected as the creator of the nation's wealth. More importantly, Prohibition appeared to be a violation of the rights and freedom of the individual so cherished by the US Constitution and the Bill of Rights. So why and how did it come into being?

Anti-Saloon League. Prohibition originated in rural and small town America. It was a crusade against liquor inspired by the misery, poverty, depravity and violence that alcohol was perceived to produce. The campaign for a total ban on alcohol was driven by a pressure group called the Anti-Saloon League whose membership was drawn from middle-class, Protestant, church-going Americans who were especially critical of behaviour and morality in the big, crime-ridden cities such as New York and Chicago. The League enjoyed the support of other middle-class **temperance** groups such as the Women's Christian Temperance Union. More significantly, it also had the very influential backing of some big business tycoons. For example, John D. Rockefeller gave both his personal support and large sums of money to the League. This was not from his own strong moral convictions, but rather because he believed that his workers would be far more productive if their minds and bodies were free from the debilitating influence of alcohol!

KEY TERM

Temperance in this context refers to those who believed in abstaining totally from drinking alcoholic drinks.

Collectively, these groups were able to exert a significant influence by voting for politicians who would then support their cause in Congress. By the time the 18th Amendment was discussed and voted on, there was sufficient support to ensure that prohibition of alcohol became law either because these politicians believed in it or because the moral pressure was so great that they did not want to be seen to oppose it. Several states already had prohibition laws on their statute books and the federal prohibition movement built on this.

It is also thought by some that the war in Europe was influential. A large proportion of America's brewers were of German origin. The anti-German feeling that was growing in America by the time the legislation went before Congress lent support to its actions. It is impossible to speculate how many politicians supported Prohibition from personal conviction. Suffice it to say that, at the Democratic Party Convention in San Francisco in 1920, delegates happily drank illegal whiskey provided by the Mayor free of charge!

Once the National Prohibition Act became law nationally, John F. Kramer was appointed the first Prohibition Commissioner. His task was to drain America dry of alcohol wherever it could be found. Subsequently, 1,500 additional agents were appointed to carry out the work. By 1930, there were around 3,000. Their task, however, was impossible since they were poorly paid, which left them open to bribery and, in some circumstances, they lacked the scientific and industrial expertise to carry out the work. They were undoubtedly overwhelmed by the criminal forces that prohibition unleashed.

What was the impact of Prohibition? The National Prohibition Act was an experiment in social engineering but it went horribly wrong. It was intended by its authors to promote morality, but it had entirely the opposite effect.

- **Crime.** It only proved how imaginative and resourceful people could be in evading the law. It increased the consumption of alcohol enormously. Crime increased catastrophically and amongst those millions of Americans who did not support it, Prohibition engendered a sense of injustice, resentment and, in some cases, rebellion.
- **Growth of soft drinks.** The imposition of Prohibition did, however, give a significant boost to the American soft drinks industry. This had been growing during the nineteenth century, especially after John Styth Pemberton developed the 'secret formula' that went into

making Coca Cola. As early as 1905, it was being marketed as 'The Grand National Temperance Drink'. Output had been increasing impressively from 17.4 million cases in the 1880s to 113 million by 1920. During the period when Prohibition was in force (1920–33), this rose to 182 million. By the time of the repeal of the prohibition laws, Coca Cola and its rival, Pepsi Cola, were well established household names and the industry was flourishing.

- **The illegal liquor business.** Notwithstanding the encouragement of the soft drinks industry, generally the impact of Prohibition was negative. Its effects were entirely contrary to the intention of the law. People, deprived of legal liquor and angered by the restriction of their rights, found other sources of alcohol. For those reluctant blatantly to defy the law, there was 'medicinal' whiskey. This could be obtained legally on prescription although, undoubtedly, these 'legal' prescriptions were dubiously obtained.

However, it is clear that vast numbers of people, especially in the big cities, were prepared to defy the law and buy illegal drink however and wherever it could be obtained. In many instances, they made their own (**moonshine**) often with devastating effects on health and well-being. This often inexpertly distilled alcohol made from corn could be lethal, causing paralysis, blindness and sometimes death. In the big cities, especially, illegal bars (**speakeasies**) appeared and multiplied rapidly, far outnumbering their legal counterparts before Prohibition. Nightclubs, restaurants and shops sold **bootleg** whiskey. Arrests for drunkenness trebled and deaths from alcoholism rose by 600 per cent. Speakeasies were owned and operated by gangs who obtained liquor partly by smuggling it into the USA from Canada, Mexico and the Caribbean (**bootlegging**) and also by establishing illegal breweries. These city gangs became notorious. Organised crime, including gambling, prostitution and narcotics, developed on a huge scale. Bribery of politicians, judges and law enforcement officials was widespread. Whilst gangland 'executions' removed some of the main criminals, 'big crime' families and organisations remained a dominant feature of US city life throughout the twentieth century.

KEY TERMS

Moonshine enabled farmers to make money from their corn crop which otherwise was of little value. They made beer by fermenting their corn. They also boiled and distilled it to produce 200 proof corn whiskey, which they sold to bootleggers.

Bootlegging is the term used to describe the illegal traffic of alcoholic drink in the USA. The term originates from the nineteenth century Midwest when traders concealed flasks of illegal liquor in their boot tops when trading with the Native Americans. In the 1920s, ships hired or owned by bootleggers anchored out to sea beyond the three-mile limit. This put them outside the jurisdiction of the law. Here they unloaded their illegal liquor into small high-powered boats that could out-run the coastguards, to carry their cargo to the mainland.

Speakeasies were illegal liquor shops or drinking clubs during the Prohibition period.

Gangs, gangsters and organised crime. Prohibition effectively transferred the provision and manufacture of alcoholic drinks from the hands of legitimate businesses into those of criminal organisations, especially in the big cities such as Chicago and New York. These were almost exclusively of immigrant origin. In New York, half were Jewish, a quarter Italian and a quarter were Polish and Irish. In Chicago, they were exclusively Italian and Irish. 'Gangster' leaders became incredibly wealthy and virtually controlled these cities. The significance of this was that crime brought political influence to groups previously without power.

Al Capone.

John Torrio and Al Capone are particularly good examples of how gangsters operated and flourished in Chicago as a result of Prohibition. Torrio was the leader of an Italian–American gang with Mafia links. He organised Chicago into gang 'territories' to reduce conflict between criminal gangs. He bought the 'protection' of Mayor 'Big Bill' Thompson and ensured political support by rigging elections. For example, in 1924, after moving the base of his illegal operations to a suburb of Chicago called Cicero, he successfully fought off police intervention to ensure the election of a town council made up of his nominees. Torrio built up a very lucrative business in bootlegging and speakeasies until 1925 when he retired to Italy taking with him his $30 million fortune from crime.

His successor in the 'business', Al Capone, was extremely violent. He was involved in every crime of vice and extortion that existed. Whilst appearing publicly alongside Mayor Thompson, politicians and officials as a city celebrity at charity events, he was extorting millions of dollars in protection money from Chicago citizens, making a fortune from speakeasies, brothels and drug trafficking, as well as indulging in gang warfare with his rivals. By 1927, his criminal activities had provided him with a fortune of around $27 million. He was driven around Chicago in an armour-plated Cadillac. In the midst of all of this, law-enforcing bodies were helpless; judges and police officials were frequently in the pay of the gangsters. In addition to all of these crimes, between 1927 and 1931, there were

227 gangland murders for which no one was ever convicted.

The most outrageous of these happened on 14 February 1929 and became known, therefore, as 'The St Valentine's Day Massacre'. Four members of Al Capone's gang, dressed as policemen, trapped seven members of a rival Irish–American gang led by 'Bugs' Moran. The captives were told to put their hands against the wall. Expecting a routine police search, they did so without hesitation. Capone's men produced sawn-off shotguns and sub-machine guns and shot them in the back. Such levels of violence angered the citizens of Chicago but Capone, himself, seemed untouchable. Finally, an **FBI** team led by Eliot Ness ensured the conviction of Capone for tax evasion for which he served 11 years in Alcatraz. He was never punished for the 400 murders that he is alleged to have ordered. The Depression that hit the USA after 1929 saw the demise of the speakeasy and bootlegging. Unemployment was so high that there was no money to spend on liquor.

KEY TERM

FBI or **Federal Bureau of Investigation** This is an agency of the US Department of Justice. Besides investigating breaches of federal law, it is also responsible for investigating organised crime and drug trafficking.

Fiorella La Guardia was a New York City politician and an outspoken critic of Prohibition. In evidence given to a Senate Committee, he had this to say in criticism:

> 'It is my calculation that at least a million dollars a day is paid in graft and corruption to Federal, State and local officers. Such a condition is not only intolerable, but it is demoralising and dangerous to organised government. The Government even goes to the trouble of facilitating the financing end of the bootlegging industry. In 1925, $286,950,000 more of $10,000 bills were issued than in 1920, and $25,000,000 more of $5,000 were issued. What honest businessman deals in $10,000 bills?'

WOMEN IN THE 1920s

> 'Flirting, kissing, viewing life lightly, saying damn without a blush, playing along the danger line in an immature way – a sort of mental baby vamp.'

This is how **F. Scott Fitzgerald**, the American writer, described his wife, Zelda, in the early 1920s. He regarded her as the personification of a 'flapper' – unconventional, wild and reckless. For so the rebellious spirit unleashed by Prohibition manifested itself, not only in the illegal consumption of alcohol and all that went with this. Another consequence was the rejection of previously held codes of social and moral conduct by some young, well-off women in the twenties who caused eyebrows to rise and produced outbursts of moral indignation from older generations of women who regarded them as brazen.

These young women interpreted liberation as having the freedom to dress and behave as they chose. This meant defying all the accepted conventions of feminine behaviour.

- They were distinguishable by their bobbed hair, loose, shorter length clothes, bare, sometimes made-up legs and often outrageous behaviour.
- They smoked, partied, drank and danced the Charleston until the early hours of the morning.
- There were hints of sexual permissiveness in their attitudes and lifestyle although this was, perhaps, more imaginary than real.
- They became inextricably linked with the popular and emerging musical craze of the twenties – jazz.
- They regarded themselves as thoroughly 'modern' – a new breed of feminists. They were also very much the products of the affluence of the 1920s.

Materialistic and impressionable, these young women were an easy prey to the aggressive advertising of the time, in magazines and on the radio, which portrayed the glamorous and extravagant as desirable and attainable: 'Ads for automobiles, cigarettes, electrical conveniences and home furnishings created a fantasy world of elegance, grace and boundless pleasure.' So, images of beautiful women driving Model T Fords and wearing fashionable clothes made these a must for the truly emancipated female.

Women's quest for emancipation in the 1920s. This popular image of the flapper was a creation of the media of the time. They did not, by themselves, represent a

KEY PERSON

F. Scott Fitzgerald was an author of novels and short stories. He named the 1920s the 'Jazz Age' and caught the spirit and mood of the time in his writing. In 1920, he married Zelda Sayre, an archetypal 'flapper'. With the money that he made from his short stories he financed his extravagant lifestyle, so much so that he and Zelda lived out the popular image of the 'roaring twenties'.

This mood and image was captured particularly in his *Tales of the Jazz Age* (1922) and *The Great Gatsby* (1925). After 1930, Zelda suffered from bouts of insanity and Fitzgerald from alcoholism. His work was never fully appreciated in his lifetime. It was only after the publication of his last work, *The Last Tycoon* (1941) and after his death, that his earlier works were reappraised and their quality recognised.

A flapper.

'Jane's a flapper . . . let us take a look at the young person as she strolls across the lawn of her parents' suburban home, having just put the car away after driving sixty two miles in two hours. She is, for one thing, a very pretty girl. Beauty is the fashion in 1925. She is frankly, heavily made up, not to imitate nature, but for an altogether artificial effect – pallor mortis, poisonously scarlet lips, richly ringed eyes – the latter looking not so much debauched (which is the intention) as diabetic . . . And finally, there are her clothes. Jane isn't wearing much this summer . . . Her dress is brief. It is cut low . . . The skirt comes just below her knees, overlapping by a faint fraction her rolled and twisted stockings . . . The corset is as dead as the dodo's grandfather . . . The petticoat is even more defunct . . . The brassiere has been abandoned since 1924 . . . '

An extract from 'Flapper Jane', an article that appeared in *The New Republic* on 9 September 1925

---

significant and enduring new **feminist** movement. In fact, other feminist groups in America regarded their materialistic emancipation as the very opposite of what they were trying to achieve. It is, therefore, misleading to focus attention exclusively on the flapper female if we wish to explore the changing role of women in American society in the 1920s. During the twenties, groups of American women continued a quest for emancipation that had begun in the nineteenth century (see below). This had included demands for the right to higher education and for access to the professions, particularly medicine and law. The success of these efforts was limited.

By 1900, there were numerous women's associations but very little evidence of female solidarity irrespective of ethnic origin or race. Women's groups were involved in a variety of diverse campaigns on a range of issues. Although women were now accepted as fully qualified doctors and lawyers, they continued to campaign for equal rights, particularly wage and labour rights. Women had campaigned successfully for the vote in several states

KEY TERM

Feminists were women who believed in women's rights and freedoms and in the equality of the sexes. They actively worked and campaigned for these to be recognised politically, socially and economically. This included the recognition of women's rights in legal issues relating to marriage and property and the right to vote.

KEY THEME

The right to vote was first granted by Wyoming in 1869, and by Utah in 1870, Washington Territory in 1883, Colorado in 1893 and Idaho in 1896.

The quest for women's rights in America during the nineteenth century

1850 First national women's rights convention. 1,000 attended.

1850 Female medical college established by Quakers in Pennsylvania amidst strong opposition.

1862 Homestead Act gave women the opportunity to own land in the West.

1862 onwards Some opportunities for black and white women to enter higher education.

1868 onwards Women workers became involved in some trade union activity to establish and safeguard their rights.

1869 Women in the State of Wyoming given the vote. **American Woman Suffrage Association** formed to get the vote for women in each state.

1872 The first African-American female lawyer is admitted to the US bar.

1874 Women's Christian Temperance Union founded. This later also campaigned for the vote for women.

1879 Female lawyers allowed to practise law in all federal courts.

1890 National American Woman Suffrage Association formed. Associations of Jewish and Coloured Women follow.

1899 National Consumer League formed to push for better working conditions and protective laws for women workers.

during the latter part of the nineteenth century, but there had been no national **suffrage** movement. This was largely because women seem to have been less interested in their political rights than in other social issues.

Suffrage. By the eve of America's entry into the First World War the campaign for women's suffrage was gaining momentum. In 1917, Jeanette Rankin of Montana had become the first woman to be elected to Congress and the National Woman's Party, led by **Alice Paul**, began a

KEY TERM

Suffrage is the right to vote in political elections.

KEY PERSON

Alice Paul was born in 1885. She gained MA and PhD degrees from the University of Pennsylvania. In 1906, she visited Britain where she became involved in militant suffragette activity. Returning to America in 1909, she became involved in the suffrage movement. In 1913, she was a co-founder of the Congressional Women's Suffrage and became an ardent campaigner for the 19th Amendment to the Constitution. After this became law, she took up the campaign for equality for women all over the world. She fought, unsuccessfully, for an Equal Rights Amendment for American women and joined other feminist activists in world peace movements.

Progress of the extension of the franchise to women in the nineteenth century
1869 Wyoming Territory
1870 Utah Territory
1883 Washington Territory
1896 Idaho
1893 Colorado

KEY EVENT

19th Amendment to the Constitution This prohibited sex discrimination in voting. It also gave Congress the power to enforce this by legislation.

more aggressive campaign to secure the vote. In January 1917, women picketed the White House enduring freezing temperatures and public hostility. Later the same year, 168 women made US history by becoming its first political prisoners when they were arrested for peaceful picketing. In prison they staged hunger strikes and were force fed. Finally, in 1919, Congress passed the **19th Amendment to the Constitution** by a narrow majority. It became law on 26 August 1920 and women were allowed to vote for the first time in the presidential election of that year. African-American women in the southern states, however, continued to experience discrimination when they tried to register to vote, as did African-American men.

KEY PERSON

Carrie Chapman Catt was born in 1859 and worked as a teacher until she became involved in the women's suffrage movement in the 1890s. She was president of the National American Woman Suffrage Association from 1900 until 1904 and again from 1915 until her death in 1947. After founding the National League of Women Voters in 1920, she became involved in the campaign for international peace. She was the leader of the National Committee on the Cause and Cure of War from 1925 to 1932.

Limited results of suffrage. During the First World War, whilst the men were away, women had taken over their work in heavy industry, manufacturing, driving transport vehicles and delivering mail. They had also earned good wages, probably for the first time. This experience had clearly had some impact on support for the movement to gain the vote for all American women. Moreover, individual women certainly did make progress in gaining political power. For example, Nellie Tayloe Ross of Wyoming became the first woman to be elected governor of a state in 1924 and in 1926, Bertha Knight Landes became the first female mayor of a city (Seattle).

These were, however, exceptions. During the 1920s, and in spite of the flapper image, the feminist movement weakened. The vote made very little difference to the majority of women. It certainly did not transform politics as some feminists expected. This was because, in spite of the educating efforts of **Carrie Chapman Catt** and the

National League of Women Voters (1920), the majority of women were fundamentally uninterested in politics or did not see politics as the means to achieving what they wanted. Although apparently liberated by mass-produced, labour-saving devices, married women were unable to resolve the conflict between work and home. Women who did not try to do both were more successful. Even then, opportunities were limited.

- Medical schools allocated only 5 per cent of places to women. Consequently, the number of women doctors actually declined in the period.
- In 1920, 47.3 per cent of college students were women, but the numbers subsequently declined.
- Whilst assembly-line production of consumer goods should, potentially, have created more jobs for women, in fact the workforce remained predominantly male.
- Numbers of women working rose by 2 million in the 1920s, but this still only represented 24 per cent of the population.
- Discrimination in wages continued, as did the view that women only worked until they married.

Feminist activists turned their attention to a variety of issues. As a result, the movement splintered. Many pursued the cause of equal rights in employment and promotion opportunities and equal pay. Others, for example **Jane Addams** and Carrie Chapman Catt, put their energies into peace movements and into other areas of social reform such as the abolition of child labour. Their efforts to get reforming legislation were unsuccessful.

Fundamentally, there were philosophical disagreements between the different feminist organisations. The real meaning of equality and equal rights for women was a particularly controversial issue. The 'old guard' of the feminist movement rejected the materialism and mass culture of the 'roaring twenties', but in the process lost the support of young women who were caught up in it. For them, freedom was the right to wear, say and do whatever they wanted.

Carrie Chapman Catt.

KEY PERSON

Jane Addams was born in 1860. Following her education in America and Europe, she became involved in social issues at home and women's issues abroad. She became president of the Women's International League for Peace and Freedom, speaking at conferences all over Europe in the 1920s. At home, she was accused of having communist sympathies by right-wing, middle-class women's organisations during the late 1920s. She won the Nobel Peace Prize in 1932 for her work for peace and her books on the subject.

A jazz group of the 1920s.

JAZZ, RAG AND 'BOOGIE-WOOGIE'

If flappers provided the distinctive images of the twenties in America, jazz was the distinctive sound of the twenties. Jazz was the new and exciting music of the time. In the speakeasies and nightclubs, its loud and **syncopated** rhythms articulated the rebellious mood of the 'roaring twenties', hence the alternative label – the 'Jazz Age'.

KEY TERM

Syncopation is a musical term describing a method of creating alternative rhythms in a piece of music by making the strong beats weak and vice-versa.

In fact, jazz was not 'new'. In its original form, it was the casual, spontaneous music of the negro slaves who were encouraged to sing at work as this was believed to increase production. They used washboards, cans, pickaxes and percussion to produce a distinctive sound.

This improvised music grew in the nineteenth century and became known by a number of terms such as 'blues', 'rag' and 'boogie-woogie'. Classical music was 'jazzed' or 'ragged' by changing the beat and creating new rhythms. The terms 'jazz', 'rag' and 'boogie-woogie' were sexual slang terms amongst African-Americans. So when jazz hit the social scene in the 1920s, it provoked moral outrage, particularly amongst the right-wing, middle-class critics of hot-blooded youth. Feminist followers of Carrie Chapman Catt complained that female singers and dancers were compromised by having to perform this immoral music. Some of the extreme feminist groups linked the spread of what they called 'negro music' to the rise in illegitimacy rates. In 1921, the *Ladies Home Journal* published an article entitled, 'Does Jazz put the Sin in Syncopation?', whilst a Methodist minister claimed that the new dances that accompanied this 'fast' music brought 'the bodies of men and women in unusual relation to each other'.

In spite of all of this, jazz and ragtime music produced some great musical figures who took these early, undisciplined sounds and rhythms and transformed them into something new and exciting. Different performers in different parts of the USA developed their own distinctive style.

- **Louis Armstrong**, the trumpeter from New Orleans, made the first recordings of jazz music that soon became international. During the 1920s, jazz moved to Chicago and New York.
- **'Duke' Ellington** moved from Washington DC to New York where he performed in the Harlem Cotton Club.
- Songwriters and composers, such as **George Gershwin**, and performers, such as **Al Jolson**, eventually made jazz respectable.

Jazz became the great attraction of night clubs and speakeasies. It was also carried into the homes of Americans by the medium of the new radio technology. Above all, jazz was a distinctively American product. This was very important to a country that was made up of so many different cultures but was struggling to find a truly national identity.

CINEMA – THE GREAT ESCAPE

'It was really an experience. You would be treated like a king or queen. You were issued into an enormous

KEY PEOPLE

Louis Armstrong was born in New Orleans on 4 July 1900. He became famous as a trumpeter, making his debut in 1917 in a New Orleans jazz band. He moved to Chicago, the jazz capital of the USA, in 1922 and remained there until 1929 except for one year spent in New York. By 1925, he had his own band and soon had a national reputation as a jazz trumpeter and singer. He is now regarded as one of the greatest of all time. Some of his recordings including 'Ain't Misbehavin' and 'Tiger Rag' are jazz classics.

Duke Ellington was born in Washington DC in 1899 and became a composer, conductor and pianist. He moved to New York in 1923 where he assembled a ten-piece band. By the time he died in 1974, he had come to be regarded, along with Louis Armstrong, as one of the most highly respected jazz musicians of the twentieth century.

George Gershwin was born in Brooklyn, New York in 1898. With his brother, Ira, who wrote the lyrics, he composed musicals and popular songs, which were a clever combination of jazz and the popular music of the day. For example, in 1924, he wrote 'Rhapsody in Blue' for piano and jazz band and in 1935, the opera *Porgy and Bess* which used folk music and jazz. He died two years later in 1937.

KEY PERSON

Al Jolson was born in 1886 in Russia (probably St Petersburg). He was Jewish and began singing as a child in the synagogue. He made his stage debut at the age of 13 and went on to become a circus performer and café entertainer. The turning point in his career came when he joined a touring company of minstrel-style singers wearing black face make-up. This became his trademark. He became a part of movie history when he starred in the first talking film – *The Jazz Singer* – in 1927. He was also a radio and recording artist.

KEY TERM

Nickelodeon. These were the first cinemas, so-called because a seat on the wooden benches cost a nickel. They were also referred to as 'flea pits', due to the dirty and unsanitary conditions inside them. They were more often found in poor areas of American cities, especially where there were large immigrant populations, and mostly were owned by immigrants.

lobby of marble and gilt with huge stairways leading up to the balconies. All the carpets were at least an inch or two thick. Everything was done in there to make you feel comfortable, to make you feel very important.'

Mary Evelyn Hults, *The People's Century*

This was the world of the cinema that came into its own in America in the 1920s. From the **nickelodeons** of the first decade of the twentieth century sprang the 'picture palaces' of the second – the New York 'Roxy', for example, and the Boston 'Metropolitan' with its 4,000 seats and 300 ushers. The uncomfortable wooden benches were replaced by luxurious seats; the hollow-sounding piano by the mighty organs. In some cinemas a full orchestra provided the musical backing for the 'silent' movies. By the end of this decade, 'talkies' had replaced the silent screen and America was exporting its films all over the world to audiences anxious to share, however vicariously, in the glamour and extravagance of the American scene. How did this all come about?

Films were a popular form of mass entertainment by the beginning of the twentieth century. By 1909, D.W. Griffiths had directed about 140 silent films, which were enjoyed in the nickelodeons. These cinemas had immigrant owners. Jewish immigrants were particularly active in the rapidly expanding entertainment industry. It is, perhaps, not surprising that almost all of the great names of the cinema that were to emerge during the 1920s were of immigrant origin also:

- **Carl Laemmle** was one of the first Jewish film tycoons.
- **Marcus Loew** (Metro-Goldwin-Mayer) was the son of an immigrant.
- **William Fox** (of 20th Century Fox) was Hungarian.
- **Louis B. Mayer** (of MGM) was born in Russia.
- The **Warner brothers** were the offspring of a Polish cobbler.

More importantly, perhaps, these ultimately successful men started from very humble beginnings:

- **Joseph Schenck**, who helped to found United Artists, ran an amusement park.
- **Sam Goldwyn** (MGM) was a blacksmith's assistant.
- **Harry Cohn** (film director) was a trolley bus conductor.
- **Sam Katz** (film director) began as a messenger boy.

Their enterprise, plus the availability of cheap real estate in Hollywood and low cost electricity, created a boom industry.

Hollywood. By 1920, around 100,000 people in the Hollywood area were employed in making films. It was soon a billion-dollar business. Moviemakers and their stars became millionaires, building themselves amazing luxury homes in the Los Angeles area. **Cecil B. DeMille**'s star, Gloria Swanson, reigned supreme in her 22-room mansion in Beverly Hills. Douglas Fairbanks, **Charlie Chaplin**, Buster Keaton, Laurel and Hardy were the legendary stars of the day. The often lavish silent films had massive popular appeal. Language was not a barrier and, through the medium of film, America projected and exported its image of affluence, extravagance, fun and fashion that were the hallmarks of the 'roaring twenties'. Its impact on attitudes and behaviour was huge.

In 1927, the movie-going world was amazed once more when *The Jazz Singer*, the first talking movie, hit the silver screen. Its star, Al Jolson, uttered the now immortal words, 'You ain't seen nothin' yet' and he was right. The film-making industry went from strength to strength. In 1928, Mickey Mouse appeared for the first time in *Steamboat Willey*, the first animated movie from the world of Walt Disney.

Throughout the Depression that hit America in 1929, the cheap entertainment provided by the cinema was an escape from the harsh reality of poverty. People who had little to wear and even less to eat still managed to find money to go to the movies. Film companies found it harder to make profits, as they now had to compete for customers who had limited amounts to spend on entertainment. Warner Brothers, for example, offered gifts as incentives to people

KEY PERSON

Cecil B. DeMille was one of the most successful film directors. He was born in Massachusetts in 1881. His parents wrote plays and both Cecil and his brother, William, followed in their footsteps to become actors and playwrights. Together with Samuel Goldwyn, they made films of successful stage plays. In 1925, Cecil became an independent film producer-director. His films included *King of Kings* (1926) and *Cleopatra* (1934). These, together with his last film, *The Ten Commandments* (1956), were famous for being vast, expensive spectaculars.

Charlie Chaplin.

to go to their movies. Nevertheless, they went. As one observer put it:

> 'It was very cheap to go to the movies in those days. But thinking about the money we didn't have, it was a very special treat. It was a difficult time for people . . . Just going and laughing for a bit at something that might be totally ridiculous was very important.'

WHAT WAS THE INFLUENCE OF THE MASS MEDIA?

Undoubtedly, the development of the mass media in the 1920s did much to create a kind of mass culture. In addition to the images portrayed in the cinema, the development of radio technology in the 1920s was also a significant influence. News, sport, entertainment and advertising were easily relayed into millions of homes. Radio became the main source of family entertainment, and a powerful force in creating the atmosphere and lifestyle of the twenties. It provided at least a flavour of what was being enjoyed by a few for the many who were too poor to partake and could only watch from the sidelines.

It is fair to say that the wild and rebellious lifestyle of the twenties was restricted to a relatively small percentage of the population. Whilst African-Americans, many immigrants, farmers and industrial workers may have listened to the radio or gone to the cinema as a form of escape, for them, the old values and attitudes remained. This was also true for millions of other Americans who rejected the mass materialism of the day and what they saw as its accompanying moral decline. Nevertheless, the mass media provided celebrities to worship and heroes to admire. In May 1927, **Charles Lindbergh**'s solo flight from New York to Paris in the *Spirit of St Louis* got full media coverage – radio, movie newsreel and newspapers – and delighted an admiring nation. With all their imperfections, the mass media certainly widened the horizons of most Americans.

The Depression that followed the Wall Street Crash in 1929 brought this unique period of American history to a

KEY PERSON

Charles Lindbergh was born in 1902 in Detroit. He became fascinated by flying and gave up university after two years to go to a flying school in Nebraska. He began flying in 1922 and, in 1927, took part in a competition to fly solo across the Atlantic. The prize of $25,000 had been offered in 1919 by Raymond B. Orteig, a wealthy Franco-American. The flight, in the *Spirit of St Louis*, took 33 hours 32 minutes. He became a hero in both the USA and Europe. This was only the first of many pioneering flights. Lindbergh and his family moved to Europe after the kidnapping and death of his 16 month old son in 1932, returning to the USA in 1939. He wrote several books. His autobiography, *The Spirit of St Louis*, won the Pulitzer Prize in 1954.

sudden and catastrophic end. Yet behind the scenes of extravagant lifestyle and colourful popular culture, there was a darker side. For besides the poverty of city and rural life, there existed intolerance and racism. This will be examined more closely in the next chapter.

SUMMARY QUESTIONS

1 Why was Prohibition imposed and what were its effects?

2 In what ways was this an age of 'liberation' for women in America?

3 a) Why was jazz controversial?
b) In what ways did jazz represent the spirit of the age?

4 Why was the cinema a 'great escape'?

5 Why was life in America the envy of Europe in the 1920s?

CHAPTER 5

America in the 1920s – a society in conflict

Almost from the moment of its birth, the United States of America had presented itself to the world as the 'land of the free'. Its Constitution and Bill of Rights cherished and protected those precious ideals of freedom and liberty for which, in the late eighteenth and nineteenth centuries, people in many parts of the world still struggled. It offered itself as a land of opportunity and opened its doors for unlimited numbers of people from all over the world to enter and escape from poverty and persecution. They came to the land of promise in search of 'the American dream'. However, from the beginning there were contradictions at work in the United States. In Article 1, section 2 of the original Constitution, slaves were counted as only three-fifths of a free person. Slavery was formally acknowledged and women and most men did not enjoy the right to vote. By the 1920s, the dream had become a nightmare for thousands of hopeful immigrants and America's liberal ideals had become even more visibly tainted with intolerance, hatred and racial prejudice.

Where did it all go wrong? There are a number of factors that help to provide an explanation:

- To some extent, the answer lies in the nature of the original English-speaking Americans and the society they had established.
- In the meantime, US entry into the First World War and its aftermath acted as the catalyst that generated reactionary attitudes and behaviour.
- In the shorter term, by the 1920s, Americans were confronting the social and economic impact of the 'open door' immigration policy.

The period provides us with a number of key events that clearly demonstrate these points in action.

WHITE PROTESTANT AMERICA

In the 1920s, in spite of the huge influx of people from other countries, the descendants of the original, English-speaking settlers were the most influential section of American society. They were predominantly Protestant and lived in the rural and small town areas of America. They were also powerfully represented politically and were, consequently, able to influence policy in state governments and in Congress. The imposition of Prohibition is a good example of this. There was bigotry among WASPs, but there was also bigotry among many of the white immigrant community as well, including Irish Catholics and East European immigrants.

Fundamentalism and the Scopes 'Monkey Trial'. A significant proportion of Protestants were either Baptists or Methodists. In 1859, **Charles Darwin** had published his **theory of evolution**. This had led to much debate in religious circles generally, but by the 1920s in America, Protestant groups were divided on their views. Some believed firmly in the description of the creation of the world exactly as it is in the Old Testament of the Bible. In 1919, these people set up the World's Christian Fundamentals Association and consequently became known as the fundamentalists. They wanted to make it illegal to teach or discuss Darwin's theories. In 1921–2, fundamentalist politicians led by William Jennings Bryan, succeeded in passing bills banning the teaching of evolution in schools. Six southern states implemented the laws, including the state government of Tennessee. The ban was seen as an infringement of individual liberty and the American Civil Liberties Union (ACLU) offered to defend anyone who wished to test the law.

John T. Scopes, a biology teacher in Dayton, Tennessee, rose to the challenge. He read out a description of Darwin's theory to his biology class, for which he was arrested and charged. His trial in Dayton reflects the impact of the media boom of the 1920s. Press, photographers and film crews descended on Dayton to witness and report the clash between one of

KEY PERSON

Charles Darwin and the theory of evolution Darwin was a British scientist born in 1809. In 1831, he took part in a scientific expedition on board the ship HMS *Beagle*. As a result of his studies, he wrote his controversial work, *Origin of the Species by Means of Natural Selection*. From this developed his ideas about the evolution of human beings and all primates, for example, apes and monkeys, from the same ancestor in early times. He wrote about this in a later work called *The Descent of Man*. This caused offence to religious organisations who rejected Darwin's theories.

KEY TERM

Fundamentalism is the strict belief in the truth of events exactly as they are described in the Bible. This belief was central to the beliefs of many religious groups in the late nineteenth and early twentieth centuries and remains so today in some religious sects.

America's leading criminal lawyers, Clarence Darrow (hired by the ACLU) and the champion of **fundamentalism**, William Jennings Bryan. The media certainly got what it came for. In cross-examination, Darrow challenged Bryan's views on biblical accuracy. His literal belief in the description of Creation, the story of Noah and the Flood and other biblical 'miracles' was completely ridiculed by the press who also exposed his ignorance of scientific interpretation, so much so, that the presiding judge stopped this humiliating cross-examination. Scopes was found guilty and fined $100, but the real point had been made.

Nevertheless, whilst the support for fundamentalism declined after the Scopes Trial, it did not disappear altogether. It survived in many of the new revivalist churches that sprang up during the twenties often with mass support. Aimee Semple McPherson's Angelus Temple, for example, in Los Angeles, seated 5,200 people. She broadcast regularly to thousands more on the radio. When she died in 1944, her Church of the Foursquare Gospel had more than 600 branches.

The assertion of white, Protestant supremacy revealed itself also in attitudes to immigrants and in racial prejudice. It manifested itself to some extent in the revival of the Ku Klux Klan (see page 64) and the political intolerance of the period. Whilst these all had their roots in the late nineteenth and early twentieth centuries, they were exacerbated by the effects of America's entry into the First World War.

WHAT WAS THE IMPACT OF THE FIRST WORLD WAR?

America's entry had significant political and economic effects that were to influence events in the post-war years. Whilst the Espionage (1917) and Sedition Acts (1918) effectively silenced any open criticism or opposition to the government during the war, there was, nevertheless, strong opposition to the war, emanating from some immigrant minorities, particularly Italian-Americans. These organisations had been involved previously in organising strikes and demands for higher wages and were quickly dubbed 'socialists' and 'anarchists'. One particularly influential anarchist Italian publication was *Cronaca Sovversiva*, edited by Luigi Galleani. The authorities were especially apprehensive of this because it accepted violence and revolution as means to securing its ends and had taken up an aggressively anti-war position before legislation had halted production. Galleani and the journal's other editors were arrested and deported at the end of the war but its supporters remained. Two of these were **Nicola Sacco** and **Bartolomeo Vanzetti** to whom we will return.

African-American migration. The First World War had boosted the US economy. America's wheat fields produced food for the warring Allies. Its wartime munitions factories created jobs for women but especially for immigrant workers and African-Americans who were being drawn increasingly into urban areas by the opportunity of work. This migration from the southern rural areas had begun in the 1890s but reached its peak in the war years when an estimated 500,000 African-Americans moved into the big cities of New York, Philadelphia, Boston, Chicago, Detroit, Cleveland and St Louis. This aggravated long-established racial tension between blacks and whites. Incidences of race riots increased between 1917 and 1919.

After the war, the closing of the munitions factories, the fall in demand for food and the effects of large numbers of soldiers returning to the workforce adversely affected large proportions of the rural and urban working population. White Americans believed that they were either being deprived of work or forced to accept lower wages because of the abundant availability of cheap immigrant and black labour. Hatred and intolerance of immigrants of Eastern European or Asian origin were accelerated by economic considerations such as these.

Impact of the Russian Revolution. The post-war years also saw the birth of international **communism**. The **Bolshevik Revolution of 1917** and its subsequently stated intention to spread communism abroad caused fear and alarm in all

KEY TERMS

Communism The communist ideology believes that the economic means of production determine the nature of society. It sees capitalism as exploitative because workers create wealth but get poor wages, while the capitalists make great profit simply by having wealth in the first place. Communism looks to create a society in which each receives according to need, people willingly co-operate together and the state withers away. In the transition from capitalism to communism there needs to be a corresponding transition period in which state socialism controls the economy. The first communist state was created in Russia after the Bolshevik Revolution of 1917. Its leader, Lenin, aimed to achieve a worldwide socialist revolution.

Capitalism Capitalism is based on the productive capacity of accumulated money and the division of labour in an efficient system of production. The laws of supply and demand dictate economic life. Government only has a minimal role and in conjunction with political liberalism this can create a system of political *and* economic freedom: they complement each other.

KEY EVENT

Bolshevik Revolution, 1917 The Bolsheviks, led by Lenin, successfully took power in Russia in March 1917. The Tsar and his family were murdered in 1918 and Lenin set about the task of destroying capitalism and replacing it with a socialist system where the vast division between rich and poor would be closed. The wealth of the nation would be shared equally and the workers would have a fair share of the profit that they had helped to create by their labour. Whilst this might have sounded reasonable in theory, in practice it led to repression, persecution and a denial of fundamental rights and freedoms.

the democratic states of the western world but nowhere more so than in America. Unrest and criticism, common in all those countries whose economies had been dislocated by the war, were quickly dubbed communist and subversive. Whilst partly explaining the isolationist foreign policy subsequently followed by US Republican administrations, this 'red scare' resulted in a virtual witch hunt in US political circles. It created an atmosphere of fear and suspicion that not only pervaded most of the decade but was also responsible for actions that were uncharacteristic of a nation pledged to liberty and freedom.

The 'Red Scare' and the Palmer Raids. The activities of communist groups in Russia and in Germany in the years immediately following the war were widely reported in US newspapers. This only helped to convince the US Attorney General, Mitchell Palmer, of the need to purge the land of what he called 'foreign-born subversives and agitators'. Palmer himself might have had good reason for his panic. In 1919 he had narrowly escaped death when a bomb, planted by anarchists, exploded in front of his house. Other leading officials in other cities of the USA had similar experiences. Whether Palmer was right to use his power and position to further his own prejudices and obsessions is another matter.

Suddenly, activities that in any other circumstances would have been seen as part and parcel of life in a free society were regarded as suspect and potentially part of a communist conspiracy to undermine the American republic. So Palmer ordered raids on magazine offices, private houses, union headquarters and public meetings on any subject that could be remotely labelled controversial. On New Year's Day, 1920, the Justice Department rounded up 6,000 'aliens', most of whom were imprisoned or expelled. He personally led the raids that were carried out in New York. During these raids, five elected members of the New York State Assembly were disqualified from taking their seats. Other state governments tried to expel elected socialists from their ranks. Palmer's personal hysteria proved to be infectious. It resulted in prejudiced perversions of justice and in dramatic changes to the immigration laws. However, Congress refused to pass a

Nicola Sacco (left) and Bartolomeo Vanzetti.

draconian sedition bill urged upon it by Palmer. Also there was a real problem with anarchists – on 16 September 1920, 38 people were killed by a bomb on Wall Street. After this things subsided, although at state level there was still persecution.

In 1920, a known anarchist, Andrea Salsedo, was arrested in New York City. He was denied his rights to receive a fair trial and to be represented by legal counsel, supposedly guaranteed by the 5th Amendment. He was imprisoned for eight weeks without contact with his family or a lawyer before his crushed body was found, on the ground, 14 floors below where he was being held by the FBI. The official explanation was that he had committed suicide. His fate alarmed his friends and associates, some of whom began to carry guns for protection. Two of these were Sacco and Vanzetti.

The case of Sacco and Vanzetti. Few events of the twenties in America have caused the same interest and heated debate as the trial of these two Italian-Americans. Amongst other things, it is seen as illustrating, more than any other event of the time, the deep divisions and prejudices in American society. It also has other implications.

On 15 April 1920 two men – Allesandro Berdelli and Frederick Parmenter – were robbed and murdered near the Slater and Morrill Shoe Factory in South Braintree, Massachusetts. They were carrying a $15,776 payroll. This kind of robbery was quite common in the years of hardship following the end of the war. This particular one, however, gained national attention because the two men who were eventually charged with the murders were known anarchists who had opposed the war, avoided military service and supported strikes. Their arrest also coincided with the high point of Palmer's onslaught on communists and anarchists.

The fairness of the trial of Sacco and Vanzetti was highly questionable. The judge, Webster Thayer, was a conservative Republican who was clearly prejudiced against the two men because they were Italian immigrants and political activists. He had already tried Vanzetti on a lesser crime of robbery at Bridgewater, not far from South Braintree. On that occasion, very few concessions had been made to the fact that Vanzetti himself, and also many of the Italian witnesses in the case could not speak very good English. When the Braintree murder trial was held, Thayer presided over that also, contrary to the usual practice. He made adverse comments about the men privately, confirming the suspicion that he was determined to see them convicted and executed. On flimsy, circumstantial evidence, the men were convicted and sentenced to death.

There followed a lengthy, seven-year struggle to prove the men's innocence and secure, at least, a re-trial. In spite of the fact that there was huge international support for the movement to free Sacco and Vanzetti, including that of many eminent literary figures of the day, the convictions and sentences were upheld. Sacco and Vanzetti went to the electric chair in 1927. News of the executions prompted riots in Paris, Geneva, Berlin, Bremen, Hamburg and Stuttgart. By 1927, they had become martyrs in a huge, left-wing, propaganda exercise. Their case had become an international ***cause célèbre*** which makes it difficult now to extricate the truth. The trial and the evidence surrounding it remain the subject of academic interest and debate today. There is still much speculation but the following points are significant.

- As Italian immigrants, they were the victims of racial discrimination. They were denied the rights to which they were entitled.
- They were also the victims of the political mood of the time. At the end of the day, this may be considered to be

KEY TERM

'Cause célèbre' This is a test case or issue that attracts a great deal of discussion across a very wide area. In the case of Sacco and Vanzetti, there is an implication that this was 'blown up' into something great in order to draw international attention, not just to the apparent unfairness of their trial, but also to the discrimination that they were experiencing because they were of Italian origin and because of their political views which, in a democracy, they had the right to hold.

the real significance of their case. Vanzetti had refused to take the stand to give evidence in his own defence at his trial in Bridgewater. He was afraid that his political activities would become a major focus and that, in reality, he would be tried for this rather than for robbery. In fact, he was sentenced to 15 years in the Charlestown State Penitentiary. This was an excessive punishment for robbery at this time.

- The evidence that condemned them to death was highly circumstantial. Their supporters claimed that vital evidence had been disregarded. Subsequent research has suggested that Sacco may well have been guilty but it remains a matter for debate.

However, the case of Sacco and Vanzetti is perhaps more important for what it tells us about American society at this time rather than for itself. The allegedly subversive activities of some immigrants and the economic effects of the 'open door' policy finally convinced politicians that immigration had to be controlled. This was backed up by pressure from the rural and small town communities that were overwhelmingly white Protestant American. President Coolidge undoubtedly spoke for them when he affirmed that, 'America must be kept American'.

WHY AND HOW WAS IMMIGRATION CONTROLLED?

In 1782, a Frenchman living in New York called Jean de Crèvecoeur, put forward the idea of the American 'melting pot'. According to him, men and women could arrive in America from any part of the world and, as a result of the experience of settlement, would receive a new nationality. They would be miraculously transformed into Americans. By the 1920s, it was abundantly clear that the 'melting pot' was not working. As thousands of immigrants poured into the USA during the nineteenth and early twentieth centuries, they not only brought with them the language, religion and culture of their origins, but they also clung to them. In the large cities, they congregated together in clearly identifiable districts – Italian, Polish, Greek, etc. There was, therefore, less possibility of these immigrants becoming assimilated into a recognisably American society. Even those who wanted assimilation found themselves rejected – the victims of intolerance and discrimination.

Between 1910 and 1920, 5,906,000 people emigrated to the USA. By the 1920s, immigrants were increasingly coming from Eastern Europe. The majority were unskilled and illiterate and consequently provided a huge pool of cheap labour. This was seen as threatening by many Americans, who felt that such cheap labour would undercut them in the labour market and would drive wages downwards. These immigrants became the main focus of the anti-immigration laws that were passed during the 1920s.

- The **Quota Act (1921)** reduced immigration from Eastern and Southern Europe drastically by establishing a quota system to regulate entry into the USA. The limit was fixed at 3 per cent per year of the foreign-born people of the same nationality who already lived in the USA in 1910. This applied to Italians and Poles (Catholics) and Russian Jews. There were, however, exceptions to this. Artists, actors, singers, lecturers, nurses and other professionals were allowed to enter irrespective of their origins. This made it clear that it was only the unskilled and illiterate Europeans that were unwelcome. Immigrants from French Canada and Latin America continued to pour into the USA. During the 1920s, the Mexican population of California rose from 90,000 to 360,000. By 1930, there were 2 million Mexicans in the USA.
- The **National Origins Act (1924)** took this a stage further by reducing once again the Eastern European quota to 2 per cent of the existing population from the same background. This Act also excluded Asian immigrants completely, which caused offence to the existing Chinese and Japanese communities in the USA. This is a very clear example of the institutional racism of the time. The Act remained in place until 1929 when a further immigration act was passed. This time figures were based on the immigrant population of the USA in 1920 when it came to establishing the quota based on 'national origins'.

Thus, immigration from Europe fell from 2,477,853 in the 1920s to 348,289 by the 1930s. The total number was reduced from 4,107,200 in the 1920s to 528,400 by the 1930s. This quota system continued to systematically reduce the numbers of people who were allowed into the USA until the 1960s.

Race riots and the re-emergence of the Ku Klux Klan. Immigration control can be seen as a passive expression of racism. The influx of foreigners combined with the existing racial tension between African-Americans and white Americans and led to more violent forms of protest. At a more extreme level, it led to the reappearance on the scene of the **Ku Klux Klan**.

Following the abolition of slavery, African-Americans had been guaranteed their civil rights by the 14th and 15th Amendments to the Constitution. The first of these gave them equality before the law and the second gave them the right to vote. Both of these had been disregarded. The southern states evaded the law and excluded blacks by imposing literacy and tax qualifications to obtain the vote. They continued to be persecuted throughout the last three decades of the nineteenth century. Almost 2,000 were killed in the south during this time by lynch mobs who hanged their victims and sometimes even burned them alive. The accelerated movement of African-Americans into the cities during the First World War years extended and increased these tensions. Their arrival resulted in serious housing shortages that adversely affected the white population. In parts of St Louis and Chicago, there was violence from time to time during 1917.

In July 1919 violence once again erupted in Chicago. A teenage black boy had accidentally drifted towards a 'whites only' beach on Lake Michigan. The people on the white beach began to stone him until he disappeared under the water. His death began a week of horrific violence that left 23 black people and 15 whites dead and 537 people wounded. This incident clearly indicates the depth and extent of the hatred and prejudice. There were similar, but smaller riots in at least 20 other cities where African-Americans were tending to cluster in ghetto areas.

KEY EVENT

Ku Klux Klan This was a secret organisation that was formed originally in Pulaski, Tennessee in 1865. It got its name from the Greek word *kuklos* which means a circle. It became particularly sinister after 1867 and directed its attention towards the former negro slaves who had gained their freedom. Its members particularly resented the political power that these black Americans had been given as they believed them to be innately inferior. They terrorised them, appearing at night in their white pointed hoods and robes, burning crosses to frighten their victims and finally flogging, mutilating or murdering them.

The Klan was forced to disband in the 1870s but re-formed in Georgia in 1915. This was a reaction to mass immigration. Its purpose was to maintain the supremacy of white Protestant Americans – Jews and Roman Catholics therefore were its victims also. Between 1919 and 1929, there were about 357 reported incidents of lynchings of black Americans, the highest numbers being in the period 1919–23. By 1929, corruption and violence brought severe criticism of the Klan and its numbers declined. It remained active through the Depression of the 1930s, however, when it attacked trade union activists.

A public lynching in Indiana, 1930. A crowd gathers to witness the killing of Tom Shipp and Abe Smith.

KEY THEME

The 14th Amendment
Much debate took place over the next 100 years as to what the Amendment actually meant. It took a long process of the 'nationalisation of the bill of rights' and the Civil Rights Campaign to achieve a situation that approximated to 'equality before the law'.

The Klan's activities. The cause of white Protestant American supremacy was taken up by the Ku Klux Klan. This formidable racist organisation had died out in the 1870s but re-formed in 1915 in Georgia. By 1920, a huge recruiting campaign was underway. This time the targets were Catholics and Jews as well as African-Americans, trade union members and anyone else that could be described as 'subversive'. Once again the hooded figures marched through the streets and the burning crosses appeared in the night. People were beaten and mutilated and generally intimidated by the Klan members. Once again, it spread terror wherever it went. By the mid-twenties, the Klan claimed a membership of between 2 and 5 millions. In some areas – Oklahoma and Oregon, for example – it had significant political power, having infiltrated the state assemblies. It certainly had the backing of many state officials until at least half way through the decade. From that point, its activities became the subject of enquiries and its membership began to decline.

CONCLUSION: THE HARLEM PHENOMENON

There is a fundamental irony that the most characteristic feature of the twenties in America – jazz – should have largely emerged from the place that perhaps best exemplifies the other side of the American dream – Harlem. This once highly fashionable corner of New York, populated by comfortably-off Americans had received the largest proportion of the migrant African-Americans coming from the South, gradually displacing its original inhabitants. By the 1920s, 87,417 blacks had arrived. Their numbers had been swelled by 45,000 Puerto Ricans and immigrants from the West Indies. The arrival of the latter increased racial tension. They were hard-working and entrepreneurial. As such they were resented by the rest of the ghetto population, leading to inter-racial violence that, by 1925, had risen by 60 per cent.

By the end of the 1920s, Harlem had become a slum. Its dense population (336 to the acre) led to a high demand for the available housing and this, in turn, to extortionately high rents and overcrowding. Standards of health and hygiene were very poor. Yet this ghetto area produced what came to be known as the 'Harlem Renaissance'. Poets, writers and musicians attracted the attention of white patrons who admired the talent of the few whilst ignoring the poverty and suffering of the masses. The ultimate irony is that when black jazz musicians entertained in the Harlem jazz clubs, negroes were banned from the audiences. Their only source of escape from relentless persecution and hardship was either through membership and support for the **National Association for the Advancement of Coloured People** (NAACP) or through the propaganda of **Marcus Garvey** and the concept of 'Black is beautiful'.

The glitz and glamour that attracted the attention of the rest of the world to the USA in the 1920s was superficial. For a short time, it hid the reality of the experience of the mass of the people, especially those who had gone there in the belief that life would be better, only to be disappointed. Freedom and equality were limited to the few. Soon the bubble would burst and, when that happened, its dark and empty heart would be fully revealed.

'A lad whipped with branches until his back was ribboned flesh: a negress beaten and left helpless to contract pneumonia from exposure and die; a white girl, divorcee, beaten into unconsciousness in her home; a naturalised foreigner flogged until his back was a pulp because he married an American woman; a negro lashed until he sold his land to a white man for a fraction of its value'.

A description of Ku Klux Klan activities from *Current History* written by R.A.Patton in 1929.

'Literally half the town belonged to the Klan when I was a boy. At its peak, which was from 1923 through 1925, the Nathan Hale Den had about 5,000 members out of an able bodied adult population of 10,000. With this strength the Klan was able to dominate local politics. It packed the police and state departments with its own people . . .'

From *Konklave in Kokommo*, written in 1949

KEY EVENTS

The **NAACP** was formed in an effort to encourage black Americans to stand up for themselves against white persecution and injustice. The organisation tried to combat discrimination and racism by using political and legal channels. It claimed to have a membership of about 91,000 in 1919.

Marcus Garvey and the Garvey Movement Garvey came originally from Jamaica. He formed the Universal Negro Improvement Association. He believed that all black people were one people and that Africa was their natural home. Africa still belonged to its European colonial rulers. He wanted it to be returned to its own black people so that they could return to Africa from wherever in the world they were living. Garvey also encouraged black people to be aware and proud of themselves. Their colour was not a symbol of inferiority but was one of strength and beauty. His plans failed but he did succeed in raising the self-esteem of many black Americans.

SUMMARY QUESTIONS

1 Is it realistic to talk about 'one American society' in the 1920s?

2 What evidence is there that America was intolerant and reactionary in the 1920s?

3 Does the case of Sacco and Vanzetti prove that the USA was racist in the twenties?

4 Why did the Ku Klux Klan re-form? How did the activities of the Klan affect Americans during this period?

5 Consider the image of America that was created by the prosperity described in the last chapter. How true was that image?

CHAPTER 6

US foreign policy in the 1920s

Isolationism. On 4 March 1921, Warren Harding was sworn in as President of the United States. In his inaugural speech he outlined his ideas on foreign policy. These were based partly on the view that if America's vital interests in the Americas or Pacific were at stake, then the USA would intervene. At the same time, his statement, 'we do not mean to be entangled', clearly indicates his apparent determination that there were to be no alliances and no commitments which would infringe America's sovereignty or limit its freedom of action. Consequently, whilst he was happy for America to be involved in negotiations on disarmament and in the setting up of the **International Court of Justice** to settle disputes between countries, he did not want the country to be involved in world affairs, particularly those of Europe.

KEY TERM

The **International Court of Justice** was established as a complementary institution to the League of Nations. The United States was more closely associated with the Court, which was intended to act as an arbitrator of international disputes, but it never became a member.

This Republican approach to foreign policy, described as isolationist (see Chapter 2), is the main reason why the United States refused to join the League of Nations, a position maintained throughout the period. This position clearly had the support of most Americans. After all, Harding was elected with a majority of 7 million votes. The extent to which American foreign policy during this period was in fact isolationist is one of the key issues for debate. The purpose of this chapter is to examine the main features of American foreign policy at this time and to suggest some tentative conclusions.

However, Harding must have realised himself that there was no going back to the 'old world order' of pre-1914 and that a new international system would have to be created, in which there would be an important role for American money and principles. He also realised that he himself was not wise enough to run American foreign policy. He was more than happy to leave this to Secretary of State, **Charles Evans Hughes** and Secretary of

KEY PERSON

Charles Evans Hughes was born in 1862. He became governor of New York State and an associate Supreme Court Judge. However, he gave up the latter to run as the Republican candidate in the presidential elections of 1916, a contest that he only narrowly lost to Woodrow Wilson. He became Secretary of State in Wilson's administration with responsibility for foreign affairs. Although he pretended to be an isolationist to please the electorate, Hughes did not believe that the USA could turn its back completely on the rest of the world.

KEY EVENT

Washington Treaty 1924
This was the outcome of the Washington Naval Conference of 1921–2. The conference met to consider naval armaments and Far-Eastern questions. Most of the leading powers, including France, Japan and Great Britain, attended. The key results of the conference were:

- the United States isolated Japan by pressurising Britain into ending the Anglo-Japanese Alliance
- Britain accepted naval parity with the United States. The ratio of ships to be built by each nation was 5 : 5 : 3 : 1.67 : 1.67 for Britain, the United States, Japan, France and Italy respectively.

Commerce, Herbert Hoover. It is their approach which helps us to understand US foreign policy at this time.

HUGHES AND HOOVER

Hughes and Hoover agreed that America could not be completely isolated from world affairs. For them, the question was about the nature and extent of its involvement. Hughes believed in the importance of American influence in the world (Pax Americana). Hoover however, stressed that although the United States should not retreat into isolation, it must remain free to act in its own interests. He also believed that individual enterprise, which was making America a wealthy nation, should be extended to other countries to make sure that they remained at peace. For Hoover, what had clearly worked in America would benefit the rest of the world. There were, therefore, two main planks to US foreign policy in the 1920s beginning with the presidency of Harding and continuing through those of his Republican successors (Coolidge 1923–9 and Hoover 1929–33):

- diplomatic involvement to maintain world peace
- economic involvement to support and encourage the development of the economies of European countries struggling in the aftermath of the First World War. This would, at the same time, provide opportunities for American investment and so would be to America's advantage.

Diplomatic involvement

The Washington Treaty System 1924. America's action here is a good example of its willingness to become involved in international affairs if the vital interests of the USA were at stake. In this case, the issue was disarmament. In 1921, the United States was becoming increasingly concerned about the growing naval power of Japan. The Americans were not only worried about the potential threat it represented in the Pacific but also the financial cost of trying to keep up with Japanese naval expansion. Late in 1921, Hughes invited the representatives of nine leading world powers to Washington to discuss this question and demanded

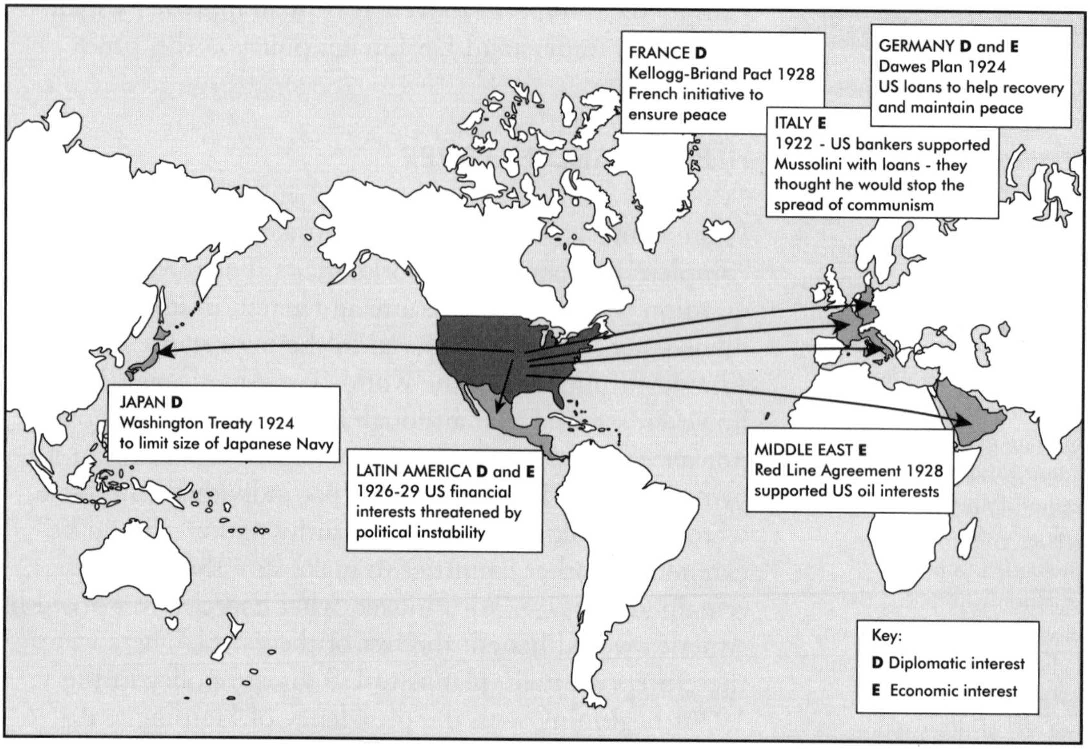

US interests worldwide in 1921–32.

significant proportionate reductions in naval power. The outcome was a triumph for Hughes. In spite of opposition from many countries, limits were finally agreed of 525,000 tons of shipping for Britain and America, 315,000 tons for Japan and 175,000 tons for France and Italy. The three treaties, which made up the **Washington System**, also brought to an end the **Anglo–Japanese Alliance of 1902** which could have resulted in Britain being dragged into a war in the Pacific against America.

The Kellogg–Briand Pact 1928. This was a result of an approach by **Briand**, the French foreign minister, to produce an agreement between the two countries that would outlaw war. **Kellogg**, the Secretary of State responsible for negotiating the agreement, suspected that this was really an attempt by France to draw America into a security system that would protect France from any future German aggression. As such, it was contrary to America's interests. However, it was an opportunity to promote peace. Consequently, Kellogg cleverly succeeded in watering down Briand's original initiative by drawing in

KEY EVENT

Anglo–Japanese Alliance 1902 This was signed in January 1902 because both countries were afraid of Russian expansion in the Far East. Japan feared that the Russians intended to take Korea whilst Britain was anxious to protect its imperial possessions in that region. It committed Britain to fight in support of Japan in the event of acts of war against it. By the 1920s, this alliance was still intact but in need of renewal.

most of the other world powers and producing a multilateral agreement that upheld the principle of world peace but that had no effective means of maintaining it.

KEY EVENT

The Kellogg–Briand Pact 1928 This is sometimes also known as the Treaty for the Renunciation of War. It was co-sponsored by the USA and France and was signed by 15 nations in Paris on 27 August 1928. By its terms, all the signatories agreed to reject war as the means to solve international disputes. It did, however, recognise the use of arms for self-defence. In practice, as a peace-keeping agreement it was useless as there were no provisions for dealing with countries that broke the agreement.

AMERICAN MONEY AND FINANCIAL CONSIDERATIONS

An important function of US foreign policy was to provide the necessary support for American financial investment leading to increased prosperity and a more peaceful world.

Post-war loans. In 1914, when the First World War began, the United States owed $3 billion to other world powers; when the war ended, the world owed the Americans $3 billion. The First World War began the process of turning the United States into a wealthy country and there was a growing realisation that this wealth could be used to create a more prosperous and thereby a more peaceful world. It was entirely in line with American thinking at this time that this new world order would be created by private banking. The role of the government would be to provide support by creating a set of rules for business to follow. There were to be, for instance, from 1921, no US loans to the Communist Soviet Union and there were to be severe restrictions on those to China. All war debts would have to be repaid but debt repayment could be used as a political threat to keep European powers in order if they proposed to do anything that would threaten American interests. When Britain, for example, attempted to force up the price of world rubber by restricting supplies from the Empire, the United States retaliated by threatening harsher repayment terms of war debts and a trade war.

KEY PERSON

Frank Billings Kellogg (1865–1937) was a US lawyer and politician. He was the US Ambassador to Great Britain between 1924 and 1925 and became Secretary of State in the Coolidge administration in 1925. He showed his skill in negotiating the Pact in such a way as to show America's support for world peace whilst avoiding any danger of active involvement in any future conflict. He was awarded the Nobel Prize in 1929 for his work to promote world peace.

Germany. Perhaps the best example of the way in which private banking helped the United States to achieve its foreign policy objectives can be found in Germany, which, in the early 1920s, represented a serious problem for America. Despite Harding's promise 'to seek no part in directing the destinies of the Old World', the creation of a stable, peaceful Germany was very much in American interests; economic and political instability increased the prospect of a Communist revolution. This dilemma reflects the limits to isolationism. Crisis talks in 1924 over German reparation payments led to the Dawes Plan, named after Charles Dawes, a Chicago banker who later became US Vice-President. The Dawes Plan provided for:

- a reduction in German reparations payments to $250 million
- a rise in those payments over the following five years as the German economy improved
- an immediate loan of 800 million marks to pump life into German production
- US bankers to provide half of the above amount, the remainder coming from foreign bankers.

Both bankers and private individuals rushed to loan money to Germany under the Dawes Plan. The problem was that the loans, originally regarded as a temporary boost to the German economy, became an important element of economic recovery and led to a dangerous reliance on American money.

The Young Plan of 1929, drawn up by Owen Young, the head of the General Electric Company, attempted to reduce the burden on Germany of reparation payments. The 1921 figure of $37 billion was reduced to $8 billion, payable over 58 years. But although this burden was being reduced, the United States continued to pump dollars into Germany at a growing rate. Between 1925 and 1929, $1.25 billion were loaned to the country as a whole plus the 800 million marks under the Dawes Plan for industrial regeneration. The dangers of this were realised when the US economy collapsed after 1929. US foreign investment ceased and loans was recalled. This was often not achieved and in 1931, Hoover placed a **moratorium** on war debts owed to the USA by foreign nations.

Other examples of US action

- Many American bankers and politicians approved of Mussolini's seizure of power in Italy. The political stability he offered could be followed by economic recovery based on American investment.

KEY PERSON

Aristide Briand (1862–1932) was a French socialist statesman. He had headed a coalition government in France during the First World War and afterwards favoured a conciliatory policy towards Germany. In 1921, he led the French delegation at the Washington Conference but was forced to resign shortly afterwards. In 1925, as foreign minister, he negotiated a security treaty with Germany and was awarded the Nobel Prize in 1926 for his efforts. In his second term as foreign minister (1926–32), he worked with Frank Billings Kellogg to negotiate the Kellogg–Briand Pact.

KEY THEME

American loans Not all loans to Germany were recalled after the Crash in 1929. One of the causal factors of the Depression was that US dollars invested in Germany began to flow back to the United States, attracted by and then further fuelling the boom on Wall Street. They partly caused the Crash.

KEY TERM

Moratorium means postponement. In this context it refers to the postponement of the repayment of war debts.

- The Red Line Agreement of 1928, negotiated by the US government, gave American oil companies access to Middle East oilfields.

Latin America. The Washington Treaty system had effectively created a situation where the military force of leading world powers would maintain order in their own regions. However much the USA wished to remain uninvolved in other parts of the world, there were no doubts in the minds of Americans that Latin America remained an area of major US influence. Of the 20 Latin American nations, all but six were influenced or controlled by US marines, US-backed politicians or both. US investments in Latin America between 1924 and 1929 more than doubled from $1.5 billion to $3.5 billion and, whilst there was considerable debate about whether this involvement was desirable, there was no lack of clarity about US policy – if American economic and political interests were threatened, then the United States would intervene. Thus, in 1926, Coolidge sent US marines into Nicaragua officially 'against Bolshevism', but, in reality, to protect President Diaz, a pro-American President, against anti-Diaz rebels. In 1929, Hoover sent arms into Mexico to back President Callas in a revolt against him mainly because he was a supporter of US oil interests in that country.

The United States did not therefore retreat from the world in the 1920s, it attempted to reorganise it. The foundations of the new structure were the Washington Treaty system and the US dollar. When the dollar collapsed after 1929, the new structure collapsed with it.

SUMMARY QUESTIONS

1 What evidence is there to suggest that the USA remained involved in the foreign policies of European states in the 1920s?

2 What were the limits of the USA's policy of isolation?

3 What role did Charles Evans Hughes play in foreign policy during the 1920s?

CHAPTER 7

America goes bust

On Thursday, 24 October 1929 share prices on the New York Stock Exchange on Wall Street fell faster and lower than ever before. By the end of the day, $4 billion had been wiped off the value of shares, 12 million shares changed hands and it took until 5 a.m. the next day to clear all the financial transactions that had taken place. Thus began the collapse of the New York stock market known as the Wall Street Crash. The crisis continued until 'Black Tuesday', 29 October, when share prices reached an all time low, falling by a further $14 billion.

Whilst the Wall Street Crash appeared to happen suddenly and unexpectedly, most historians agree that it was the result of serious underlying weaknesses in the American economy that had been ignored in the boom years of the 1920s. As well as examining the events of the Crash, this chapter looks at the underlying weaknesses in the American economy that caused it. It also examines how the Crash led to the Great Depression.

WHAT WERE THE UNDERLYING WEAKNESSES IN THE AMERICAN ECONOMY?

These were:

- unequal distribution of wealth
- farming problems
- trade problems
- stock market speculation and a general lack of economic regulation
- international debt and monetary matters and reparation payments.

Unequal distribution of wealth

Whilst American economic prosperity in the 1920s was fairly widespread, this wealth was unequally distributed. Sixty per cent of American families had an income of less than $2,000 per year, the minimum thought necessary for survival. There were, therefore, significant differences between the wealth of the rich, middle-class Americans and the rest who made up over 50 per cent of the population. The top 5 per cent of wealthy Americans earned one third of the total personal income. How had this come about? The high profits created by gains in productivity had been paid out to investors whilst the workers received comparatively small wage increases.

However, there were weaknesses in the American economy which were to have important consequences in the late 1920s and early 1930s.

- The American banking system was not integrated. This meant that bankers stood on their own. When the system of credit began to collapse, so individual banks which were overexposed collapsed.
- There was little regulation of the economy, which meant that excessive consumer borrowing and overspeculation were not dampened down.
- The international economy was still in the process of recovering from the impact of the war. However insular the American economy attempted to be, it was still affected by international trends. War debts, reparation repayments, the Depression and inflation in Germany (Europe's largest economy) did have an impact.

This concentration of potential buying power in the hands of a relatively small proportion of the population was to have seriously adverse effects on the domestic market for goods produced in American factories. Only the well-off could afford to buy. Consequently, as output increased, it was not matched by a proportionate increase in consumer buying power. The only way that the less wealthy could manage to buy cars, radios, telephones and other mass-produced goods was by taking advantage of credit facilities. In the process, large sections of the population borrowed far in excess of what they could realistically afford. Their ability to repay depended entirely on their wages. Eighty per cent of Americans had no savings at all at this time. Clearly, the Republican view, voiced by Coolidge, that the interests of business and those of the nation were the same was not correct. Whilst the American economy had prospered in the 1920s, the wealth was not equally distributed amongst those who created it.

Farming problems

Perhaps the unequal distribution of wealth is best illustrated in farming, where farmers in South Carolina were earning only about 10 per cent of those in California, as the table below shows.

Average monthly earnings of US workers in 1929

	$
Farmers in South Carolina	129
Town workers in South Carolina	412
Town workers in New York	881
Fruit farmers in California	1,246

The problems faced by American farmers such as over-production resulting from mechanisation, the creation of food surpluses and falling prices have already been mentioned in Chapter 3. The situation of many of them was made worse by their attempts to find a solution to these problems. In the 1920s, American farmers borrowed $2,000 million in mortgages. Whilst these mortgages were easy to obtain from banks willing to offer cheap loans, the farmers had virtually no chance of repaying them. Many were evicted and the workers they employed were sacked as a result.

Trade problems

The protectionist policy of the Republicans, characterised by high tariffs on imported goods, may have encouraged the consumer boom of the 1920s but it had dangerous side effects. The most important of these was retaliation by other world trading powers against US goods. This meant that American goods could not be cheaply exported to other countries. In the longer term, this adversely affected American manufacturing industry. Mass production meant that eventually output would be greater than the demand from the home market alone. As goods could not be sold abroad, this would lead to stock-piling at home and, consequently, to cutbacks in production. Eventually, this would hit employment, profits and, ultimately, the value of shares. Protection also meant that there were no export markets for surplus US food. As the 1920s progressed, the situation of the US farmers, in particular, worsened.

Stock market speculation

It is a popular but mistaken view that most Americans were playing the stock market in the 1920s. The number is thought to be about 1 million active speculators with many more having stocks and shares.

Whilst the actual number playing the markets is important, what is more significant is that many of the shares which were changing hands were doing so with borrowed money. The practice of buying shares on credit, 'on the margin', worked well as long as prices were rising, but when the price rise started to slow down or prices fell, problems began to set in. The way in which 75 per cent of the purchase price of shares could be borrowed encouraged excessive speculation, which kept prices artificially high. Easy credit policies on the part of the Federal Reserve Board plus tax cuts made more money available for speculation and resulted in a situation where, by the summer of 1929, loans from bankers had reached $6 billion. The complete lack of stock market regulation by government or any other agency encouraged more and more speculation. In 1925, the market value of all stocks stood at $27 billion but by October 1929, it had reached $87 billion.

Thus, William Payne was able to state in 1929 that, 'it had become so easy to make money on Wall Street that it had ceased to be a gamble'. Payne may have been correct in describing events up to that moment. What was to happen next was to prove him wrong, for:

> 'The Everest of the 1929 stock market was a mountain of credit on a molehill of actual money.'
>
> Paul Johnson, *History of the American People.*

1927: SIGNS OF A GATHERING STORM?

Perhaps with the advantage of hindsight, 1927 has now come to be regarded as the year in which storm clouds began to appear over the American economy – signs of troubles ahead, which were largely ignored.

This was the year in which:

- the sales of new motor cars went down
- fewer new houses were built
- the rise in industrial wages slowed down
- for American farmers, grappling with the effects of over-production, earnings decreased.

Whatever problems may have existed, these were not reflected on Wall Street, where speculators continued to indulge in the buying and selling of stocks and shares with the same fervour and enthusiasm as they had shown throughout the 1920s, despite an attempt by the Federal Reserve Board in July 1928 to dampen speculation by increasing interest rates. The Board also warned member banks not to lend money for stock market speculation – difficult to achieve when speculation yielded up to 20 per cent interest. Speculators were encouraged to continue in their activities in 1928 by what appeared to be signs of economic recovery, but the underlying trend was not good. In early 1929, the construction industry again experienced difficulties; in fact, between 1928 and 1929, there was a 25 per cent decline in house building. From 1927, throughout the US economy, unemployment had been rising and as the market became glutted with goods, prices fell. Thus, key indicators of economic activity such as employment, house building and price levels suggested that there were problems ahead.

Why then did Wall Street ignore them? Perhaps there was a blind confidence that nothing could go wrong and that what were temporary setbacks would soon be overcome. Whatever the thinking of those speculators involved, they were about to receive a great shock, the disastrous effects of which they could never have imagined.

STOCK RISE JUSTIFIED

3 July 1929

STOCK PRICES BREAK ON DARK PROPHECY

BABSON PREDICTS 'CRASH' IN STOCKS

6 September 1929

HAZLEWOOD WARNS BANKERS ON CREDIT

2 October 1929

STOCK PRICES WILL STAY AT HIGH LEVEL FOR YEARS TO COME, SAYS OHIO ECONOMIST

13 October 1929

FISHER SEES STOCKS PERMANENTLY HIGH

MITCHELL ASSERTS STOCKS ARE SOUND

16 October 1929

STOCKS GAIN SHARPLY BUT SLIP NEAR CLOSE

VIGOROUS RECOVERY MARKS MOST OF DAY AND MANY ISSUES SHOW NET ADVANCES

23 October 1929

THE WALL STREET CRASH: WHAT HAPPENED?

Although 24 October, known as 'Black Thursday', is widely accepted as the day that the Wall Street Crash began, the US stock market had, in fact, been behaving erratically throughout the mid and late summer of 1929. This is reflected in the headlines from *The New York Times* during that fateful summer. A headline on 3 July 1929 referred optimistically to the way in which returns on stock were in line with industrial activity, whilst, on 6 September, the same newspaper reported a drop in stock prices following predictions of a big slump.

By 2 October, warnings were sounded about the banks being over-generous in extending credit. By mid-October, however, *The New York Times* tried to reassure its readers generally, and the financial community in particular, that there was no cause for anxiety. Even as late as 23 October, the paper was reporting good news for shareholders.

But this level of optimism was misplaced. On Tuesday 24 October, panic set in and prices dropped alarmingly as more and more investors tried to sell their holdings. As soon as the New York Stock Exchange opened its doors at nine in the morning, stockbrokers started selling shares in large numbers. By midday, shares in even the largest companies had gone down dozens of points. By the end of the day, the Stock Exchange had lost $4 billion.

PRICES OF STOCKS CRASH IN HEAVY LIQUIDATION. TOTAL DROP OF BILLIONS

PAPER LOSS $4,000,000

2,600,000 SHARES SOLD IN THE FINAL HOUR IN RECORD DECLINE

MANY ACCOUNTS WIPED OUT

BUT NO BROKERAGE IS IN DIFFICULTIES AS MARGINS HAVE BEEN KEPT HIGH

Thursday, 24 October 1929

On Friday, 25 October, the paper was reporting that, although the situation was difficult, attempts were being made to stop the slide. These attempts continued on Saturday, 26 October and cost US bankers $40 billion.

WORST STOCK CRASH STEMMED BY BANKS

LEADERS CONFER, FIND CONDITIONS SOUND

Friday, 25 October 1929

CAUTION ADVISED BY STOCKBROKERS

Saturday, 26 October 1929

The final crash. Over the weekend of 26–27 October, the situation worsened. Many brokers who had sold shares 'on the margin' had borrowed money from banks to buy the shares in the first place. The banks were now demanding repayment of their money. To repay the banks, the brokers in their turn had to ask their customers for repayment of debts; the only way in which their customers could repay was to sell shares – at any price. Panic-stricken brokers and investors sold over 16 million shares in one day. The average price of shares fell 40 points and stock prices slumped by $14,000,000.

STOCK PRICES SLUMP $14,000,000 IN NATION-WIDE STAMPEDE TO UNLOAD

Tuesday, 29 October 1929

STOCKS COLLAPSE IN 16,410,030 – SHARE DAY

Wednesday, 30 October 1929

By early to mid November, there was a growing realisation amongst many Americans of what had actually happened during that last week in October. On Wall Street, millions of dollars had been wiped off the price of shares to the extent that, between 29 October and 13 November, over $30 billion disappeared from the value of the American economy. Many individual Americans suffered personal financial ruin. Whilst on 19 December *The New York Times* was proclaiming that 'The worst is over', there was also a recognition that the ease with which speculation had been made possible was the cause of the Crash.

How share prices dropped

	3 Sept. ($)	13 Nov. ($)
American Can	182	86
Anaconda Copper	162	70
Electric Bond and Share	204	50
General Electric	396	168
General Motors	182	36
New York Central Radio	505	28
United States Steel	279	150
Westinghouse E & M	313	102
Woolworth	251	52

It is an often-quoted statistic that, during the panic selling of shares on 24 October 1929, eleven ruined speculators committed suicide. A popular joke at the time runs like this, 'Did you hear about the fellow who engaged a hotel room and the clerk asked him whether he wanted it for sleeping or for jumping?' Whatever the accuracy of this figure, J.K. Galbraith in *The Great Crash* offers more detailed statistics in the table below.

Number of suicides per 100,000 of population 1926–33

Year	New York City	United States
1926	13.7	12.8
1927	15.7	13.3
1928	15.7	13.6
1929	17.0	14.0
1930	18.7	15.7
1931	19.7	16.8
1932	21.3	17.4
1933	18.5	15.9

THE WALL STREET CRASH AND THE GREAT DEPRESSION

What were the causes of the Depression?

The Wall Street Crash did not, by itself, cause the Great Depression. It was the 'trigger' for general economic collapse because it had a disastrous knock-on effect on the US banking and financial system. Consequently, the Crash had a tremendous impact on a large number of Americans.

The banks. It is important to understand that American banks were not part of a national organisation but often only existed locally or statewide. Many of these banks tended to be small, lacking the funds to meet unusual demands. In the 1920s, they used the money deposited by their customers and lent it out liberally to enable speculators to make quick profits for themselves on the stock market. The easy terms banks offered for loans encouraged the high level of borrowing that resulted in the wild speculation that led to the Crash of 1929.

The Crash resulted in many personal tragedies for small investors whose speculations, however understandable, had been foolish, However, of greater importance were the heavy losses sustained by many banks. For, in the immediate aftermath of the Crash, those who had savings deposited in the banks, rushed *en masse* to withdraw their savings, fearful that they, too, might be lost. Faced with this run on the bank and unable to recover loans from bankrupt speculators, many banks were forced to close their doors and declare themselves bankrupt (see the table below). Consequently, many savers also lost their money.

Bank failures

	1929	1930	1931
Number of banks closed	659	1,352	2,294
Total deposits lost	$200 m	$853 m	$1,700 m

Businesses collapse. The failure of the banking system ruined any chance of a speedy recovery from the Crash. Unable to obtain the necessary bank loans to tide them

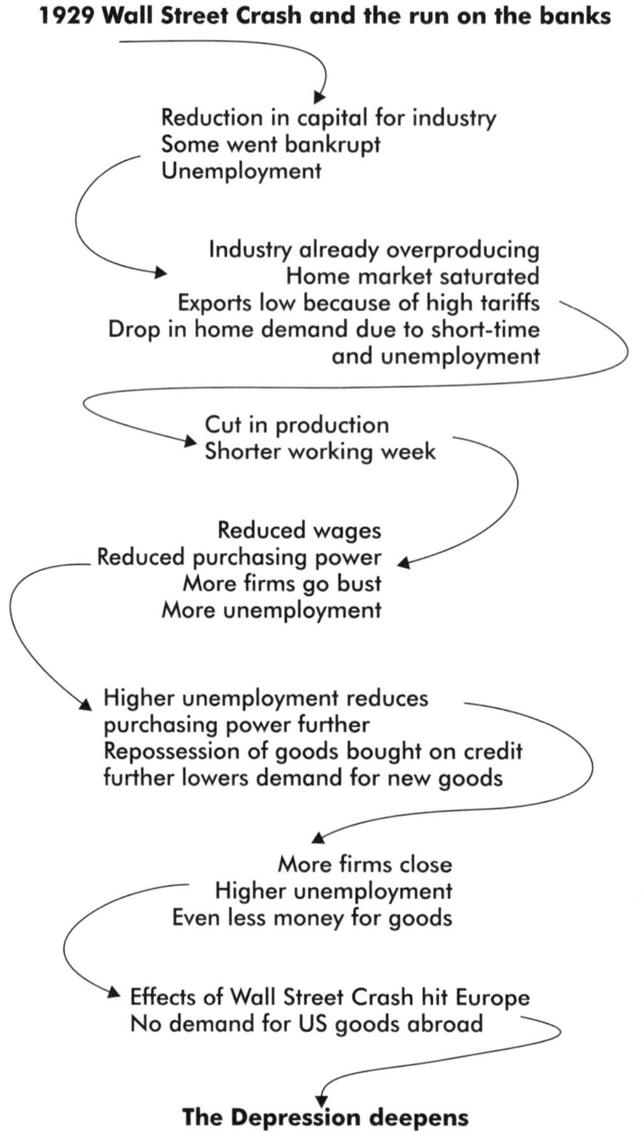

The link between the Wall Street Crash and the Great Depression.

over, many businesses were forced to close. Workers who may have saved for a 'rainy day' now found themselves with nothing and there was no 'dole' of any kind to help them through these difficult times. Thus, although it was not until 8 June 1932 that share prices hit their lowest level, the USA was already moving swiftly into a downward spiral of severe economic depression. Its industries were largely producing consumer goods, but workers without jobs bought less. The subsequent fall in demand led to a shorter working week and, ultimately, unemployment, further reducing consumer spending power. Repossession

Percentage of labour force unemployed 1926–33	
1926	1.8%
1927	3.3%
1928	4.2%
1929	3.2%
1930	8.7%
1931	15.9%
1932	23.6%
1933	24.9%

Farm income 1926–33 ($000,000s)	
1926	13,302
1929	13,938
1933	7,107

Farm wages (per day)	
1926	$2.40
1929	$2.30
1933	$1.15

Industrial production (baseline 100)	
August 1929	114
March 1933	54

Average weekly earnings ($)	
1929	25
1932	17

of goods bought on credit also reduced the demand for further production and entrepreneurs found it increasingly difficult to raise the money needed to run their companies. Consequently, as purchasing power fell dramatically and companies were forced into closure, the US economy was rapidly squeezed to half the size it was prior to the Wall Street Crash.

America had faced economic depressions before in 1873, 1893, 1904, 1907 and 1921. The Great Depression that hit the USA in 1929 was different from these in its length and in the extent of the poverty that it brought to the American people.

The main features of the Great Depression

- Gross National Product (i.e. the value of goods produced plus income from abroad) slumped from $104 billion to $59 billion in 1932.
- Farm prices fell by 60 per cent between 1929 and 1932.
- Wheat prices plunged from $1.04 per bushel to 51 cents.
- 5,500 banks had closed their doors by 1933.
- 20,000 companies went bankrupt.
- Unemployment soared from 3 per cent in 1929 to 25 per cent in 1933. These figures represent a daily increase of 12,000 reaching a total of 13 million by 1933. Many others who were in work were facing cuts in wages and a reduction in working hours.
- National income fell by half from $80 billion in 1929 to $40 billion in 1932.

The human cost

Millions of Americans suffered during the Great Depression, none more so than the farmers. Facing a massive fall in food prices, they reduced production, halving it in the period from 1929 to 1932. Thousands of American farmers lost their livelihoods and their farms. Industries connected with farming also went bankrupt.

Unemployment and its consequences

Unemployment made individuals and families destitute (see the tables). This was particularly acute in the industrial cities such as Chicago where there was a 40 per cent rate of

The unemployed, New York, 1932.

unemployment. Here a local relief organisation gave the most desperate a meagre $2.40 per week for an adult and $1.50 for a child (a dozen eggs cost 28 cents). Immigrant communities, black and Mexican Americans were particularly badly affected.

- Homelessness was a massive problem. Unable to pay rents, thousands of families were forced to take shelter in makeshift 'homes'. These 'shanty towns' grew up in the cities and became known, sarcastically, as 'Hoovervilles' after President Hoover who seemed to be doing very little to deal with the crisis.
- Ill health was an inevitable long-term consequence of this experience – inadequate medical care, poor diet and even malnutrition became commonplace. The drop-out rate in high schools escalated. By 1933, approximately 300,000 children were out of school.
- The suicide rate had risen and families were breaking up under the pressure of trying to survive.
- Finally, deprived of their pensions and robbed of their savings, older adults had very little to live on or to look forward to.

The impact abroad

KEY THEME

Reparations The collapse in the repayment of reparations was to have an important impact on the US economy. US dollars were withdrawn from Germany, Germany was thus unable to pay reparations to Britain and France, Britain and France were as a result unable to repay war debts to the United States.

The Wall Street Crash and the subsequent Depression sent shock waves throughout the whole world economy. American banks had lent money to aid post-war recovery and development in many countries, Germany being a prime example. When the US economy collapsed, the first reaction of many American bankers was to call in these loans to keep themselves afloat. US money was being used to finance economic development and the ability of countries to repay the loans depended to a large extent on the success of these enterprises. The sudden loss of financial support from America led to economic collapse abroad. As many world countries also sank into depression, they could not repay the loans. Consequently, US banks were unable to recoup the money they had loaned to aid their own recovery.

HERBERT HOOVER AND THE GREAT DEPRESSION

By the beginning of 1932, Herbert Hoover, US President since March 1929, had come to realise that his efforts so far to combat the effects of the Great Depression had failed. Although a follower of Republican ideals and principles, Hoover had rejected the view of many in his party that the Crash and subsequent Depression were part of a natural economic cycle, the terrible effects of which would simply have to be borne until better times arrived. To ease the suffering faced by many Americans, Hoover pinned his hopes between 1929 and 1932 on the '**voluntarist**' approach.

KEY TERM

'Voluntarism' The term describes Hoover's efforts to persuade businesses to take action to deal with the economic crisis without the government passing laws to force them to act. For example, he wanted them to agree not to cut production or lay off workers.

'Voluntarism' in action

- Business leaders were summoned to the White House and pledged themselves there to maintain wages and employment. This was essential to overcome the Depression.
- Seeing unemployment as a local issue, Hoover called on municipal and state governments to create public works projects.
- In October 1930, he established the Emergency Committee for Employment to co-ordinate voluntary relief agencies.
- In 1931, he persuaded the nation's largest bankers to establish the National Credit Corporation to lend money to smaller banks to make loans to businesses.
- He cut taxes at home. This meant that a family man with an income of $4,000 had his tax cut by two thirds.
- He increased government spending to $2.2 billion in 1931.

The failure of 'voluntarism'. Hoover's voluntarist strategy failed dismally. Unemployment continued to rise. In 1931, US Steel, General Motors and other large business corporations broke their pledges and cut wages. Other support for the unemployed failed. Public charities and local welfare agencies faltered. In Philadelphia, for example, as the jobless total rose to 300,000, the city actually cut relief payments to $4.23 per family per week and in June 1932 suspended them altogether. By this time many Americans were becoming disillusioned with

Hoover and the Republicans. As early as November 1930, the Republicans had not only lost eight Senate seats but also control of the House of Representatives.

Early in 1932, with an election looming and voluntarism having so obviously failed to meet the crisis, Hoover changed his tactics. More decisive intervention was clearly required. In January, Congress provided $2 billion in funding a new agency, the Reconstruction Finance Corporation (RFC), to make loans to large economic organisations such as railroads and insurance companies. In February, Hoover signed the Glass-Steagall Act, allocating $750 million of government gold reserves for loans to private businesses. In July, he signed legislation authorising the RFC to give $2 billion to state and local governments for **public works** programmes.

KEY TERM

Public works These were programmes funded from taxation with the purpose of getting people back to work, for example road building. Once in work, they would have money to spend on manufactured goods and this in turn would stimulate industrial growth.

The failure of intervention. Whether these initiatives represented a real change both in thinking and policy on the part of Hoover is a matter for debate. What is more important is that they failed to stop the rapid rise in unemployment and to help the millions of Americans who were suffering as a result. Why did they fail? The popular view is that the measures taken by Hoover were 'too little, too late' and came nowhere near to tackling the enormous problems which the American economy faced. There is some truth in this view but it does not go far enough.

The reality is that, for the measures to succeed or even to be implemented, Hoover needed the support and co-operation of a number of bodies and agencies away from Washington. If the American economy was going to recover:

- state governments would need to keep up their spending to support the economy at a local level
- farmers would need to cut their production
- employers would need to keep their workers on the payroll
- the banking system would need to be reformed and general economic regulation was needed.

Hoover also needed to be sure that financiers would invest government money in private enterprises and that bankers would give their customers credit to revive their damaged businesses. None of these needs was met because the American people, as a nation, had lost confidence in their economy, in themselves and in the ability of Republican politicians to lead them out of the Depression.

The President's Emergency Committee for Employment. This provides a good illustration of the difficulties in which Hoover found himself. Its main concern was with the provision of poor relief for the millions of unemployed. In tune with the thinking of the President, it saw no role for federal (central) government, but spent much of its time appealing to state and local agencies to raise money for relief from their own communities. Even if the Republicans had been advocates of federal action, it is difficult to envisage how a national system of relief could have operated in a country where there was no precedent for this kind of social spending on the part of the government. After all, there was no national education system, no national police force and, in 1929, federal spending was only 2.5 per cent of **GNP**.

Action to deal with the nation's economic problems was further hindered by the deeply held Republican belief in the importance of the balanced budget, the idea that state and national governments should not spend more than they receive in income. This view, coupled with their strong commitment to low taxes, left Hoover and the Republicans unable to do very much either to help those suffering the effects of the slump or to put the economy back on the road to prosperity.

Thus, by early 1932, the American public viewed Hoover as a president who appeared not to care about their plight and the difficulties they were experiencing. His belief in 'self-help' may have worked in the rural, farming communities that were once the main feature of American society, but it was no longer applicable in a country that was now increasingly urban and industrial. Although Hoover was elected unopposed as Republican candidate in the forthcoming presidential election, even his most ardent supporters must have been gloomy about his prospects of success. In the summer of 1932, these prospects worsened

KEY TERM

Gross National Product (GNP) This is the total income of a country made up of production at home and income from trade and investments abroad.

KEY THEME

Economic reform The alternative for Hoover was to reform using the ideas of British economist J. M. Keynes. He believed that governments could help their economies to recover by investing in schemes which would create jobs. The wages for these jobs would stimulate demand in the economy.

as bitterness and resentment grew among the unemployed and in some instances, erupted into violence.

MOUNTING DISCONTENT

The bonus marchers. By the spring of 1932, anger and resentment were mounting among the unemployed and, in some instances, threatening to turn into violence. Those evicted for non-payment of rent, and without enough food for their families, threatened to take food from stores unless they were given it at no cost. The bread lines, made up of unemployed Americans who had lost everything, became places of discontent where those preaching violence received a sympathetic hearing.

In the late spring, veterans of the First World War, who were without work and whose families were hungry as a

Bonus marchers and police fight in the Hooverville in Washington, summer 1932.

result, began a march on Washington demanding the payment of a veterans' bonus approved by Congress in 1924 but to be paid 20 years afterwards. The sum voted by Congress was $3,500,000,000 and it is easy to understand why, in 1931, Congress received a proposal to pay the bonus immediately. Clearly, the money would provide an important lifeline for those veterans and their families who were suffering so much. Thus, the purpose of the 20,000 marchers was to lobby Congress to approve the proposal. In mid-June, Congress rejected it. In protest, several thousand 'bonus marchers' and their families stayed on and built settlements of tents and packing crates on Anacosta Flats in the south-western part of Washington DC, threatening to stay there until their demands were met.

The Anacosta Flats incident. The extent to which the 'bonus marchers' were part of a communist conspiracy to overthrow the Republican government has been overplayed by its supporters. Certainly, there were plenty of agitators attempting to whip up the veterans into more violence but whether this justified the action taken is doubtful.

On 28 July, Hoover, having ordered the veterans to be confined to the Flats, now approved a plan to evict them. Army Chief of Staff, General Douglas MacArthur and his aide, Major Dwight D. Eisenhower were in command of the operation, but Major George Patton was the cavalry commander who led the attack. One thousand armed soldiers, equipped with tear gas, tanks and machine guns, drove the veterans from the camp and burned it to the ground. Two veterans were killed and as many as a thousand were injured.

What is the significance of this incident? Both the veterans and the army used a great deal of propaganda to support their respective positions and stories of soldiers bayoneting children were contrasted with government warnings of an impending communist revolution. What is really important about this whole episode is that it cast Hoover in a very bad light. The idea of an American president ordering troops into action against fellow Americans, particularly those who had risked their lives in war, shocked millions. Hoover was seen as cruel and insensitive to the distress which so many were experiencing, whilst the desperate plight of the marchers was a terrible comment on the depths into which the American economy had sunk. On 8 November, presidential election day, American voters would have the opportunity to pronounce their verdict on Hoover's presidency. The terrible events on Anacosta Flats in July only served to damage further his failing fortunes.

CONCLUSION

Whilst Hoover was returned unopposed as Republican candidate for the presidency, party members must have realised that, in the forthcoming election, they faced defeat. Although they praised his efforts to deal with the effects of the Depression, they knew that he had become widely unpopular. The mocking use of the term 'Hoovervilles', for example, was a reflection of this. They must also have recognised that election defeat would not only bring to an end the period of their ascendancy but also the political career of probably the most brilliant Republican politician of the century so far. Hoover was a great humanitarian Quaker who was just overwhelmed by the Depression. He was a pragmatic politician, but his pragmatism did not stretch to the kind of radical measures necessary to halt the onward march of the Depression.

SUMMARY QUESTIONS

1 What were the weaknesses in the American economy in the 1920s?

2 What problems faced American farmers in this period?

3 What were the warning signs that the economy was in danger?

4 Describe the sequence of events that led to the Wall Street Crash.

AS SECTION: THE UNITED STATES OF AMERICA: 1933–45

INTRODUCTION

The Great Depression was a watershed in the political, social and economic life of the United States. In 1932 the American electorate finally lost confidence in the Republicans and voted overwhelmingly for the former Democratic Governor of New York State, Franklin Delano Roosevelt for President. Using cleverly focused rhetoric, he was able to convince the people that the Depression could be defeated, that they had 'nothing to fear but fear itself'. He promised them a 'new deal' that would put them back on the road to prosperity and they believed him.

Roosevelt was elected by a large majority and then re-elected on three further occasions to become the first president to hold office four times in succession. During this time, he asked for and received the power to take action to help Americans find work and to restore prosperity. He reacted to the weaknesses in the economic infrastructure (the banking system, for example) and took emergency action to restore confidence in financial organisations in order to attract investment. He set up a number of agencies that came to be known as the 'Alphabet Agencies' to help vulnerable sectors such as agriculture, and provide short-term employment. In this way, he hoped to stimulate consumer demand and consequently revive manufacturing industry.

KEY TERM

Special powers In his presidential inauguration speech, Roosevelt asked for powers equal to those a president would have in times of war. These powers would allow decisions to be made without as much scrutiny from Congress.

His actions were controversial. He frightened some right-wing politicians who saw his assumption of **special powers** as an attack on democracy. He alarmed businessmen who considered his policies to be hostile towards them. When he attempted to introduce more lasting social reform after 1935, he was accused of being a socialist and anti-capitalist. Nevertheless, he was supported by many ordinary Americans. In spite of the fact that he was ultimately drawn into war against Hitler and Japan and that many of his schemes were only marginally successful, a large percentage of the electorate still believed in him. He left a political and economic system in the USA that would never be the same again.

In this part of the book, the character, actions and impact of Roosevelt are described, and students can use the information to arrive at their own conclusions.

- **The Great Depression and its impact.** It is important to set the arrival of Roosevelt onto the political scene against the background of the Depression. The seriousness of this situation helps to explain and justify the actions that Roosevelt took.
- **The New Deal.** Roosevelt was given unprecedented powers by Congress to implement an emergency programme of measures to stimulate the US economy and to alleviate the suffering caused by the Depression. Some of these were job-creation schemes. To carry out his plans, Roosevelt appointed talented and committed individuals including the first female Secretary of Labor, Frances Perkins.
- **Opposition to the New Deal.** This was partially directed at Roosevelt himself. Coming as he did from a wealthy background, businessmen and the better off who found themselves paying high taxes to finance his schemes believed that he had betrayed his own class. The Supreme Court also struck down some of his reforms as unconstitutional.
- **The struggle to preserve peace and neutrality.** Roosevelt was a cautious internationalist in politics. In economics he turned away from the international economy at the London World Economic Conference in 1933 in favour of concentrating on domestic economic reform. However, Secretary of State Cordell Hull began a modest reorientation back to economic internationalism by sponsoring the 1934 Reciprocal Trade Relations Act through Congress which delegated powers to the Executive (see page 6) to negotiate reciprocal tariff reductions.

- **The War and the legacy of the New Deal.** America's involvement in the Second World War transformed Roosevelt from a national to a world leader. He did not survive the war to continue his domestic programmes in the post-war period. His domestic achievements must, therefore, be judged largely by what had been achieved by 1941. Roosevelt's legacy is not so much what he achieved in real terms but in the changes that he brought about in the responsibilities of government and in the expectations that the American people had of their President. There were other areas of real impact, including:
  - economic regulation at a national/federal level;
  - labour and welfare reforms;
  - agricultural reforms;
  - the creation of a modern bureaucracy.

CHAPTER 8

Franklin Roosevelt and the launch of the New Deal

Franklin Delano Roosevelt is probably the best-known American president of the twentieth century. He was inaugurated in March 1933, re-elected for three more terms and died in office in April 1945, shortly before the surrender of Germany in the Second World War. During his terms as president, Roosevelt attempted to bring an end to the Great Depression. This he achieved to an extent. When the Second World War began, he initially attempted to keep America out of the conflict. However, after the Japanese attack on Pearl Harbor and the German declaration of war shortly afterwards, Roosevelt had no alternative but to take his country into the war. Subsequently, he came to be regarded by many as a great wartime leader.

However, Roosevelt was not universally popular. His policies at home were criticised by the Republicans as a waste of public money and an attack on individual liberty, whilst those on the **political left** attacked his policies for not doing enough to tackle the real problems facing the American people. Nevertheless, he was elected in 1932, and re-elected in 1936 and 1944, and on each occasion with a comfortable majority. This was proof of his popularity with the millions of ordinary Americans who had suffered most during the Great Depression.

KEY TERM

Political left Politicians who wanted substantial reform, particularly social and economic reform.

Presidential election results 1932–44

Year	Republican candidate	Votes for Republican	Votes for Roosevelt
1932	Herbert Hoover	15,759,266	22,815,785
1936	Alfred Landon	16,697,583	24,751,597
1940	Wendell Wilkie	22,304,755	27,243,466
1944	Thomas Dewey	22,006,278	25,602,505

What sort of a politician was Roosevelt? What were his aims and ideals and how were they formed? An examination of his early life and formative years will give some help in answering these questions.

FRANKLIN DELANO ROOSEVELT

His early life

Franklin Roosevelt was born on 30 January 1882, at the family estate in Hyde Park, New York. The Roosevelts were of Dutch origin and had already produced one US president, Theodore, a Republican who was President from 1901 to 1909. They were a wealthy family and Franklin was brought up in a comfortable and loving home. Amongst other things, his early educational experiences instilled in him the idea that those from rich, privileged backgrounds had a duty to help those who were less fortunate. After passing the New York State bar examination, he became a lawyer on Wall Street. By 1910 however, he was bored and restless and looking for a change of direction. Consequently, he turned to politics.

Roosevelt's early political career

In 1910, he was elected to the New York State Senate representing the area around Hyde Park. He found politics much more exciting than the law. Following a broadly progressive approach, Roosevelt supported reform, particularly women's suffrage and laws setting a maximum working week of 54 hours for boys between 16 and 21 years old. In 1912, he supported Woodrow Wilson for the Democratic presidential nomination.

Assistant Secretary to the Navy. Following his election, Wilson rewarded Roosevelt for his loyalty by giving him the position of Assistant Secretary to the Navy, which he held until 1920. Roosevelt was highly effective in running the navy during the First World War. He supported America's involvement in the war and believed in the USA maintaining a large navy. In 1918, he travelled to the Western Front. Following his belief in honest government, he opposed price-fixing by those bidding for defence

KEY PERSON

Franklin D. Roosevelt 1882–1945

Education. He was educated by governesses until 1896 when he went to Groton School, Massachusetts. There he was instilled with Christian values and a sense of the importance of public service. His academic record was not particularly distinguished. Between 1900 and 1904, he was a student at Harvard University, graduating with a BA degree in law. Until 1907, he went to law school at Columbia.

Family. Whilst at Harvard, he met and, in 1905, married Eleanor Roosevelt, a distant cousin. They had six children, one of whom died in infancy. Eleanor was a great support to him throughout his political career.

Illness. In August 1921, tragedy struck when Roosevelt contracted polio, a life-threatening illness at that time. Although he survived and fought back into active politics, he remained badly paralysed and largely confined to a wheelchair. He suffered great pain and discomfort for the rest of his life.

contracts and showed great political skill in dealing with admirals, employers and trade unions.

Vice-presidential candidate. So effective was his work with the US Navy that in 1920 he was chosen by the Democrats to run for the vice-presidency with James Cox, the presidential candidate. Unfortunately, the Democrats' beliefs in progressive ideals and their support for the League of Nations were no longer popular with the voters, and Cox and Roosevelt were well beaten by the Republicans, Harding and Coolidge. Roosevelt decided to leave politics and formed a law firm in New York City.

Governor of New York State. By 1924, Roosevelt was again active in the Democratic Party, a party now in the political wilderness with the Republicans in power. In 1928, with Hoover and the Republicans sweeping to victory, Roosevelt went completely against this trend by being elected Governor of New York State. Here he laid the foundations for his future presidential policies. He now had the opportunity to try out some of his progressive ideas.

- Schemes for reforestation were initiated.
- Working hours for women and children were regulated.
- Old-age pensions were introduced throughout the state.
- In 1931, when the Depression was serious, Roosevelt became the first governor to set up an effective system of relief across the state. It was directed by Harry Hopkins, later to be his closest adviser in Washington.

Into his administration, he drew talented politicians like James Farley and Frances Perkins to carry his progressive schemes forward. In a series of 'fireside chats' over the radio, Roosevelt was able to use the new medium to explain his policies to the electors. In 1930, they responded by re-electing him by 750,000 votes, the largest margin in the history of the state of New York.

THE PRESIDENTIAL ELECTION OF 1932

In June 1932, when the Democrats met in Chicago to select a candidate to fight the forthcoming presidential

Roosevelt giving one of his 'fireside chats' on the radio in 1933.

election, Roosevelt stood out as the strongest contender. This was largely because the policies he introduced as Governor of New York State had helped to lessen the problems caused by the Depression there, even if they had not always solved them. Even so, it took four ballots before he finally gained the nomination and then only after his aide James Farley had made a deal with his main opponent, John Garner. As a result of this deal, Garner accepted the nomination for the vice-presidency.

The election campaign. In the election campaign, Roosevelt did not always appear to have clearly thought out how he was going to lead America out of the Depression.

- Certainly, he promised to increase relief for those suffering hardship and to offer work creation programmes, but without much idea of how they were to be funded.
- He was in favour of conservation, old-age pensions, unemployment insurance and the repeal of prohibition.
- In some speeches, he attacked Hoover for spending too much but, in others, he promised to spend more money himself on relief.
- In a speech at Pittsburgh in October 1932, he spoke in favour of reducing federal government spending and

balancing the budget, but seemed uncertain about whether taxes would have to be raised.

Why was Roosevelt successful? In view of the comment from Carey McWilliams and others like it, we may well wonder how Roosevelt came to be elected at all. A number of reasons can be suggested:

- The Depression was so bad that whoever stood against Hoover would have been elected. Hoover was not responsible for the Crash and the Depression that followed, but someone had to take the blame.
- Unlike Hoover, Roosevelt was ready to experiment with policies to bring down unemployment and to get the American economy moving again. His period as Governor of New York State proves this and makes his outlook different to many Republicans who believed that the Depression was part of a natural cycle which must be allowed to take its course.
- Roosevelt, unlike Hoover, projected confidence and optimism that things certainly could get better. His 'fireside chats', talking directly to ordinary Americans, were very popular and millions were made to feel that he had compassion for them and that he knew they wanted change.
- His promise to end Prohibition made him popular, whereas the Republicans called for it to continue.

Whatever the reasons for his election in 1932, Roosevelt gained an impressive victory. He captured 22,815,785 votes compared with 15,759,266 for Hoover and took the **Electoral College** by 472 to 59. In both houses of Congress, the Democrats achieved large majorities, ensuring that any measures introduced by Roosevelt to combat unemployment would easily become law.

THE 'LAME DUCK' MONTHS

Because it was common practice that a newly elected president must wait four months before taking office, Hoover continued to govern even though the electors had voted him out. For this reason, the four months from the

'My first reaction to Roosevelt was very adverse. I remember particularly my great disappointment in a 1932 speech he made at the Hollywood Bowl . . . He didn't have a ghost of an idea, really, on what the Depression was all about. He was going to balance his budget, he was going to do all sorts of things, unrelated to the problems he had to face . . . He had no program. He was pressured into doing the fine things he did.'

Carey McWilliams, a magazine editor, speaking in an interview.

KEY TERM

Electoral College This is the system, embodied in the American Constitution, whereby the American people are involved in the election of their President and Vice-President. They vote for members of an electoral college depending on their own political views. Each state has its own electoral college made up of individuals nominated by the political parties – mainly the Democrats and Republicans. Once elected, the college members meet to cast their votes for the candidates for the two offices. The successful candidate will usually have received the votes of the majority of members of the electoral college.

election until Roosevelt was inaugurated on 4 March 1933, are known as the 'lame duck' months.

This period was, however, one of considerable activity, as Hoover tried desperately to revive the economy and to stop the rise in unemployment. His announcement in December that he would cut taxes was followed by his promise to:

- reduce government spending by $800 million
- reorganise the banking system
- reduce spending on weapons
- continue to make available loans for businesses through the Reconstruction Finance Corporation.

All these policies failed. During the four months, unemployment reached 15 million and those working found their wages cut. Strikes spread and in many cities, as companies went bankrupt, buses and trains stopped running and gas and electricity supplies were cut off. The worst aspect was the banking crisis.

- In February 1933, banks throughout the country started to close, simply because so many customers were taking out savings from their accounts that the banks did not have enough cash to pay them all. Whenever this occurred, panic spread as other savers rushed to

Key events:

1932	Oct.	Roosevelt became President	The 'lame duck' months
1933	Feb.	Banking crisis	
	4 Mar.	Roosevelt inaugurated	
	9 Mar.	Emergency Banking Act	'The Hundred Days'
	15 Mar.	Economy Act	
	20 Mar.	Beer Act	
	31 Mar.	Civilian Conservation Corps	
	12 May	Federal Emergency Relief Administration	
		Agricultural Adjustment Administration	
	18 May	Tennessee Valley Authority	
	16 Jun.	Public Works Administration	
		National Recovery Administration	

withdraw money from their banks before the same happened to them.

- By the beginning of March 1933, every bank in America was closed.

This 'run on the banks' illustrates the complete lack of confidence of millions of Americans in their economy and in Hoover's ability to do anything to improve the situation. This is the reason why his policies failed and explains why, in early March, both the political and economic situation in America had reached such a desperate point.

Inauguration. On 4 March 1933, Franklin Roosevelt was sworn in as US President. His speech on this occasion makes interesting reading. It contains a number of dramatic phrases, many of which have become well known, for example, 'Let me first assert my firm belief that the only thing we have to fear is fear itself'. He began by painting a grim picture of the state of the country at that moment with high unemployment and widespread poverty. But the people, he said, were not to blame. They had been badly led and the economy had been mismanaged by those without vision who had been following their own financial interests. Therefore, according to Roosevelt, a moral crusade had to be launched to revive the nation. But it had to be a crusade based on action to put people to work, action in which the federal government had a part to play.

Emergency power. In parts, the speech sounded more like a 'call to arms'. There were very good reasons why it did. Roosevelt wanted to convey the idea to those listening that America was at war against unemployment and the poverty that it caused. If victory were to be achieved, then his leadership had to be supported by 'the great army of our people'. There was another reason why Roosevelt used the idea of America being 'at war'. During the First World War, the Trading with the Enemy Act was passed which gave President Wilson extraordinary power to take action without asking for congressional ratification. The aim of this Act was to allow the President to act quickly in an emergency. The Act was not cancelled at the end of the war and Roosevelt stated in his speech that he intended to use it to deal with the crisis facing the nation. On 6 March, two days after his inauguration, he ordered all the banks to stay closed so that a strategy to salvage the situation could be developed. While he may have been attacked by his opponents for abusing his powers, he nevertheless proved his determination to tackle the great problems facing the country at this time.

THE HUNDRED DAYS

The period from 4 March until 16 June 1933, is known as 'The Hundred Days'. During this time, Roosevelt used all his powers under the Trading with the Enemy Act to deal with the most dangerous crises facing the nation, the most serious being the banking crisis.

The banks and banking. On his second day in office, he ordered all banks to close. On 9 March, Congress accepted his request and passed an **Emergency Banking Act**. The accounts of all banks in the country were to be inspected and only those with properly managed accounts and plenty of cash would be allowed to reopen. On 12 March, Roosevelt spoke directly to the American people in the first of his 'fireside chats' as President. He assured them that the banks were now safe and that there was no longer any reason for withdrawing money. They believed him. When the banks reopened the following week, more money was deposited than had previously been withdrawn. Because Roosevelt was new and willing to be proactive in trying to tackle the nation's problems, the Americans were prepared to give him a chance and put their trust in him; the banking crisis was over.

Pay cuts. The determination to act, which Roosevelt displayed over the banking crisis, was illustrated further on 15 March with the passing of an **Economy Act**. The pay of all those working for the government and the armed forces was cut by 15 per cent, whilst the budgets of all government departments were cut by 25 per cent. Nearly $1 billion were saved and available for spending in other areas.

KEY THEME

Consumer demand
Although cutting wages does not seem to be the best way to promote consumer demand, Roosevelt's administration hoped that by lowering wages it would enable the government to redistribute the money in such a way that it increased net consumer demand.

The end of Prohibition. The Economy Act made Roosevelt popular, but nowhere near as popular as he was on 20 March with the passing of the **Beer Act**. The manufacture and sale of beer was legal again and Prohibition was ended. Many new jobs would now be created and the government would gain money from the tax on beer.

Roosevelt had begun his presidency in spectacular style and had shown himself ready to act decisively to deal with the major problems facing the nation at this time.

THE NEW DEAL

Shortly after Roosevelt was inaugurated as President, he spoke to the nation and announced his plans for a 'New Deal' for the American people. The idea of a New Deal, as far as Roosevelt was concerned, was born when he was governor of New York. Faced with the problems of the Depression, he collected together a 'brains trust' predominantly of Columbia University professors to think up ways of reducing unemployment and the suffering that resulted. Some of their ideas were put into action quite successfully.

When he became President, these professors joined Roosevelt's government and developed further the work they had begun in New York. In simple terms, Roosevelt set out to deliver what he termed 'the 3 Rs':

- **relief** for those suffering the terrible effects of the Depression
- **recovery** of the country by help in the creation of jobs
- **reform** by passing laws to make sure that the economic disaster of 1929–32 did not happen again.

The New Deal was a collection of policies to make 'the 3 Rs' work for the American people. But Roosevelt realised that if these policies were to succeed, the federal government must be involved in the economy and it must be accepted that taxes must rise to finance, in particular, schemes to create jobs.

Summary of the 'alphabet agencies' created during 'The Hundred Days', 1933		
31 March	Civilian Conservation Corps (CCC)	Young men lived in camps run by the army. They did useful conservation work such as tree planting and were paid $1 a day. By August 1933, 250,000 young Americans had received work. (See Chapter 10.)
12 May	Federal Emergency Relief Administration (FERA)	Had $500 million to give to the hungry and homeless. $1 was given to the state government for every $3 FERA spent on relief. (See Chapter 9.)
	Agricultural Adjustment Administration (AAA)	Helped farmers increase their profits by adjusting the amount of crops that they grew. (See Chapter 10.)
18 May	Tennessee Valley Authority (TVA)	Planned to build 16 dams on the river in the Tennessee Valley for irrigation and to generate electricity. Thousands of jobs created. (See Chapter 10.)
16 June	Public Works Administration (PWA)	Created work for unemployed industrial workers by public works schemes, for example bridges. (See Chapter 9.)
	National Recovery Administration (NRA)	Employers were persuaded to pay fair wages and charge fair prices. (See Chapter 9.)

The 'alphabet agencies'. Central to the New Deal were the 'alphabet agencies', organisations set up by the government and financed by taxes which were intended to help those suffering as a result of the Depression. By 1935, there were large numbers of these agencies covering every aspect of American life and activity. The first and arguably the most important of these were formed during 'The Hundred Days'. Their work is summarised in the table and examined in greater detail in later chapters.

SUMMARY QUESTIONS

1 In what ways did Roosevelt's background and early political career prepare him for the presidency?

2 What were the main features of Roosevelt's election campaign in 1932?

3 What was so 'revolutionary' about 'The Hundred Days'?

4 What were the main features of the 'New Deal'?

CHAPTER 9

A New Deal for the unemployed and industry

If the economy of the United States was going to be revived, then the Roosevelt administration had to tackle the problem of mass unemployment, decisively and quickly. With unemployment as high as 25 per cent in 1933 and likely to rise with the approach of winter, measures had to be taken to reverse this alarming trend. As early as 16 May, within 'The Hundred Days', the **Federal Emergency Relief Administration** (**FERA**) was born. The details of how this system of relief would work were left to **Harry Hopkins** who was put in charge of the FERA. His outlook and ideas are crucial to understanding not only the workings of this agency, in particular, but a lot of Roosevelt's reforms in general.

HARRY HOPKINS AND THE CIVIL WORKS ADMINISTRATION

Hopkins believed that the unemployed should be given work, not dole. According to his thinking, work relief was better than dole because it gave the unemployed self-respect. It was good for their morale and could result in the completion of a number of socially useful projects.

Those who opposed this idea, including some Democrats, argued that:

- work relief was more costly than paying dole
- the Public Works Administration already existed to create jobs – what was the point in duplicating its work?

Hopkins was so close to the President that those who argued against him were wasting their time and in November 1933, Roosevelt created a new agency with Hopkins in charge, the **Civil Works Administration** (**CWA**).

KEY PERSON

Harry Hopkins (1890–1946) was born and educated in Iowa and eventually took up social welfare work in New York where he met Roosevelt in 1931. Hopkins became an adviser to Roosevelt whilst he was Governor of New York State and was to become Director of the Works Progress Administration in 1935 and Secretary of Commerce between 1938 and 1940. He was the President's closest aide, actually living in the White House from 1940.

Harry Hopkins.

Through the winter, the CWA spent $1 billion on short-term projects for the unemployed. Within two months of its creation, work had been found for 4 million Americans, who received 40 cents per hour if unskilled and $1 if skilled. They built or improved thousands of kilometres of roads, thousands of public buildings and hundreds of local airports. Those who criticised Hopkins doubted whether some of the jobs actually existed and laughed at reports of researchers studying the history of the safety pin or of others using balloons to scare pigeons away from public buildings. Such jobs were labelled 'boondoggles' (the plaits made from leather by American cowboys to pass away the time when they had no work).

KEY THEME

Civil aviation Throughout the 1920s and 1930s the civil aviation industry grew into an important sector of the American economy. The industry was based in California.

Hopkins was unmoved either by these criticisms or those that claimed he was wasting millions of dollars of public money. His view was that as long as money was circulating around the economy, it must be doing good. When, at the end of the winter, the CWA was disbanded, 4 million Americans found themselves, once again, without work. But at the very least, they had been helped to survive the winter, something that could not have been guaranteed under the Republicans.

HAROLD ICKES AND THE PUBLIC WORKS ADMINISTRATION

KEY PERSON

Harold Ickes (1874–1952) was born in Blair County, Pennsylvania and educated at Chicago University. From 1933 until 1944, he served as Secretary of the Interior and was in charge of the Public Works Administration.

Unlike Hopkins, **Harold Ickes**, who was in charge of the Public Works Administration (PWA), was very careful with the government's money. He believed that the schemes organised by the PWA should have a lasting value for the nation and he would never have accepted any proposal which sounded at all like a 'boondoggle'. Because of this, he was often seen as slow and indecisive and became the least popular of the New Dealers although others saw him as acting in the public interest.

Not only did Ickes and Hopkins have different ideas about the New Deal, there was rivalry between them. Ickes had considerable political ambitions and possibly hoped to become vice-president. He was more liberal than Truman who replaced Roosevelt in 1945. Ickes resigned in 1946, disillusioned with the appointment to the Cabinet of a number of conservative politicians.

The Public Works Administration. Under Harold Ickes, the main aim of the PWA was to create work for skilled workers, always ensuring that there was value for money. It was set up on 16 June 1933, within 'The Hundred Days' with a budget of $3.3 billion. Between 1933 and 1939, the PWA:

- built 70 per cent of the nation's schools and 35 per cent of its hospitals
- constructed four big river dams, including the Grand Coulee Dam in Washington State
- was responsible for the electrification of the railway from New York to Washington
- constructed 50 airports.

With Ickes in charge, there was no waste of money but, in other respects, the PWA's success was limited. It was only ever intended to create work for skilled workers and the problem of the millions of unskilled workers remained. But there was perhaps a more serious problem. Because Ickes was so concerned to give the taxpayers value for money and subjected all proposals to the closest of scrutiny, the money available was extremely slow to trickle through into the economy. This was really the opposite of what the New Deal had intended.

HARRY HOPKINS AND THE WORKS PROGRESS ADMINISTRATION

To help the millions of unskilled workers, in 1935 Harry Hopkins set up the Works Progress Administration (WPA), which in 1937 became the Works Project Administration. Between 1935 and 1939, it became the country's biggest employer, giving work to an average of 2 million people each year. The building of La Guardia airport in New York owed much to the work of the WPA.

In addition, there were other projects which included:

- the Federal Writers Project – unemployed writers were paid to write guide books on American states and cities.
- the Federal Art Project – painters produced pictures for display in schools and public buildings
- the Federal Theatre project – thousands of actors were employed to tour the country performing plays and shows
- photographers, including the great Dorothea Lange, were paid by the WPA to tour America producing a unique photographic record of the state of the nation at that time.

Roosevelt, however, had a clearer and more positive view of the aims of the work of the WPA than did its critics:

'The WPA should preserve not only the bodies of the unemployed from destruction but also their self-respect, their self-confidence, and courage and determination . . . the projects should be useful . . . of a nature that a considerable portion of the money spent would go into wages . . . to give employment to those on the relief rolls.'

As one might imagine, the WPA had many critics, particularly those who were quick to produce a picture of millions of workers 'leaning on shovels' whilst being paid out of public money.

The extent to which the PWA and the WPA created new and lasting jobs, and whether or not they gave value for money, will be considered later. But the intention in setting them up was very clear. By creating employment opportunities it gave workers wages, which meant money to spend. By spending this money, the demand for goods from factories would increase which, in turn, would create more jobs. At the same time, those in work would gain more self-respect and increased self-esteem, as well as the confidence to believe that for them and the country, things could get better.

A NEW DEAL FOR INDUSTRY

KEY THEME

Trade union weakness The trade union movement was weak for a number of reasons which included:

- federalism, which made it difficult to have a national trade union movement
- successive waves of immigration, which provided cheap labour
- the role of the courts, which protected employers over the freedom of contract.

The problems of industry. From the beginning of the twentieth century, employers in the United States were in a very powerful position. Workers trying to improve their pay and conditions found it very difficult. Amongst many employers, there was a strong determination to stop trade unions and their activities. In the Ford factories, for example, men were employed to spy on their fellow workers and those suspected of even attempting to discuss their grievances with others were sacked or physically intimidated (i.e. beaten up). The situation was so bad that, in some places, workers found talking together were fired. To try to improve their working conditions, workers were forced to negotiate with their employers individually, which put them at an immediate disadvantage. When they did attempt to join together in 'collective bargaining', the employers often used the courts to stop them. The results were that, generally, the employers prospered, but the workers struggled to improve their pay and conditions. Even in the years of prosperity, between 1923 and 1929, when industrial profits rose by 72 per cent, those of industrial workers rose by only 8 per cent, so that by 1929, 5 per cent of the population with the highest income received about one third of all personal income.

The situation worsened with the onset of the Great Depression in 1929. As the demand for goods dropped, factory owners cut their production and sacked workers.

An official enquiry in Connecticut in 1932 reported on:

'the existence of over a hundred sweatshops hiring young girls for as little as 60 cents to $1.10 for a 55 hour week. A family of six, including four children, were found stringing safety pins on wires late into the night for $4 to $5 a week.'

In this situation, conflict between employers and workers increased. Strikes, sit-ins and workers breaking into and occupying their factories became increasingly common. In response, employers called in the police or, even worse, employed their own groups of strike-breakers. There were, therefore, some very violent scenes in many factories across America, which became more serious as the Depression worsened. This was a major problem for Roosevelt to address early on in his presidency.

The National Recovery Administration (NRA). In 1933, Roosevelt appointed as Labor Secretary, **Frances Perkins**, the first woman in American history to hold a Cabinet post. In many ways, Perkins was the driving force behind the New Deal. In the early months, when Roosevelt himself was uncertain about what to do, she supplied many of the ideas and showed how they could be put into operation. Plans for federal aid to the states for unemployment relief and programmes of public works to create jobs owed much to her thinking, as did the creation of the Civilian Conservation Corps. The National Labor Relations Act and the Social Security Act and her contribution to their creation will be considered later, but working conditions and insurance, pensions and child labour were areas of policy in which she was particularly interested. The **National Recovery Administration** (NRA) was set up to deal with some of these issues.

Frances Perkins.

KEY PEOPLE

Frances Perkins was born in Boston in 1882. After graduating from Mount Holyoak College, she worked as a social worker in Worcester and as a teacher in Chicago. In 1910, she took a master's degree at Columbia and became secretary of the Consumers' League. This work brought her into contact with progressive politicians such as Robert Wagner and Alfred Smith.

When Smith became New York governor in 1919, Perkins joined the Industrial Board. In 1924, she became its chairman and succeeded in obtaining a reduction in the working week of women to 54 hours. In 1929, when Roosevelt became New York governor, Perkins became Industrial Commissioner. She was, therefore, a natural choice to become Labor Secretary in 1933, a position she occupied until Roosevelt died in 1945.

General Hugh Samuel Johnson Born in Kansas in 1882, Johnson graduated from the United States Military Academy in 1903. He fought with General Pershing in Mexico in 1916 and by the end of the First World War, had reached the rank of brigadier general.

On 16 June 1933, on the last of 'The Hundred Days', Congress passed the **National Industry Recovery Act (NIRA)**. It set up the National Recovery Administration which aimed to foster co-operation between the different sides of industry by developing agreed codes of practice about such issues as production limits, wage levels, working hours, prices and trade union rights. The idea was that agreement would be reached within each industry or trade association. To provide a framework for these negotiations, Congress passed laws which:

- set a 40-hour week for clerical workers, and a 36-hour week for industrial workers
- established a minimum wage of 40 cents an hour ($12.5 per week)
- abolished child labour
- gave workers the right to organise trade unions and take part in collective bargaining.

To administer the NRA, Roosevelt appointed **General Hugh Samuel Johnson**. Johnson threw himself into leading the NRA with great energy and enthusiasm, despite his weakness for alcohol and his indiscretion. He gave the NRA wide publicity, organising spectacular parades of those involved, aimed to encourage more and more workers and employers to join its programmes. Membership of the NRA was voluntary but those companies which accepted the codes developed by the various trade associations could place the NRA blue eagle symbol in their factories and on the packaging of their goods. This put great pressure on many companies to join the scheme since those which refused were often seen as unpatriotic and selfish. By early 1934, 557 codes had been drawn up and accepted and about 23 million people were working under them.

The NRA achieved a considerable improvement in the working conditions of many Americans. Shorter working hours, minimum wage levels and the right to join trade unions represented considerable progress. However, there were many drawbacks:

- Many companies seemed more interested in obtaining the blue eagle symbol (the symbol of NRA approval)

A poster promoting the NRA.

than in making sure they followed the NRA's codes of practice and there were many violations. Henry Ford refused even to sign the NRA code of practice.

- At the same time, many of the actual codes drawn up by trade associations seemed to favour the employers more than the workers.

In 1935, the Supreme Court ruled that if Congress were allowed to make laws like the NIRA then there could be no limit to the jurisdiction of the federal government. This would damage the very idea of federalism which was based on the idea of *divided* sovereignty (federal government and state government) and parallel systems of government (federal and state). If the NIRA was upheld, in other words, there was little of nothing left for state governments to govern. So the issue was about striking down a law of Congress that asserted federal right to regulate economic activity within states.

The National Labor Relations Act, 1935. On 5 July 1935, Congress passed the National Labor Relations Act. According to Frances Perkins, all the credit for this important law should go to **Robert Wagner**, and not to Roosevelt for whom it had no appeal.

KEY PERSON

Robert Ferdinand Wagner was born in Germany in 1877. His family emigrated to the United States in 1885 and settled in New York. In 1900, after graduating from the New York Law School, he was admitted to the bar. He became active in the Democratic Party and was eventually elected to the state senate. His main interest was in industrial working conditions and the trade union movement.

In 1919, he became a justice in the New York Supreme Court, a position he held until 1926 when he was elected to the United States Senate. Here, he failed in his attempts to persuade Congress to pass laws to help trade unions and the unemployed. In 1933, Roosevelt appointed Wagner the first chairman of the National Recovery Administration and it was in this capacity that he began work on laws to improve labour relations.

Although workers in the United States had the right to join trade unions and to go on strike, this was a limited freedom as employers also had the right to dismiss them because they had joined unions and had gone on strike. Because it was easy, during the Depression, for employers to find workers to replace those sacked, people were reluctant to join unions and by 1933, only 10 per cent of the workforce was unionised. The National Labor Relations Act established the rights of workers to join unions and bargain collectively through the representatives they had elected and not those chosen by the employers, which sometimes happened. Workers now had legal protection from their employers and union membership started to rise. The Act also set up a three-man **National Labor Relations Board** which had the power to bargain on behalf of workers and to stop companies from using blacklists and company unions. This Act increased the role of the government in labour relations and led to a growth in union membership and power.

WOMEN, THE DEPRESSION AND THE NEW DEAL

The Depression undoubtedly had a very adverse effect on the cause for female equality and emancipation. The 1920s had seen a trend towards more women, especially married women, in the workplace. As unemployment levels rose after 1929, there was increased resentment towards women taking jobs that might otherwise have been filled by men. This resentment was particularly directed at married women who were unfairly accused of going out to work for 'pin money' (i.e. to buy themselves luxuries). In a poll taken in 1936, 82 per cent said that women should not work. In reality, many were often struggling to supplement a low income earned by the male breadwinner, or to make ends meet where fathers and husbands were unemployed. Discrimination against married women at work continued throughout the 1930s and some states even imposed legal restrictions on women working. By the end of the 1930s, however, the number of married women in the workforce had risen from 11.7 per cent to 15.6 per cent.

Discriminatory attitudes failed to take into account the 2 million unmarried women who, by 1932, were unemployed, homeless and roaming the streets in search of food and shelter. Where women were heads of households, they were frequently obliged to earn money at home by taking in laundry or lodgers. There was also less opportunity for educated women to enter jobs such as teaching, social work, librarianship or book-keeping which had been growth areas before the Depression. Instead, women were increasingly taking up clerical occupations throughout the 1930s. By the 1940s, one third of white American women were working in the clerical sector. Whilst Chinese-American women were slowly entering this sector, African-American women were denied even these opportunities. They were forced by prejudice and poverty to work in domestic service. Only about 1.3 per cent of African-American women were white-collar (i.e. clerical) workers. Economic opportunities for Native American women did not exist.

Most women were discriminated against as evidenced by the gap between male and female earnings. Women tended to accept this situation, although trade union membership increased particularly during this period from 265,000 to 800,000, suggesting that some were becoming more active in defence of their rights. In some assembly-line industrial concerns, the slogan, 'Same work, same pay', was beginning to be heard. Male trade unionists, however, upheld the traditional view that a married woman's place, at least, was very definitely in the home.

Eleanor Roosevelt.

KEY PERSON

Eleanor Roosevelt was born in 1884. She was the niece of the former President, Theodore Roosevelt. She married Franklin in 1905. They had six children. However, Eleanor was determined to pursue a career of her own. She became actively involved with a number of organisations attempting to improve the position of women, for example, the League of Women Voters and the Women's Trade Union League.

During the Depression she became active in organisations attempting to bring relief to impoverished workers and to provide youth employment. She also supported groups opposed to racism and publicly demonstrated her opposition to discrimination. In 1938, for example, she attended a conference in Alabama where blacks and whites were segregated. She deliberately placed her chair between the two groups.

What did the New Deal do for women?

'Get into the game and stay in it. Throwing mud from the outside won't help. Building up from the inside will.'

This was the advice given to women by the First Lady, **Eleanor Roosevelt.** To this extent, the Roosevelt presidency did at least give to women a role model, a woman who was a mother and grandmother but who was, nevertheless, very active in many aspects of public life. Beyond this, her husband's New Deal policies did not directly improve the position of women. The New Deal programme was about stimulating the economy by increasing purchasing power. This meant reducing unemployment and boosting the numbers of wage earners. In this context, women's rights were fairly irrelevant. The focus was on the male breadwinner.

The minimum wage. Government intervention to fix minimum working hours and wages through the National Recovery Administration (1933) and the Fair Standards Act (1938) helped some women whose level of pay was below the new minimum, but in many cases, it only confirmed the pay differentials to which women had been previously subjected. Hence, by 1939, a female school teacher still earned 20 per cent less than her male colleagues doing the same job.

Social and welfare reforms. In so far as it achieved anything for women, the New Deal did seek to alleviate family stress by the introduction of welfare benefits, especially to the old and to poor families through the **Social Security Act (1935)**. This included **Aid to Dependent Children** that was especially helpful to mothers with young families who were unable to work and who were desperate. However, there was often discrimination in administering this benefit. In some places it was paid only to white families, leaving African-American women struggling to survive. Young mothers, applying for aid to unsympathetic administrators, frequently found the experience humiliating. There was still a view amongst the better-off that poverty was the result of idleness or waste, a view expressed in a letter to Eleanor Roosevelt in 1936: 'Personally, I have found that the more you give to the lower classes, the more they want.' The provision of this kind of welfare support was also strongly opposed by many politicians in Congress.

The plight of minorities. Some reference has been made to the plight of African-American women and the failure of the New Deal to support them. The situation of families of minority groups, Mexican as well as African-American, was particularly acute throughout the 1930s.

- In addition to the discrimination faced by women seeking welfare benefit and their inability to find better paid work, the discrimination against African- and Mexican-American men in the workplace had an impact on their wives and families. In the competition for jobs in industry, white men were given preference.
- The agricultural policies of the New Deal resulted in the eviction of large numbers of Mexican- and African-American farmers. As these began to flood into cities in search of work, racist tensions rose. In one city, notices around the place read, 'No niggers, Mexicans or dogs allowed'.
- Lynchings and serious miscarriages of justice increased. In the face of discrimination, African-Americans, particularly, began to resist. Some of their women became active in this cause. They formed the **Association of Southern Women for the Prevention of**

Eleanor Roosevelt and Mary McLeod Bethune.

SOME KEY WOMEN

Grace Abbott set up and worked through the Children's Bureau to provide support for homeless and neglected children.

Ellen Sullivan Woodward was appointed director of Women's Work in the Federal Emergency Relief Administration. She organised training programmes for women and particularly stressed the need for black women to benefit from New Deal policies.

Nellie Taylor Ross became the first woman Director of the Mint.

Frances Allen became the first woman judge on the US Circuit Court of Appeals.

Molly Dawson supported the New Deal because she believed that economic improvement and social welfare were the best means of advancing the cause of women. She was the leader of the Democratic Party's women's section and worked hard to encourage women, especially African-American women, to use their right to vote. In the 1936 elections, she gathered 15,000 women volunteers who distributed 80 million flyers to people's homes to explain and promote the New Deal.

KEY PERSON

Mary McLeod Bethune was appointed Director of Negro Affairs and spoke up on race and gender issues in the administration of the New Deal. The daughter of former slaves, she was the highest-ranking black appointee in the Roosevelt administration.

Lynching and received support from Eleanor Roosevelt. Other similar women's groups were established to oppose lynching, rape and racism. However, attempts to make lynching a federal crime failed to be passed by Congress in 1935 and again in 1938. Roosevelt, himself, did nothing to intervene in this process, although his wife demonstrated her opposition to racism on several public occasions.

- Some black women formed self-help groups for African-American families who were struggling to survive. The Alpha Kappa Alpha's Mississippi Health Project, for example, provided health care each summer from 1935 until 1942 for poor black communities. The Housewives League of Detroit, formed in 1930, agreed to buy goods from black businesses.

Native Americans. The New Deal did seek to try to help Native Americans. The Indian Reorganization Act gave Native American women formal political rights. It also provided them with opportunities for training as domestic workers and seamstresses and stimulated interest in native arts and crafts. A small number had the opportunity for education. Gladys Tantaquidgeon, for example, became an anthropologist and worked for the government's Indian Bureau where she specialised in promoting and encouraging traditional Indian arts and crafts. The Reorganization Act also attempted to protect the land

A Seminole woman using a Singer sewing machine to produce traditional clothing.

rights of Native Americans and, in doing so, it reinforced male dominance in Indian tribal communities.

Women in public service. The Roosevelt administration did provide opportunities for individual women to hold office and to make their mark. Roosevelt was the first US President to appoint a woman to a position in his Cabinet, Frances Perkins. He also appointed the first woman ambassador and increased the number of female federal judges. However, these women invariably used their positions to pursue social or welfare issues and were not obvious supporters of feminist aspirations for sexual equality and female emancipation. When America was plunged into the Second World War at the end of 1941, the women of America found new opportunities for advancement.

SUMMARY QUESTIONS

1 How important were the following to the success of the New Deal:
   a) Harry Hopkins
   b) Harold Ickes
   c) Frances Perkins?

2 What was the purpose of the National Recovery Administration? What did it achieve?

3 How were women affected by
   a) The Depression
   b) The New Deal?

CHAPTER 10

A New Deal for the farmers and the land

THE PLIGHT OF THE FARMERS

In 1932, the magazine, *New Republic* described the problem in agriculture:

'Beginning in the Carolinas and extending clear into New Mexico are fields of unpicked cotton that tell a mute story of more cotton than could be sold for enough, even to pay the cost of picking. Vineyards with grapes still unpicked, orchards of olive trees hanging full of rotting fruits and oranges being sold at less than the cost of production.'

Oscar Heline, a farmer from Iowa, described what he saw:

'We had lots of trouble on the highway, people were determined to withhold produce from the market – livestock, cream, butter, eggs, what not. If they could dump the produce, they would force the market to a higher level. The farmers would man the highways, and cream cans were emptied in ditches and eggs dumped out. They burned the Trestie Bridge, so the trains wouldn't be able to haul grain.'

Of all the groups who suffered the effects of the Great Depression, it was the farmers who suffered most. The First World War badly damaged European agriculture, a situation which American farmers turned to their advantage by increasing their own production and selling their surpluses on world markets. Many enjoyed considerable prosperity as a result, but by the 1920s this was coming to an end. As agriculture in Europe recovered, American farmers found it increasingly difficult to find markets for their produce. By the late 1920s, many found themselves in great difficulties even before the Wall Street Crash and the Depression which followed. The farmers were also victims of their own productivity and the lack of regulation in agriculture until the New Deal. Those who tried to solve their problems by maintaining or increasing production levels only made matters worse. Prices fell even lower, wiping out any profits that remained.

The difficulties faced by the farmers had serious effects:

- By 1933, average farm incomes, which in 1929 were $13,938, had plummeted to $7,107.
- In the same year, one farmer in 20 had been evicted from his land for not keeping up mortgage repayments.

Many were facing a desperate situation. In 1933, the farmers' union leader, Ed O'Neal, warned that unless something were done to help, 'we will have a revolution in the countryside within less than twelve months'. Certainly, the situation in Iowa, the heart of American farm country, was particularly bad. Here, an organisation called the Farm Holiday Association was active in stopping the movement of produce to market.

Signs of unrest. In April 1933, angry farmers in Iowa, masked with blue handkerchiefs, broke into a court-house where Judge Charles Bradley was signing orders for the eviction of farmers from their land. They dragged him onto the street, smeared him with tractor grease and attempted to hang him, even reaching the point of placing a rope around his neck. Although they abandoned their efforts when he refused to be intimidated, the situation was considered so serious that the state was placed under martial law. Many Americans were very shocked by what had happened. Clearly, incensed and angry farmers in a number of states represented not just a threat to law and order but a major challenge for Roosevelt to face, immediately after he was sworn in.

HENRY A. WALLACE AND AGRICULTURAL ADJUSTMENT

Shortly after taking office, Roosevelt moved quickly to deal with the desperate plight of the farmers. As Secretary of Agriculture, he appointed **Henry A. Wallace**, in many ways the ideal person for this difficult task since he came from a farming background.

The crucial issue facing Wallace was that of farm surpluses – American farmers were producing too much and the resulting low prices made it impossible for many to survive. This was not a new problem and the traditional way of dealing with it was by 'dumping'. The government bought the surpluses from the farmers and then sold them cheaply on world markets. Whilst this may well have disposed of the surpluses, it seriously damaged trade relations with other countries, whose own farmers were having to compete with cheap imports. Wallace believed that the way to deal with the problem was to raise prices by cutting production. On 12 May 1933, within 'The Hundred Days', Congress passed the **Agricultural Adjustment Act** which set up the **Agricultural Adjustment Administration.**

KEY PEOPLE

Henry Agard Wallace (1888–1965) was born in Adair County, Iowa into a family of well-known American farmers and agriculturalists. His grandfather had founded an influential farmers' magazine, *Wallace's Farmer*, which he himself had edited. Henry was also interested in the scientific aspects of farming and developed several new strains of hybrid corn. The family was Republican and his father had served as Secretary in Harding's Cabinet.

In 1928, Henry Jr resigned from the Republican Party in disgust at the failure to help the farmers and, in particular, at the opposition of Hoover to any programmes of assistance. Wallace was later to become Vice-President (1941–5) eventually falling out with Roosevelt who switched his support to Harry Truman as his running-mate for the 1944 presidential election. Wallace also ran as an independant in 1948 for the presidency and was critical of the Truman administration's policy towards the Soviet Union, which he thought was too aggressive. However, in 1933, his experience made him an excellent choice as Agricultural Secretary.

The Agricultural Adjustment Administration (AAA)

- The aims of the AAA were to raise commodity prices to pre-1914 levels by 'adjusting', effectively reducing, the size of farm crops. If smaller amounts of farm produce were sold at market, prices would rise.
- To encourage farmers to take fields out of production, financial compensation would be offered. (This is now known as 'set-aside' and is practised in the European Union.) The money for this would be raised by a tax paid by the food processors, who in turn would pass this on to the consumer in the form of higher prices.

By the early summer of 1933, many crops had been planted. Consequently, the AAA decided that if the new policy were to succeed, some of the crops already in the ground would have to be destroyed. Cotton farmers were therefore encouraged to plough 10 million acres of their crop back into the ground and received generous compensation for doing so. A similar fate befell the tobacco harvest. However, the decision to slaughter 6 million piglets to boost pork prices prompted a public outcry. Some of the meat was used to supplement the diet of the unemployed in the cities. Nevertheless, the idea of millions of piglets being slaughtered was too much for many Americans to bear and there was strongly voiced opposition to the plan. Wallace, whilst angry, remained unmoved, declaring:

> 'To hear them talk, you would have thought that pigs were raised for pets.'

Criticisms of the AAA. This incident highlights an important moral issue related to this policy. Many Americans found themselves asking why crops were being destroyed and animals slaughtered when millions were starving throughout the country and in so many other parts of the world. Wallace and Roosevelt blamed the 'profit system' for making it impossible to distribute the abundance of America to both the rest of the world and to starving people in the United States. For such a distribution to take place, they argued, there would have to be a dramatic change in the structure of the American economy – in the meantime, nothing could be done.

KEY THEME

Structural changes in the economy Poor people needed money to buy food, therefore welfare would need to be increased or there would have to be some other form of redistribution of wealth.

Partly as a result of the policies of the Agricultural Adjustment Administration, overall farm incomes doubled between 1932 and 1936, although this was also due to droughts and dust storms which damaged production in many areas (such catastrophes further reduced production which caused prices to rise). There were also other agencies such as:

- the **Farm Credit Administration** which made credit available to farmers at low interest rates
- the **Farm Security Administration** which financed farm ownership for tenant farmers.

The AAA was cancelled in 1936 by the Supreme Court, but Congress passed a second Act, under which the government would make payments to farmers who would devote part of their land to 'soil conserving' crops. By 1940, 6 million farmers had joined the programme and were receiving subsidies that averaged more than $100 a year for each farmer.

Assessing the achievements of the AAA. It is important to realise that:

- financial compensation was paid on the basis of acres left uncultivated and not to individual farmers on the basis of their need
- the system was voluntary and depended on farmers themselves meeting together to decide how many acres should be taken out of production
- the farmers also supervised each other to ensure that promised reductions in production actually occurred.

All these processes tended to result in the larger and better-off farmers controlling the running of the AAA in their own areas and benefiting most from it.

The system of compensating farmers for taking land out of production did little to help those farmers with small plots of land or tenant farmers struggling to pay their rents. But the difficulties were even worse for those actually employed on the land. As more acres were taken out of production and crops were destroyed, farmers needed fewer workers.

KEY THEME

The AAA and the Supreme Court Until 1937, when the Supreme Court stopped striking down congressional laws as unconstitutional in the sphere of economic regulation, the Court had read the 14th Amendment (among other constitutional provisions) as protecting economic rights against government regulation. As far as the AAA was concerned, the Court struck down some of its provisions as unconstitutional because the Act gave the federal government powers of economic regulation which, in the view of the Court, were not constitutionally lawful, i.e. the Court was protecting economic rights from a clear *laissez-faire* perspective.

Erskine Caldwell, an American writer, visited a family of sharecroppers in 1933:

'In one of the two rooms a six-year old boy licked the paper bag the meat had been brought in. His legs were scarcely any larger than a medium-sized dog's legs, and his belly was as large as that of a 130 pound woman's . . . On the floor beside an open fire lay two babies, neither a year old, sucking the dry teats of a mongrel bitch.'

The sharecroppers were among the victims of this. They numbered 3 million, half of whom were black, and found themselves having to leave the land and seek work in other parts of the country.

It would therefore be fair to conclude that the Agricultural Adjustment Administration had limited success in dealing with the problems faced by American farmers. Clearly, those who owned the larger, well-established farms gained considerable amounts of money in compensation for cutting production, and farm incomes did rise in the years up to 1940. It is equally evident that the AAA did nothing to improve the lives of millions of farmworkers, many of whom were black and who continued to exist in conditions of poverty and starvation.

THE DUST BOWL

The experience of living through a dust storm must have been terrifying, as Avis Carlson describes:

'The impact of a dust storm is like a shovelful of fine sand flung against the face. People caught in their own yards grope for the doorstep. Cars come to a stand-still, for no light in the world can penetrate that swirling murk...In time the fury subsides. If the wind has spent itself, the dust will fall silently for hours. If the wind has settled into a good steady blow, the air will be thick for days. During those days as much of living as possible will be moved to the basement, while pounds and pounds of dust shift into the house. It is something, however, to have the house stop rocking and mumbling.'

The suffering of the farmers was made much worse for those on the Great Plains by the climatic disaster of 1934 and 1935 which resulted in 'The Dust Bowl'. During the First World War, to satisfy the demand for grain from European countries at war, American farmers grew wheat on land normally used for grazing animals. This intensive farming destroyed much of the vegetation cover. The summers of 1934 and 1935 were particularly hot with temperatures in Oklahoma rising to 100° for 36 consecutive days, turning the topsoil into dry dust. Then came the winds, dispersing the dust not only over the immediate area but reaching the Eastern seaboard, landing on Washington and even falling on ships 300 miles out in the Atlantic. The map on page 126 indicates those states most badly affected and it is evident that farmers in a large area suffered.

The effects of the dust storm. Once the wind had ceased and the dust had settled, the farmers could assess the damage done. In many ways, the land was dead, with deep cracks running through it and surrounding hills badly eroded. Most important of all, there were no signs of bird or animal life, a grim omen for the farmers of the troubles to come.

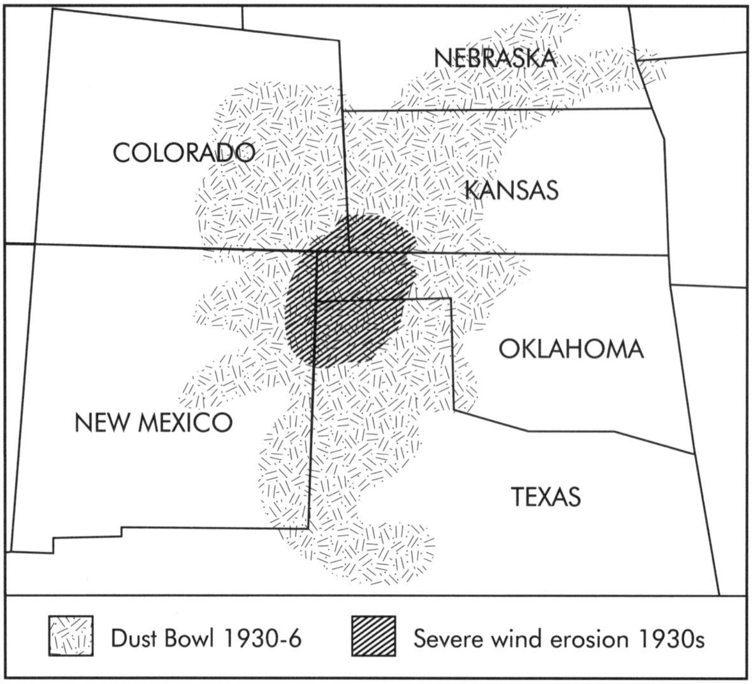

The areas affected by dust storms in the 1930s.

Tens of thousands of farming families, facing ruin, packed their belongings into their small cars and trucks and joined in the migration to the charity camps of California, seeking a new beginning to their lives. They were labelled 'Okies' and 'Arkies', terms used for all such migrants, not just those from Oklahoma and Arkansas. Their sufferings and their journey west are described by John Steinbeck in *The Grapes of Wrath*, written in 1939, and were captured by the photographer Dorothea Lange.

> The cars of the migrant people crawled out of the side roads onto the great cross-country highway, and they took the migrant way to the West. In the daylight they scuttled like bugs near a shelter and to water. And because they were lonely and perplexed, because they had all come from places of sadness and worry and defeat, and because they were all going to a new mysterious place, they huddled together; they talked together; they shared their lives, their food, and the things they hoped for in the new country.
>
> John Steinbeck, *The Grapes of Wrath* (1939)

A migrant family, photographed by Dorothea Lange, who compiled a visual record of the Depression for the Farm Security Administration.

Between 1935 and 1940, 350,000 refugees arrived in California from stricken areas of the Midwest. In many cases, they received a hostile welcome. Their presence was clearly seen as a threat to Californian farmers who themselves were struggling to survive. They were often branded as lazy, irresponsible and untrustworthy. They were thought to have too many children. The key question was whether they would receive special help from the federal government or whether their plight would be dealt with as part of a general policy of neglect of the New Deal alphabet agencies. In many ways, it was the latter rather than the former which proved to be the case.

Help for the 'Okies' and 'Arkies' was largely limited to the existing 'alphabet agencies'. However, Roosevelt supporters argued that the state of American farming did improve significantly during the last five years of the decade. Certainly, the doubling of food prices between 1932 and 1937 was good news for those farmers who had managed to hang on to their land. The many government programmes to promote soil conservation and electrification were also welcomed. There was also a very real way in which farmers, through their involvement in the running or the AAA, were becoming more important politically. However, it is not always easy to see how these benefits were shared by the 'Okies' and the 'Arkies' or by the sharecroppers and the millions of other unemployed farmworkers.

THE TENNESSEE VALLEY AUTHORITY (TVA)

The problem. Together with the Dust Bowl, the Tennessee Valley represented the biggest environmental problem facing Roosevelt during his presidency. Every spring, the River Tennessee flooded, washing away millions of tons of topsoil and destroying farms in its path. In summer, there was hardly any water in the river at all and the land became parched. The situation was not helped in many parts of the valley by generations of poor-quality farming. Forests, which had been stripped of their timber, were often not renewed. This, together with the overgrazing of animals and over-farming for crops, increased the rate of soil erosion.

The Tennessee Valley occupied an area as large as England and Wales, around 40,000 square miles. It covered, or at least touched, seven states and 2.5 million people lived within its boundaries. As the farming problems grew worse, many of them slipped further and further into poverty, so that by 1933, half were living on dole money paid out by the states involved. The poor quality of life of many of those in the valley is illustrated by the statistic that, in that year, only 2 per cent of the farms actually had electricity. Few would disagree, therefore, with Roosevelt when he described the valley as 'the nation's number one economic problem', or with the view that solving it represented possibly the greatest challenge to his presidency.

The solution. The idea of building federally-owned dams on the Tennessee River to stop the flooding and provide cheap electricity for the people of the valley was nothing new. During the First World War, a $145,000,000 hydro-electric plant and two munitions factories had been built at Muscle Shoals. After the war, Senator Norris of Nebraska, a liberal Republican, introduced a bill to convert the plant and factories for peacetime purposes. Supported by other liberals, the bill passed through Congress but aroused considerable opposition, mainly from two sources:

- The private electricity companies wanted the bill wrecked because they feared competition from cheap electricity.
- The Republicans argued against it on the grounds that since the power-producing plants would be government owned, this would be an example of socialist planning, which they strongly rejected.

The bill, which had passed through Congress twice, was vetoed by Coolidge and Hoover, much to the disappointment of Norris, but he was able to stop the dams being sold off to private companies.

Roosevelt very much agreed with what Norris had been trying to achieve and realised that a series of dams along the river, providing cheap electricity, would stimulate one of the poorest regions of the United States. On 18 May 1933, within 'The Hundred Days', Congress passed the **Tennessee Valley Act** which created the **Tennessee Valley Authority (TVA)**, one of the most successful agencies of the New Deal, which still exists today. The munitions factory was converted to a chemical plant manufacturing fertilisers and the hydro-electric plant produced power for parts of seven states (Virginia, North Carolina, Georgia, Tennessee, Kentucky, Alabama and Mississippi). The TVA produced many benefits for the people living in its area and for the country as a whole.

- Using wide powers, the Authority built a series of dams on the Tennessee and Cumberland Rivers and their tributaries. At the touch of a button, the sluice-gates could be closed to hold back the river when it threatened to flood. Controlling the water was the key to the success of the scheme. Building and maintaining the dams created thousands of jobs. Even today, the Authority employs 24,000 people.

- The dams were also used in the production of cheap electricity. Powerful turbines, built into the walls of the dams, were driven by jets of water released from the lakes behind them. Electricity began to reach thousands of poor families, who were able to enjoy electric lighting in their homes for the first time, together with new household products such as refrigerators. By 1945, 75 per cent of farms in the Tennessee Valley had electricity. (Remember that, in 1933, the figure had been 2 per cent.) By 1940, sales of electrical appliances in Tennessee averaged $46 per household, compared with $32 in the country as a whole.
- The dams played a massive role in the economic development of the valley. Industrialists, realising that cheap electricity was available, were encouraged to build new factories, creating many new opportunities for employment.
- Behind the dams, new lakes were created which were ideal for water transport. Locks built into the sides of the dams meant that ships could now travel up the river, carrying coal, steel and other products to the factories of the region. In all, the TVA was responsible for adding 650 miles of navigable river to the inland waterway system. This meant that products made in the valley could reach wider markets.
- On the newly created lakes, recreational facilities for local people were developed and on their banks, model farms developing new methods of soil conservation were begun, attempting to educate the farmers in the valley in improving the quality of their farming.

There is, therefore, considerable evidence to suggest that the TVA was one of the most successful agencies of the New Deal. It created thousands of jobs and stimulated the recovery of the whole region. Even so, it attracted criticism. For supporters of *laissez-faire* economic thinking, it was socialism at work, with all the evils of state planning. However, those who gained employment as a consequence were not too worried what it was called. The fact that cheap electricity produced by the TVA might be used to produce plutonium for developing the atom bomb or that

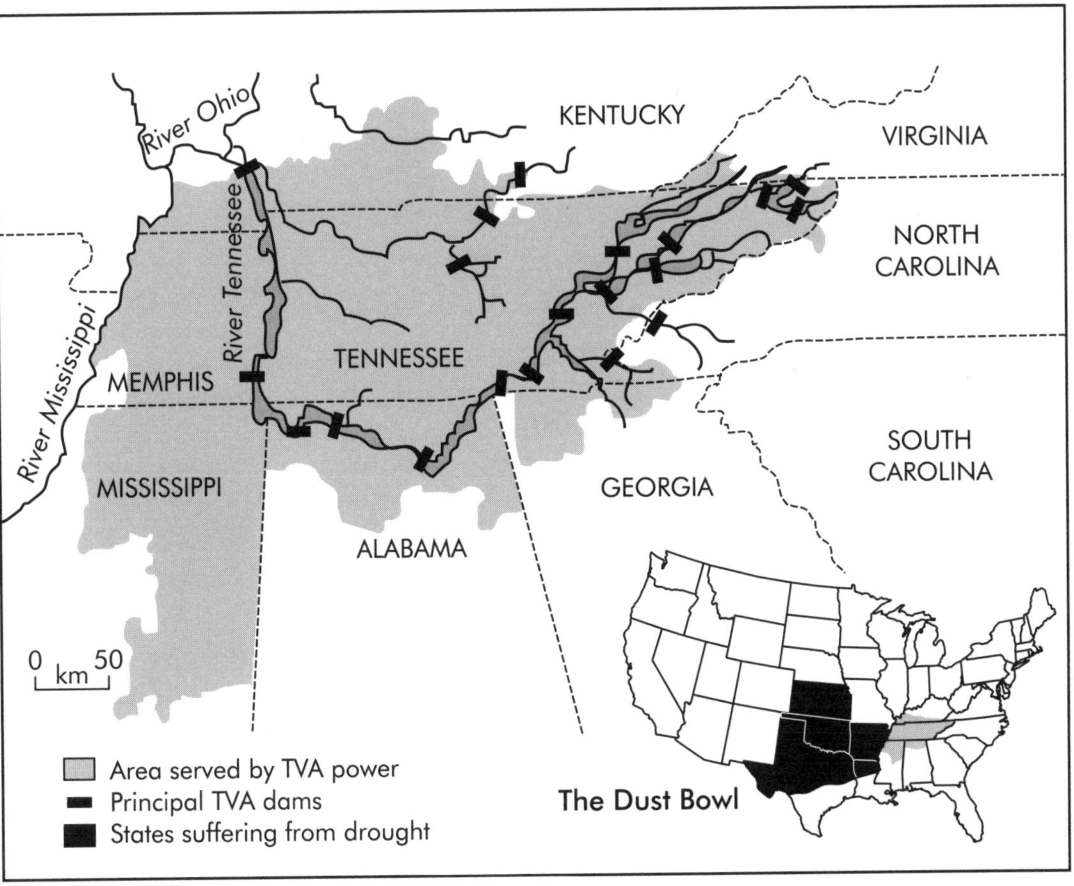

The Tennessee Valley and its dams.

many black Americans were excluded from many schemes did not matter too much to the thousands enjoying their benefits. They had come to regard Roosevelt as their 'friend in the White House'.

THE CIVILIAN CONSERVATION CORPS (CCC)

Like the TVA, the Civilian Conservation Corps was one of the great symbols of the New Deal. It provides an excellent example of the compassion that Roosevelt felt for the young unemployed, as well as of his love of the American countryside, where he was born and brought up.

The CCC was formed on 31 March 1933, the first of the 'alphabet agencies'. It was part of the Works Progress Administration and was designed to tackle the problem of young unemployed men between 18 and 25 years of age.

Throughout the country, CCC camps were set up and organised on army lines with officers in charge. The men were set to work on a range of projects aimed to conserve and improve the environment. These included:

- planting thousands of trees in America's vast forests
- building public parks
- draining swamps to fight malaria
- restocking rivers with fish
- working on flood control projects
- building forest trails
- clearing up beaches and camping grounds
- restoring historic battlefields.

The period of time spent on a CCC project was normally six months, but this was often extended. The pay was $30 per month with $22 of it being sent home to families to help them survive the Depression.

- Some of the first to join the CCC were army veterans, but by the summer of 1933, 300,000 young American men were working on various projects.
- They lived in 13,000 camps, where they received food, clothing and shelter.
- Between 1933 and 1941, over 3 million men served in the CCC.
- In the Midwest, the agency planted more than 200 million trees to stop soil erosion; around half the cultivated trees in America today were planted in the New Deal years.

Was the CCC successful? The extent to which the CCC was successful in solving the problem of unemployment amongst young male Americans is a matter of considerable debate. Roosevelt, himself, was much taken by the whole idea and, according to Frances Perkins, exaggerated its benefits. He had no real idea of what was involved in setting up the various schemes and, as might have been expected from a President, left it to others to deal with such problems as trade union opposition to what they regarded as schemes run on cheap labour. The unions were, to some extent, pacified when it was decided that the camps where the young men were to live would be built by union labour.

The experience of members of the CCC. The truth is that those young men who joined CCC programmes had widely differing experiences. Some found themselves on exciting projects in beautiful surroundings and had little difficulty finding work afterwards, often precisely because they had accepted the firm discipline on which these schemes were based and had become reliable workers. Others, like Blackie Gold (quoted below), were unable to find any permanent work and found themselves rejoining CCC schemes where the work became monotonous:

> 'I was at CCC's for six months, I came home for fifteen days, looked around for work, and I couldn't make $30 a month, so I enlisted back in the CCC's and went to Michigan. I spent another six months there planting trees and building forests. And came out. But still no money to be made. So back in the CCC's again. From there I went to Boise, Idaho, and was attached to the forest rangers. Spent four and a half hours fighting forest fires.'

SUMMARY QUESTIONS

1 Why were the farmers particularly badly hit by the Depression?

2 What was the role of Henry Wallace in Roosevelt's agricultural policies?

3 Did the New Deal really help farmers?

4 Why was the Tennessee Valley a particular challenge for Roosevelt? How successful was he in solving its problems?

5 What did Roosevelt do for the young unemployed?

CHAPTER 11

The Second New Deal and the presidential election of 1936

In January 1935, in his State of the Union address, Roosevelt outlined his plans to broaden the work of the New Deal. He stated his wish to:

- enlarge the scope and extent of federal relief
- give assistance to the rural poor
- support workers organising themselves into trade unions
- provide welfare benefits for older Americans and disadvantaged groups
- introduce stricter regulation over business
- tax the rich more heavily.

Whilst some of these ideas were merely extending the policies which Roosevelt began in 1933, others went much further. The idea that the federal government should help workers to form trade unions or become involved in setting up social security systems was new and likely to attract much opposition. At the same time, Roosevelt needed to revive those policies and agencies that had been previously opposed or declared unconstitutional by the Supreme Court. We can, therefore, refer in early 1935, to the creation of a Second New Deal which, in many ways, was more radical than the first and placed an even greater emphasis on welfare. As such, it prepared the way for the presidential election in 1936 and a Democrat victory.

The work schemes organised by the **Works Progress Administration** and the **Public Works Administration** were very costly to set up and maintain. Thus the national debt, which in 1933 stood at $21 billion, had risen to $43 billion by 1940. However, Roosevelt appears never to have become a convinced Keynesian **deficit spender**.

KEY TERM

Deficit spending is spending with the aim of stimulating demand in an economy, even if it means running up a deficit.

- In 1937 he cut back WPA expenditure and only when visible hardship and unemployment grew was massive WPA expenditure renewed.
- 1938 is usually seen as the point when Roosevelt re-embraced deficit spending, but this was simply an expedient way to ameliorate harsh conditions.
- By 1940 the economic prosperity levels of 1929 had still not been restored despite all the flurry of New Deal measures. However, a boost now came in the form of rearmament government spending and orders from Britain and France. The latter, and a sort of enforced Keynesian-defence spending, pushed the United States into its economic miracle of the Second World War.

THE SECOND NEW DEAL

These are the main features of the Second New Deal:

- The **Resettlement Administration**, set up in May 1935, offered loans to small farmers to buy their own farms and made it possible for sharecroppers and tenants to resettle on productive land. Although it lasted for only two years, it made sure that the public and the politicians remained aware of these important problems.
- The **Rural Electrification Administration**, also set up in the spring of 1935, gave low-interest loans to companies and farmers' co-operatives to extend electricity to the 90 per cent of rural America that did not already benefit from it so that by 1941 40 per cent of American farms were using it.
- In January 1936, when the Supreme Court declared the AAA unconstitutional, Congress passed the **Soil Conservation and Domestic Allotment Act** which paid farmers to reduce the production of those crops which depleted the soil such as wheat and cotton and replace them with grasses which conserved the soil.
- The **National Labor Relations Act** (known as the Wagner Act) of July 1935 is examined in detail in Chapter 10. The work of the National Labor Relations Boards, which the Act created, was clearly intended to help the workers improve their conditions at the expense of the employers and was one of the most radical aspects

of the New Deal. By 1939, the total union membership had risen to 9 millions compared with 3.3 millions in 1933.

- The **Banking Act** of August 1935 increased the control of the Federal Reserve Board over the banks and money supply and was clearly intended to avoid a repeat of the banking crisis of 1933.
- The **Public Utilities Holding Company Act**, also of August 1935, restricted gas and electric companies to one geographical region and was a great blow to the large public-utility empires which had prospered so much in the 1920s.
- The **Revenue Act** increased personal taxes at higher income levels, raised corporate taxes and boosted levies on gifts and estates. Whilst there were many ways in which the rich could reduce their tax burden, this Act does illustrate very well the way in which the New Deal was on the side of the poor and aimed to improve their lives, at the expense of the rich.

The Social Security Act, 1935

When it came to introducing social security schemes, the United States lagged far behind Britain and Germany where schemes had been introduced much earlier in the century. In 1935, for instance, only 27 of the 48 states had introduced old-age pensions and only one, Wisconsin, had a scheme of unemployment insurance. Frances Perkins and Harry Hopkins pressed Roosevelt to implement a social security system throughout America. Eventually Congress passed a Social Security Act in 1935.

KEY POINT

States of the Union Hawaii and Alaska now make up the 50 states of the Union.

The Act introduced a compulsory system of old-age pensions and a joint federal–state system of unemployment insurance. To finance the scheme, both employers and employees paid a 3 per cent payroll tax. Because the schemes were paid for out of contributions and not taxes, no payments were actually made until 1942. The unemployment benefits which were paid tended to be rather low because they were worked out as a percentage of income whilst working and not on what unemployed people needed to survive. The benefits were paid for 20 weeks at most and ranged from $10 to $85 per week.

Weaknesses of the scheme. The system introduced by the Social Security Act had many weaknesses.

- There were no sickness benefits because the health insurance clauses were opposed by the doctors who wanted to keep health provision private.
- Pensions and benefits did not extend to farm labourers, casual workers and domestic servants, the very groups who needed them most.

But despite these imperfections, the Act was of great importance, mainly because it was so much better than anything that existed before. For the first time, help for the unemployed and the aged was available through the government and not through local, voluntary charities. Pensions were paid on retirement at 65 and money was also available to the states to pay for help for the disabled and maternity care. The Social Security Act was possibly the most important and most radical of all the New Deal laws. It was attacked by many but it laid important foundations which could be built on in the future.

> Perhaps Roosevelt's landslide victory was best explained by Harold Ickes when he wrote:
>
> 'In my view, the outstanding thing about the campaign was the lack of influence of the newspapers. With over eighty per cent of the newspapers of the country fighting Roosevelt, it is remarkable that he should have swept everything as he did...In my judgement, they voted for the President because they believed that he had some interest in and concern for the welfare of the common man. The very bitterness of the assault upon the President by the newspapers reacted in his favour.'

The presidential election of 1936

In June 1936, the Democrats met to select a candidate to contest the forthcoming presidential election. Their decision was never in doubt. Roosevelt was renominated. Opposed by the Republican, Alfred Landon, Roosevelt was criticised throughout the campaign for wasting money and for failing to balance the federal budget. Many businessmen were angered by the National Labor Relations Act and attacked him for giving too much power to the trade unions.

For his part, Roosevelt made the election a class issue, portraying himself and the Democrats as being on the side of ordinary Americans against the rich and the forces of big business. The vast majority of American newspapers opposed Roosevelt, but nothing they did seemed to make any difference. When the election came, he gained a landslide victory with a majority of 8 million votes and won every state except Maine and Vermont. In addition, the Democrats won three-quarters of the seats in the Senate and four-fifths of those in the House of

Representatives. In his inaugural speech, after being sworn in as President for the second time in January 1937, Roosevelt promised much more reform, building on the success of his first four years. In fact, very little was actually achieved. The reasons for this will be explained in the next chapter.

SUMMARY QUESTIONS

1 In what ways did the Second New Deal aim to extend the provisions of the first?

2 What were the main issues in the presidential election of 1936?

CHAPTER 12

Opposition to the New Deal

The landslide victory which Roosevelt won in 1936 can obscure the fact that Roosevelt had political enemies and that not everyone benefited from the New Deal. He had many critics and opponents throughout his presidency. Some of these attacked his New Deal policies with great personal bitterness. In particular, his battles with the Supreme Court, during his second term, slowed down the pace of reform and were a major factor in bringing the New Deal to an end. It is possible to identify opposition to Roosevelt and attacks on the New Deal coming from:

- conservative politicians from within both the Republican and Democratic parties and from businessmen
- individuals, such as Huey Long, Father Charles Coughlin and Dr Frances Townsend
- the Supreme Court.

OPPOSITION FROM CONSERVATIVE POLITICIANS AND BUSINESSMEN

As might be expected, the Republicans were strong opponents of the New Deal. Not only were they the traditional opponents of the Democrats, they were also the party which represented the interests of America's rich families and large business corporations.

- They attacked the New Deal because of the huge government expenditure of its many programmes organised by the various agencies.
- They also complained that much of the money spent was being wasted and that real, lasting jobs were not being created.
- In particular, of course, they attacked Roosevelt for raising personal taxes on higher income earners through the Revenue Act, which hit the rich hard.

KEY THEME

The Republican and Democratic parties in the 1930s Some of the wealthy and well-to-do were Democrats, e.g. Roosevelt himself, Henry Morgenthau and Henry Wallace. But the South was always different. Here the Civil War had cut across class and wealth divisions which operated elsewhere – the South was Democratic because the Republican Party was the party of Lincoln and the North.

- They were also critical of high budget deficits, which Roosevelt maintained in order to pay for the various programmes.
- But what angered many Republicans about New Deal policies was that the New Deal represented intervention in the economy, controlling, for example, production targets, wage levels and working conditions. The Republicans were also the party of big business and Roosevelt's economic regulation threatened their profits. This factor should not be underestimated in its importance.

KEY THEME

Roosevelt and capitalism
Roosevelt, it is now generally believed, intended to make capitalism more acceptable by making it more accountable to the people and by regulating it. In this he succeeded. Thus it could be said that Roosevelt saved capitalism from itself.

The New Deal, therefore, was perceived as a threat both to capitalism and individual liberty, and furthermore it was not working. In late 1934, for example, there were still 11 million Americans unemployed and although national income was rising, it was still well below 1929 levels.

In 1934, the **American Liberty League** was founded to preserve individual liberty, threatened by the New Deal. As expected, it was backed by many wealthy businesspeople, but what was surprising was that it was also supported by Alfred Smith and John Davis, both of whom had previously stood as Democratic presidential candidates. There was clearly a Conservative wing within the Democratic Party which, as early as 1934, was worried about the direction in which Roosevelt was taking the party. These Conservative Democrats, many from the South and representing farming areas, may have been happy to support New Deal policies like the Agricultural Adjustment Act, but certainly not the Wagner Act with its encouragement of trade unions. Thus, as New Deal policies became more radical after 1935, more and more Democrats found it difficult to support them, causing splits within the party.

OPPOSITION FROM INDIVIDUALS

Huey Long and the 'Share our Wealth' Movement. Huey Long joined the US Senate in 1932 and became a supporter of Roosevelt and New Deal policies. He soon formed the view, however, that not enough was being done

Huey Long.

KEY PEOPLE

Huey Pierce Long (1893–1935) was born in Winnfield, Louisiana. He trained and practised as a lawyer and then entered politics. Between 1928 and 1930, he served as Governor of Louisiana and supported the small farmers who were suffering so much from falling prices. When the Great Depression hit the state, he spent public money on road building, hospitals and free schoolbooks. He was a skilled public speaker but those who opposed him were dealt with violently by his supporters and often removed from the political scene. Elections were often rigged, the police bribed and Long became virtually a dictator in Louisiana.

Charles Edward Coughlin was born in 1891 in Hamilton, Canada, of Irish Catholic, immigrant parents. Ordained to the priesthood in 1916, he became pastor of the Shrine of the Little Flower at Royal Oak, Detroit, in 1926. During the late 1920s, he became a radio broadcaster, commenting weekly on political rather than religious matters and attracting both a wide audience and a large correspondence. On the eve of the Wall Street Crash in 1929, he denounced Hoover, godless capitalists, Jews, communists and international bankers, all of whom he blamed for the economic troubles which were about to begin. He was considered by some to be a proto-fascist.

to help the poor and became a strong and potentially dangerous critic of Roosevelt. He began the 'Share our Wealth' movement, which had a very radical programme:

- He promised that, if elected President, all personal wealth over $3 million would be confiscated.
- The money would be used to give every family between $4,000 and $5,000 to buy a home, a car and a radio.
- He also promised free education, a minimum wage, old-age pensions, houses for war veterans and cheap food for the poor.

Some of these policies were clearly wild promises, which could not be kept. Long was certainly a colourful, populist politician, well known for exaggeration, but some of his ideas had been implemented in Louisiana. He claimed that, in 1935, his movement had 7.5 million members, organised in 27,000 branches, but then he did exaggerate! Nevertheless, he did intend to stand against Roosevelt as a third party candidate in the presidential election of 1936 and would have done so had he not been assassinated in 1935.

Long was a colourful if corrupt politician. He was a strong and very vocal critic of Roosevelt, who could have seriously damaged his chances of re-election in 1936 had he lived to stand against him.

Father Charles Coughlin. In 1933, Father Coughlin supported Roosevelt with the slogan 'The New Deal is Christ's Deal', but this ended in 1934 when one of Coughlin's main backers was accused of profiting from illegal foreign exchange operations. In 1935, he formed the National Union for Social Justice, promising work and fair wages for all and used the Union as a platform to attack Roosevelt whom he labelled 'anti-God'. By 1936, Coughlin was head of the organisation and, in the presidential election of that year, supported William Lemke from North Dakota as Union Party candidate. Lemke was not a serious threat to Roosevelt, polling less than 900,000 votes. Coughlin remained active until 1942 but was eventually silenced by his superiors who were angered by his anti-Semitic views.

The importance of Coughlin lies in the fact that at the height of his influence, 40 million Americans listened to his weekly broadcasts. This was the largest radio audience in the world and much larger than the number who listened to Roosevelt's 'fireside chats'. His appeal to urban, lower middle-class Americans and his attacks on the New Deal could have caused serious problems for Roosevelt but, fortunately for the President, they were not transferred into votes.

Dr Francis Townsend. Francis Townsend was a Californian doctor. His plan to improve the New Deal was possibly the most original of all. He appealed mainly to the old, who in 1934 benefited little from the policies which Roosevelt was introducing. He formed an organisation called 'Old Age Revolving Pensions, Limited'. Through this, he proposed to pay $200 a month to every citizen over the age of 60, provided that he or she was retired from work and that all the money was spent within a month, when another $200 would be paid. Townsend believed that his scheme could be financed by a 2 per cent tax on business transactions. The aim was that by encouraging people to retire, jobs would be freed for others to fill. By 1935, the 'Townsend Clubs' had 5 million members, but the whole project collapsed in 1936 when his partner, Robert Clements, was found guilty of stealing money from the funds. However, it is interesting to note that even after the passing of the Social Security Act in 1935, many older Americans still did not receive old-age pensions.

OPPOSITION FROM THE SUPREME COURT

Of the many battles which Roosevelt fought over the New Deal, his clashes with the Supreme Court of the United States were the most serious and threatening. It was inevitable that these clashes would occur because the Supreme Court was dominated by Republicans and its nine judges were likely to oppose New Deal policies.

Two cases illustrate the problems Roosevelt faced.

KEY THEME

Supreme Court judges are nominated by the President. Their politics reflect those of the President. From 1861 to 1933 there were only 16 years of Democrat presidents. Therefore the Supreme Court was dominated by Republicans.

- **The 'Sick Chickens' case** (*Schechter Poultry Corporation* v. *United States*) of May 1935. In Brooklyn, New York City, four Jewish brothers, the Schechters, ran a poultry business. In 1933, they signed the NRA code accepting NRA rules of fair prices, fair wages and fair competition. In 1935, the NRA took them to court for selling a batch of diseased chickens unfit for human consumption. They were convicted for breaking NRA rules by selling the chickens and for not following regulations on workers' wages and hours of work. The Schechters appealed against their conviction and on 27 May, the Supreme Court declared illegal the NRA code they had signed. The Schechter case struck down that part of the NIRA which claimed to use the interstate commerce clause as justification or authorisation for federal government to regulate economic activity. The Supreme Court argued that if this were upheld there would no longer be an effective division between state and federal governments. The federal government could extend its power into every area and there would be nothing left for the state government. Therefore it was protecting federalism as enshrined in the Constitution. This judgement was a death blow to the NRA, because if the poultry code was illegal, then all other NRA codes were illegal and 750 codes were, in fact, immediately scrapped.
- ***The United States* v. *Butler et al.*** In this case, in January 1936, the Supreme Court angered Roosevelt even further by declaring the Agricultural Adjustment Administration illegal. In the judgement of the nine justices, giving help to farmers was a matter for each state government, not the federal government. The result was that all help to farmers ceased.

Of the sixteen cases concerning the 'alphabet agencies', which were tried by the Supreme Court, the judges declared that in eleven Roosevelt and Congress had acted unconstitutionally. They therefore declared unconstitutional, for example, an Act regulating prices and working conditions in coal mines and a New York state law setting a minimum wage for women. Although it was possible to get round these judgements by introducing new laws, the attitude of the justices to the New Deal angered

Roosevelt to such an extent that he decided to act against them after his election victory in 1936.

Reform of the Supreme Court. On 5 February 1937, Roosevelt began his attempts to reform the Supreme Court. Realising that many of the justices were ageing, Roosevelt proposed that if a judge did not resign six months after his seventieth birthday, then the President should be allowed to appoint extra judges up to a total of six. Roosevelt made two serious errors with this proposal which was not passed by Congress.

- It was seen by many as a deliberate attempt to destroy the Constitution and to 'pack' the Court with judges who were likely to support him – which is exactly what it was, despite Roosevelt's claim that it was not.
- His second error was his failure to consult with the senior members of his own party before launching his reform plans, which resulted in many Conservative Democrats opposing them.

In March/April, 1937, the Supreme Court reversed the Schechter decision and in May declared legal the system of old-age pensions and unemployment insurance introduced in the Social Security Act. Although the New Deal was saved, some damage had been done to Roosevelt's reputation as an honest, straight-dealing politician. Most important of all was the way in which the pace of reform had slowed down, virtually to a standstill, because Roosevelt was too busy fighting the Supreme Court. The Democratic Party was now divided, making it more difficult to get New Deal laws through Congress.

KEY THEME

'The switch in time that saved nine' Shortly after this some of the older judges resigned and Roosevelt was able to make new nominations and get more liberal justices on to the Supreme Court.

TOUGH OPPOSITION

Roosevelt's massive election victory in 1936 was the signal for many **trade unionists** to increase their efforts to form single unions for each major industry and to step up the pressure for higher wages and better conditions. In fact, the Committee for Industrial Organisation had donated $770,000 to the Roosevelt campaign and was expecting

KEY TERM

Trade unions are organisations of and for labourers. They claim to represent the cause of the worker and to campaign for better working conditions, higher wages and to fight against (wrongful) dismissal.

help with their efforts to extend unionism throughout American industry.

At the end of 1936 and beginning of 1937, the Union of Auto Workers forced General Motors to shut down through a highly publicised 'sit-down' strike, with the factory occupied by the workers. The company accepted trade unions at its various factories and was followed soon afterwards by many others, including US Steel.

What angered many employers was not just the wave of unrest across the country but also the way in which Roosevelt seemed to side with the workers, whilst at the same time attacking the Supreme Court. Although, by 1940, there were still only 28 per cent of non-agricultural workers in trade unions, many employers became hardened further in their antipathy towards Roosevelt.

In June 1937, Roosevelt, worried by the possibility of inflation and under pressure to balance the budget, cut government spending. This hit the WPA and the PWA particularly badly. In addition, the federal government was taking large sums from the people in social security taxes. As the demand for goods fell, unemployment rose from 14.3 per cent to 19.1 per cent. In the nine months from August 1937, the **Federal Reserve Board**'s index dropped by over a third. It was as if all that the New Deal had achieved had been wiped away in a few months. Reports of people starving were becoming more widespread and the number on relief in Chicago increased from 50,000 to 120,000.

KEY TERM

Federal Reserve Board. This was the organisation in the US that sought to protect the banking system. It established a national system of reserve cash that was available to help struggling banks.

In April 1938, Roosevelt changed course and Congress granted his request for $1,000,000,000 for the PWA and $1,400,000,000 for the WPA. Slowly, the economy began to recover but, to many Americans, the President did not seem to be as much in command of the economy as he had been in earlier years. Between December 1937 and November 1938 his Gallup Poll support dropped from 62.1 per cent to 54.0 per cent (although these figures show considerable support given the circumstances).

Although in terms of major activity the New Deal had effectively come to an end, there were some important Acts passed in 1937 and 1938:

- In 1937, the **Wagner–Steagall Act** set up the United States Housing Authority making money available for low-cost housing.
- Also in 1937, the **Farm Tenancy Act** set up the Farm Security Administration making loans available to farm tenants and sharecroppers.
- In 1938, a new AAA law granted subsidies for food products and soil conservation.
- Also in 1938, the **Fair Labor Standards Act** introduced maximum hours and minimum wages for workers engaged in commerce between states and regulated child labour.

These Acts were passed through Congress with great difficulty. In 1938, the Republicans had increased the number of their representatives in both houses of Congress and many Conservative Democrats no longer supported Roosevelt. Whilst the New Deal was clearly coming to an end, the attention of many Americans was moving from domestic problems towards the worsening situation in Europe.

AN ASSESSMENT OF ROOSEVELT AND THE NEW DEAL

A great deal of controversy surrounds the effectiveness of Roosevelt and the New Deal. It is a subject that generates heated debate, with opinions sharply divided. To many richer Americans, Roosevelt was evil. His New Deal policies were seen as an attack on individual freedom and liberty and threatened to turn the United States into a communist state. Others saw it as potentially developing into national socialism.

The feelings that these richer Americans had for the President were summed up in April 1936 in *Time Magazine*:

'Regardless of party and regardless of region, today, with few exceptions, members of the so-called Upper Class frankly hate Franklin Roosevelt.'

At the other extreme, there were millions of ordinary Americans who worshipped him, almost like a god. They wrote to him directly at the White House as if he were an old friend – see the letter in the box on page 147. This

Dear Mr President,

This is just to tell you everything is all right now. The man you sent found our house all right and we went down the bank with him and the mortgage can go a while longer. You remember I wrote you about losing the furniture too. Well, your man got it back for us. I never heard of a President like you, Mr Roosevelt. Mrs _______ and I are old folks and don't amount to much, but we are joined with those millions of others in praying for you every night. God bless you, Mr Roosevelt.

letter does illustrate the way in which Roosevelt, with his direct appeal to the people, was a different type of president from those who preceded him. Even those who hated him could not ignore him.

WHAT DID ROOSEVELT ACHIEVE?

With the help of the evidence, it is possible to arrive at a balanced assessment of the New Deal and what Roosevelt achieved.

- **Employment.** Historians are agreed that the New Deal did not end unemployment in the United States, it brought only a partial economic recovery. By 1939, manufacturing production had returned to the level of 1929 but 9.5 million Americans were still unemployed – 17 per cent of the working population. It was not until 1941 that full employment and prosperity returned to America, a result of rearmament following the outbreak of the Second World War. However, the New Deal did mitigate the worst effects of the Depression on the most vulnerable – a remarkable achievement given the prevailing political and economic beliefs of the time which were so reluctant to see government taking the kinds of initiative Roosevelt took.
- **The role of government.** The New Deal was the beginning of a new role for the US government. Under Roosevelt, the government now had a responsibility to look after the welfare of all its citizens, regulate capitalism and ensure the economic prosperity of the country.
- **The bureaucracy.** Roosevelt created a large modern bureaucracy which is needed for a modern national government.
- **The Constitution.** The constitutional context was changed such that economic regulation was no longer considered in itself to be unconstitutional.
- **Compassion.** Roosevelt showed compassion and set an example of care for all people in the United States which his successors would find difficult *not* to follow in some degree.

- **Welfare.** The New Deal began basic welfare provisions, e.g. the Social Security Act, and turned the idea of welfare into law.
- **The role of the President.** The New Deal was closely identified by many with Roosevelt himself. His personality and character are, therefore, of great importance. On occasions, his administrative skills were weak. Nevertheless, the image of him in partnership with the people in a crusade to restore the nation's greatness was a very strong one. His appeal lay also in his practical approach to the country's problems. The New Deal was about helping those who were suffering and creating jobs for the people. In 1933, Roosevelt and the American people embarked on an experiment and there would be mistakes, but the people did not seem to mind. After years of very little happening, the country was at least on the move again.
- **Morale.** In many ways, Roosevelt restored the morale of the nation. Much has been made of his 'fireside chats' where he spoke directly to the American people. In fact, in 12 years as President, he made only 27 broadcasts, whereas in four years Hoover made 21. What was perhaps important was the difference in what they had to say.

As a result of Roosevelt's presidency and New Deal policies, the actual office of president started to become more powerful. This was not entirely welcomed by politicians, especially those who were opposed to Roosevelt's policies. However, it has continued to grow in importance since those years, together with the federal government in Washington. This is significant in the context of American federalism.

CRITICISMS OF ROOSEVELT

There were, however, clear limitations on what the New Deal achieved.

- **NRA.** The New Deal did not fundamentally redistribute income within the United States, whilst the policies on agriculture failed to help the worst-off. Some of the

KEY EVENT

The voyage of the 'St Louis'. In June 1939, the *St Louis*, carrying 900 émigré German Jews, anchored off the coast of Florida having been refused entry to Cuba, their original destination. Their appeals for permission to enter the USA were refused and the ship turned back to Europe. There the passengers were interned in camps where conditions were atrocious. Once Hitler occupied these European states, they once again fell foul of his destructive policies. Approximately 700 of the *St Louis*'s original passengers subsequently died in the extermination camps.

'alphabet agencies' achieved very little. The National Industrial Recovery Act, for example, probably did more harm than good by attempting to enforce industrial relations by legislation, rather than encouraging negotiated systems within individual organisations.

- **Housing.** No solution was found to the housing shortage caused by the Depression. The government introduced a very limited programme of house building which was inadequate to meet the need.
- **Discrimination.** Although more Catholics, Jews and African-Americans than ever before worked in federal jobs, nothing was actually done to improve the civil rights and the working and living conditions of black people. Discrimination, prejudice and anti-Semitism continued unabated. Although Roosevelt appointed individuals from all of these minority groups into key political positions, he often appeared passive in the pursuit of reform on racist issues even though minorities were becoming more assertive. One example is the move to legislate against lynching. Another is the fact that, although immigration quotas stood at 180,000 in the 1930s, only 75,000 German Jews, struggling to escape from Nazi persecution in Germany, were allowed to enter the USA.
- **Women.** With the exception of a few, nothing was done to encourage the changing role of women in the period. In fact, propaganda and legislation frequently reinforced the domestic and maternal role of women. This appeared to receive overwhelming support nationally.

A balanced assessment is therefore possible of Roosevelt and the New Deal and perhaps many would agree with the view of Joseph Alsop when he said:

> 'I do not believe that the real essence of Roosevelt's achievement on the home front is to be found in the list of new federal agencies he created . . . Instead, the very essence of his achievement . . . is derived from the combined impact of all his domestic reforms. On a very wide front and in the truest possible sense, Franklin Delano Roosevelt included the excluded.'

SUMMARY QUESTIONS

1 Where did the opposition to Roosevelt come from and why?

2 How successful was the development of trade unionism in America in the 1930s? (You will need to draw information from earlier chapters on the New Deal to answer this question fully.)

3 In what ways did it become more difficult for Roosevelt to extend his New Deal policies by the end of the decade?

4 Consider the reasons why Roosevelt's presidency 1933–9 is a controversial subject amongst historians.

CHAPTER 13

Foreign policy and the coming of war

Roosevelt's personal views of the role of the USA in foreign affairs are not straightforward. In his early political career he appeared to favour internationalism, but by the time that he stood for election as president, it is clear that he had embraced certain features of isolationism. Had he not done so, he almost certainly would not have gained the Democratic nomination to stand as the party's candidate in 1932, because economic rather than international policies were the key for a successful nomination. Once elected, the urgency of resolving the country's desperate financial difficulties took over. Roosevelt was pledged to his 'New Deal' policies and was not prepared to take any action that might threaten their success. He was a consummate politician and thus very sensitive to how lack of public and political support limited possibilities for international action. He was also very aware of how his Democratic predecessor, Woodrow Wilson, had seen his internationalist ambitions frustrated by lack of domestic political support. Roosevelt was determined not to repeat Wilson's error. He was always an internationalist, but was sensitive to the constraints imposed by lack of political and public support.

'Good Neighbor' policy. This was the nearest that Roosevelt got to pursuing an internationalist policy. In order to protect America's frontiers, he entered into friendly agreements with Latin America significantly reducing, but not completely removing, American influence. His decision to withdraw US troops from Haiti (occupied since 1914) and the Dominican Republic made him very popular in South America as did his decision to surrender America's right to intervene in Cuba. The USA also began to relinquish close control of the Panama Canal. In 1936, the US government agreed to allow Mexico to nationalise its oil fields even though some of these belonged to the USA. Favourable compensation terms were agreed.

Trade agreements. Roosevelt appears to have failed to recognise the significant contribution that America's protectionist trade policies had made to the collapse of the economy in 1929. In 1933, he sent his Secretary of State, Cordell Hull, to an international conference in London, assembled to agree strategies to stabilise world currencies and reach tariff agreements. Hull was a firm believer in free trade. He was convinced that this was the way to revive world trade and so rescue all those countries hit by economic depression. The USA could play a vital part in this. But, at a crucial point in the talks, Roosevelt sent one of his advisers, Raymond Moley, to London to tell Hull that he would not support any measures that might adversely affect the success of his New Deal policies. Hull had no choice, therefore, but to withdraw from the talks.

KEY THEME

Hull and free trade Hull believed that discriminatory tariffs and monetary arrangements were 'evil' in that they demonstated political discrimination between states or groups of states. Such discrimination caused a sense of injustice and tension that eventually led to international conflict and war. For example, the British imperial preference system, and policies of economic self-sufficiency in the Soviet Union, Nazi Germany, Italy and Japan all seemed to Hull to be significant causes of war.

In 1934, however, when the value of the dollar was at a more competitive level, Roosevelt supported Hull in Congress to secure the passage of the Reciprocal Trade Agreements Act. Congress agreed to allow the Roosevelt administration to lower tariffs by 50 per cent with those countries who agreed to reciprocate. Between 1934 and 1938, Hull negotiated reciprocal treaties with 18 other countries, mainly in Latin America but also with Britain in 1938. Generally, these only favoured the USA as they increased exports. America did little to contribute to the revival of world trade because imports remained at a low level.

The Neutrality Acts. Between 1935 and 1939, Congress passed a series of Neutrality Acts that made it virtually impossible for Roosevelt to give aid of any kind to warring states, even if he had wanted to do so. The first Act (1935) empowered the President to place an embargo on shipments of arms from America to the belligerents. Under this legislation, both sides in any dispute were equally regarded as 'belligerents'. It removed the distinction between aggressor and victim. The following year, a second Act stopped loans to countries engaged in war and in 1937, the terms were extended to include the supply of raw materials.

However, Roosevelt still managed to pursue internationalist aims despite the neutrality laws, for example:

- when war broke out between Italy and Abyssinia, he invoked the neutrality laws to stop the flow of supplies to Italy
- when Japan started its war with China in 1937, Roosevelt avoided invoking the neutrality laws so that the United States could continue to supply *matériel* to China.

War on the European horizon. Throughout these years, Roosevelt accepted the terms of the Neutrality Acts and did not use his powers to modify their implementation. Indeed, he failed to make any gesture that might have contributed towards reducing the risk of war. The USA, therefore, like the Allies in Europe, failed to make a move to enforce the terms of the Treaty of Versailles when Hitler blatantly ignored them by rearming and marching into the Rhineland in 1936. At home, he appeared unsympathetic to the plight of German Jews as news of their systematic persecution was relayed to Washington from the US ambassador in Berlin. The damage had been well and truly done before he agreed to ease the US immigration laws to enable more emigrants to enter the country. But Roosevelt did pass the trade agreement with Britain in 1938 that was seen as politically important.

Japanese aggression in China. If anything in the outside world troubled Roosevelt at this time, it was Japanese aggression towards China. In spite of apparently pursuing an isolationist policy throughout the inter-war years, the USA did take a particular interest in Asia. American missionaries and technicians worked in Burma, Siam (Thailand) and Korea as well as China and Japan. Asians in these countries were taught by Americans and governments were advised by them. In 1937, Japan went to war against China. The USA responded by placing an embargo on goods going to Japan – oil, rubber and iron. However, this embargo was slow in coming.

The outbreak of the Second World War. When war finally broke out in Europe in 1939, Roosevelt realised that the USA would not be able to remain neutral for long. Hitler's rearmament programmes meant that Germany was well placed to fight a full-scale war. The Allies, on the other hand, having followed a policy of appeasement, were much less well prepared for war when it came. US neutrality, therefore, affected Britain and France much more than Germany.

By 1940, Roosevelt knew that it was only a matter of time before America would be at war. He clearly supported Britain in the war and did not hide the fact that he was an enemy of Hitler. A Selective Service Act was passed allowing young men to be conscripted in peacetime and a defence programme was introduced to produce 50,000 planes a year. The Neutrality Acts were amended in stages by Congress. US neutrality was compromised by

- the 1940 destroyers-for-bases deal with Great Britain
- the **Lend-Lease** Act
- the US Navy assisting British convoys
- the Atlantic Conference in 1941 with Churchill
- the increasing severity of US sanctions against Japan.

In spite of the news from Europe, by 1940 only 7.7 per cent of Americans favoured voluntary entry into the war. In May 1941, 79 per cent was still opposed. However, the bombing by the Japanese of the US naval base at Pearl Harbor in December 1941 propelled America into the Second World War. On the home front, the country was mobilised for wartime production. It marked the end of America's isolationism – a policy to which it would never return.

KEY TERM

Lend-Lease The Lend-Lease Act 1941 allowed Roosevelt to send aid to countries whose defence was vital to that of the United States. Under its terms, Britain received $28.94 billion.

Whilst Roosevelt had not been totally inactive in the years since 1939 and had begun to mobilise the USA for possible involvement in the war, the country's economic and industrial potential now became fully harnessed to ensuring success.

- The 'alphabet agencies' were quickly replaced by a plethora of government bodies organising and

KEY EVENTS

Examples of wartime agencies set up to mobilise production:

War Production Board

War Manpower Commission

National War Labor Board

Office of Defense, Health and Warfare

Office of Price Administration

Office of Production Management

War Shipping Administration

Office of War Mobilisation

Office of Scientific Research and Development

Federal Public Housing Authority

War Food Administration

Office of Defense Transportation

Board of Economic Warfare

Office of the Lend-Lease Administration

Foreign Economic Administration (FEA) (1943)

administering wartime production. These were run by Roosevelt's New Deal administrators, such as Harry Hopkins. Increasingly, business people were brought in to help – many only accepted $1 per year for doing so ('dollar a year men'). One example of such businessmen was Leo Crowley, who ran the FEA.

- Government spending ran at $250 million a day.
- America's advanced methods of mass production, along with big business, were rapidly harnessed to the production of ships, tanks, aeroplanes, guns and ammunition (by 1945, shipbuilders were producing a cargo ship a day).
  - By 1945, the USA was the world's leading manufacturer of weapons and ammunition. It had also, of course, manufactured the world's first nuclear bomb.
  - Production of raw materials rose significantly.
  - Big business also managed to mass produce penicillin for the first time. As one contemporary observed:

    'If you are going to try to go to war in a capitalist country, you have to let business make money out of the process or business won't work.'
- Japanese control of sources of natural rubber led the USA rapidly to develop its own synthetic rubber industry. Within two years, it was producing 80 per cent of its needs.
- The war also reversed the fortunes of the nation's farmers. Across the board, wages rose higher than prices and the value of farm property rose over the period to $20 billion.
- The combined effect of full-scale production and the numbers of men drafted into the armed forces was to end unemployment and redistribute wealth with surprising speed. Apart from the 1 million African-Americans and 75,000 Native Americans who joined the armed forces, more job opportunities arose for minority groups.
- The money earned by wartime industry raised the standard of living amongst all Americans working on the home front. As profits soared, consumer purchasing power rose by 50 per cent.

Increase in production of raw materials 1940–5	
Increase in raw steel production	20%
Increase in rayon and acetate yarn production	55%
Increase in fuel oil production	44%
Increase in wheat flour production	27%

Increase in farm production 1940–5	
Increase in corn production	477 million bushels
Increase in wheat production	324 million bushels
Increase in rice production	500 million pounds

The production of arms and ammunition 1942–5	
Military aircraft	300,000
Tanks	86,000
Machine guns	2.6 million
Bombs	6 million tons
Cargo ships	5,000
Warships	86,000

'THE JANES WHO MAKE THE PLANES': WOMEN IN WARTIME AMERICA

Once again, war provided women with the opportunity to show what they could do. They left their aprons behind and donned their overalls or boiler suits to operate cranes, weld the hulls of ships, fit out ships, work in munitions factories, drive taxis, buses or trains, become electricians or tend blast furnaces. Over 6 million women entered the workforce between 1942 and 1945. Of these, 75 per cent were married women. However, although the National War Labor Board authorised equal pay for equal work, discrimination in wages continued. Women earned about 65 per cent of the wages paid to men doing the same work.

For the first time, women also entered the armed forces – 300,000 of them.

- Auxiliary services were formed to the army, navy, airforce, nursing and coastguard services.
- General Eisenhower, Supreme Commander of the North Africa and European campaigns, employed women auxiliaries in his campaign headquarters.
- As in England, some women joined the Land Army, much to the consternation of the farmers!

Nevertheless, underpinning the efforts of women on the home front was a persistent propaganda campaign emphasising the short-term nature of the wartime situation. Women had responded to the national emergency, but afterwards they should return to their traditional role. In 1945, a poll showed that only 18 per

Women at work in a munitions factory during the Second World War.

cent of Americans believed that women should work. Clearly, some of this propaganda was based on the concern that there must be jobs for demobilised soldiers when the war ended.

But the war had also disrupted family life significantly. The divorce rate in the USA doubled and delinquency rates amongst teenage youngsters rose alarmingly. After the end of the war large numbers of women did return to the home. Others took advantage of the opportunities that had been offered in the war years to study law, medicine and engineering. Many recognised their own potential and the advantages that work could bring.

PROSPECTS FOR PEACETIME

The post-war years would put to the test the long-term effects of Roosevelt's New Deal and of the spirit unleashed at home by the experience of war. Minority groups recognised the fundamental irony of fighting for a nation that went to war to establish justice and freedom abroad when it tolerated racism and inequality at home. The demand for civil rights would be a feature of post-war America. Workers who had joined trade unions in large numbers in the war years were unlikely to continue to be deterred from demanding their rights. Continued economic growth and development would challenge post-war administrations. The USA would have to decide its future role in the world.

SUMMARY QUESTIONS

1 In what way was Roosevelt's foreign policy a) similar to b) different from that followed by US presidents in the 1920s?

2 What do you consider to be the turning point in Roosevelt's foreign policy that led to US involvement in events in Europe?

AS ASSESSMENT: BOOM AND BUST 1917–32 AND THE UNITED STATES OF AMERICA 1933–45

Source questions – some general points

Source questions assess your understanding of the nature and use of historical evidence. In responding to them, you demonstrate your understanding of the process of writing history. In the examination, it is vital that you respond specifically to the source material that you are given. The following general points are only to help you to develop the thinking skills you need to respond to this part of the paper. They do not provide answers by themselves.

Use all the sources. It is helpful to take a little time to read **all** of the sources before you begin work on them. This gives you the sense of what the exercise is all about as well as information that might help you to focus your answers.

- You will gain an overall picture of the kind of evidence you have been given to work on (e.g. primary/secondary sources, critical/ congratulatory, sarcastic/cynical, balanced/biased etc.).
- You can also begin the process of recalling your **knowledge** of the subject and of the people providing the evidence, as you read. This will help you to recognise the significance of times and dates, to decide if the sources are all talking about the same thing at the same time (e.g. differing views on the effects of Prohibition may depend on whether the authors are referring to the cities, the rural areas or the whole of the USA).

Content. You will be asked to use the content of the sources. This may involve giving an explanation of a significant word or phrase. It could be related to the details of an event or a judgement of an individual.

- You might be asked to compare the content of two or more sources. As part of this process, note the **differences and the similarities.**
- Use your knowledge of the period or subject to identify things that are **missing** from one but contained in another. This is where you have to begin asking yourself questions. Why are there omissions? Has the detail been deliberately or accidentally omitted? If the omission is deliberate, why has it been left out? What other explanations might there be for two sources on the same subject to be different? These questions take you a little deeper into your enquiry.

Origin of the source. To begin to answer these questions, you need to use your knowledge of the author to provide you with the information you need. Do you know if the author was a supporter or a critic of the person/decision/event that the source is about? Then place your knowledge of the author in the context of your general knowledge; for instance, you **know** that Congress was critical of Wilson's Fourteen Points and that Republicans favoured a return to isolationism; you **know** that there were many groups of Americans that were highly critical of Roosevelt and his New Deal. You will need to use this kind of information if you are asked to account for the differences between sources and also if you are beginning to think about how **truthful** or **reliable** a source might be. By itself, however, this level of enquiry might not be enough to help you move into these two areas. As soon as you start asking questions, the answers generate more questions and take you deeper into your investigation.

- **Motivation/purpose.** In addition to recognising the particular bias of an author, you may need to consider the motive or purpose for what has been written. An extract from a newspaper article, for example, may have been written deliberately to encourage readers to think in a particular way; the writings of a member of the Ku Klux Klan will be written deliberately in a style that will arouse readers' racist feelings.
- **The language of bias.** The style in which a source is written can help you to make decisions about the purpose/motive/attitude of the author. Look carefully at the words used, particularly descriptive terms. Assess the tone of the passage. Is it angry/sarcastic/overly enthusiastic or supportive?

Considerations such as these will inform your thinking when you have to make judgements about how truthful or reliable a source might be. Remember that even if the evidence is biased, it remains of value to a historian since it can inform about the range of values and attitudes at a time in the past, but balanced interpretations can only be produced on the basis of a range of sources.

Sources exercise in the style of Edexcel/OCR.

Exercise 1 Racism and prejudice in the 1920s

Reading. Before you begin, read Chapter 5 (pages 55–67).

Source A

The Klan don't hate nobody! In fact, the Klan is everybody's best friend. Southern whites, occupying that super-position assigned to them by the Creator, are justifiably hostile to any race that attempts to drag them down to its own level! Therefore let black man be wise in leaving the ballot in the hands of a dominant sympathetic race.

From a speech given in Georgia in 1954 by Dr E.P. Pruitt,
Grand Dragon of the Federated Klans of Alabama.

Source B

When my mother was pregnant with me, she told me later, a party of hooded Ku Klux Klan riders galloped up to our home in Omaha, Nebraska, one night. Surrounding the house, brandishing their shotguns and rifles, they shouted for my father to come out. My mother went to the front door and opened it. Standing where they could see her pregnant condition, she told them that she was alone with her three small children, and that my father was away, preaching in Milwaukee. The Klansmen shouted threats and warnings at her that we had better get out of town because 'the good Christian white people' were not going to stand for my father's 'spreading trouble' among the 'good' Negroes of Omaha with the 'back to Africa' preachings of Marcus Garvey.

From the *Autobiography of Malcolm X* (1965).

Source C

The Klan was a super-secret organisation; masked and mysterious, with a tradition of violence for which a generation of legend had achieved a high measure of social approval. The attainment of its . . . goals, which were to protect God, Country, Home, Womanhood, the South and White Supremacy, was of paramount urgency . . . Its greatest selling point was the protection of traditional Americanism.

An extract from David M. Chalmers, *Hooded Americanism: The History of the Ku Klux Klan* (1981).

Source D

Mississippi: The white farmer has not always been the lazy, slipshod, good-for-nothing person that he is frequently described as being. Somewhere in his span of life he became frustrated. He felt defeated. He felt the despair and dejection that comes from defeat. He was made aware of the limitations of life imposed upon those unfortunate enough to be made slaves of sharecropping. Out of his predicament grew desperation; out of desperation grew resentment. His bitterness was a taste his tongue would always know.

In a land that has long been glorified in the supremacy of the white race, he directed his resentment against the black man . . . He released his pent-up emotions by lynching the black man in order to witness the mental and physical suffering of another human being . . . When his own suffering was more than he could stand, he could live only by witnessing the suffering of others.

An extract from Erskine Caldwell, *You Have Seen Their Faces* (1937). Caldwell was an investigative journalist. With his wife, the photographer Margaret Bourke-White, he made a study of poverty in the southern states in the mid-1930s.

Source E

By the mid 1920s, estimates of membership in the Klan and its auxiliary, Women of the Klan, ranged from two million to five million. The revived Klan, its targets not only blacks but Catholics, Jews, and immigrants, thrived in the midwest and far west as well as the South . . .

Klan bigotry varied from region to region. In the South the anti-black theme loomed large, but Klaverns in the North and West more often targeted Catholics and Jews. In the southwest the Klan focused on violators of prohibition and traditional morality . . .

The Klan filled important needs for its members. Although riddled with corruption at the top, the organisation consisted primarily of ordinary people, not criminals or fanatics. The Klan's promise to restore the nation to an imagined purity – ethnic, moral and religious – appealed powerfully to ill-educated and deeply religious Americans . . . Klan membership, moreover, bestowed a sense of importance and group cohesion on people who doubted their own worth.

Taken from Paul S. Boyer, *The Enduring Vision. A History of the American People*, published in the USA (1995).

Questions

1 Study Source A. According to this source, what is the attitude of the Ku Klux Klan towards African-Americans?

How to answer this question. The question is asking you to show that you understand the source. Therefore you must do the following:

- Provide some explanation which answers the question.
- Extract brief quotes from the source to back up what you are saying.

Style. Use your own words but, where appropriate, use short quotes from the source to support what you are saying. An answer to this kind of question should read like this:

In this source, the Grand Dragon suggests that African-Americans should, therefore, accept their inferior position, surrender their right to vote, they should become 'political eunuchs', in other words, powerless, allowing the 'dominant sympathetic race', that is white Americans, to rule them.

2 Study Source B. Use the source and your own knowledge to answer this question. Why has the preaching of 'back to Africa' ideas by the father of Malcolm X so angered the Ku Klux Klan?

How to answer this question. The question is asking you to explain the key term of 'back to Africa'. The question is asking for your knowledge about this and its significance in the context of the beliefs and attitudes of the Ku Klux Klan. (Your answer to the previous question should help to inform your answer to this question.) Therefore you need to respond with a thorough explanation which takes in at least some of the following points:

- An explanation of the meaning of 'back to Africa' and the work of Marcus Garvey, in particular, covering the emphasis on racial pride and assertiveness.
- Recognition that this ran contrary to the beliefs and attitudes of the Ku Klux Klan who preached the inferiority of African-Americans and their subservience to their white American 'masters'.
- Reference to the fact that the Ku Klux Klan threatened the parents of Malcolm X because they regarded his father's preaching as subversive and threatened white control of the local African-American population.

3 Study Sources C, D and E. To what extent is rural poverty an explanation for the increased support for the Ku Klux Klan in the 1920s?

How to answer this question. You need to look for reasons for increased support for the Ku Klux Klan. The question asks you to use the sources and you need to focus on what they say in your answer.

Plan. Before you write you need to come to some kind of conclusion about how you will answer the question. An example might be along the lines of the following:

- Only to a certain extent was rural poverty the reason for increased support for the Ku Klux Klan. The Klan's increased support was partly due to the moral atmosphere in post-war America that responded to the claim of the Klan that it would uphold so-called 'American values'.

Style. Make sure that you quote from the sources when making your point. Below is an example of the style you might adopt in answering this question.

In the 1920s the United States was swept by a wave of insecurity about foreigners. This was seen in the 'Red Scare' phenomenon in the early part of the century. Therefore the factor of rural poverty is not enough to explain the Klan's appeal. In Indiana where the Klan was most popular, many were attracted by what Source C describes – the 'greatest selling point was the protection of traditional Americanism'.

4 Study Sources A, C and D. How valuable are these sources to a historian studying the beliefs and impact of the Ku Klux Klan?

How to answer this question. When answering a question about the value of a source you should try to avoid generalisations about the type of source and you should attempt to concentrate on more than just its content. You should therefore ask yourself the following questions:

- What is the situation of the author of the source?
- What is the purpose of the author in producing the source?
- What are the limitations of each source as well as its positive points?

Style. Try to refer to the sources when possible to back up your ideas. To gain top marks you need to ensure that you cover all of the sources. Below is an example of the style you might choose to use.

The Ku Klux Klan craved respectability as part of their campaigns and Source A is an example of this. In the source, Pruitt is attempting to present the Klan as a rational and reasonable organisation. However, the limitations of the source are clear, Pruitt is attempting to justify the exclusion of African-Americans from the electoral process. The value of the source is in what it reveals about the aims of the Klan as well as their methods.

5 Use your own knowledge and Source E to explain the influence that the Ku Klux Klan had on American society in the 1920s.

How to answer this question. This question asks you to analyse the impact the Ku Klux Klan had on society. To reach full marks you will need to do the following:

- Look for a variety of influences exercised by the Klan. Prioritise your most important influences.
- Use information from both the source and your own knowledge.
- Plan your line of argument first and what you are going to put in each paragraph.

Exercise 2 Boom and Bust

Read the sources carefully and then answer the questions which follow.

Source A

People were speculating. Now who are you going to blame aside from them selves? It's their fault. See my point? If you gamble and make a mistake . . . it's your fault. Way back in the 1920s, people were wearing $20 silk shirts and throwing their money around like crazy . . . In 1929, I had a friend who speculated.

He'd say 'What's a good bet?'
I'd say 'We're selling high-grade mortgage bonds on Commonwealth Edison.'
'Oh hell – 5% – I can make 10% on the Stock Market.'
He was buying at great risk and thought he was rich. The government had nothing to do with that – it was people.

Adapted from an interview with Martin de Vries.

Source B

Selected prices of stocks floated on Wall Street, 1927–9.

Stock	*August 1927*	*August 1928*	*September 1929*
American and Foreign Power	$23.86	$38.00	$167.75
American Telephone and Telegraph	$169.00	$182.00	$304.00
Detroit Edison and Co.	$151.00	$205.00	$350.00
People's Gas Chicago	$147.13	$182.86	$374.75

Source C

Happiness lies not in the mere possession of money; it lies in the joy of achievement, in the thrill of creative effort. The joy of work must not be forgotten in the mad chase for short-term profits. Recognition of the falsity of material wealth as the standard of success goes hand in hand with the abandonment of the false belief that public office and high political position are to be valued only by the standards of pride of place and personal profit; and there must be an end to selfish and callous conduct in banking and business.

Adapted from Roosevelt's inaugural address, March 1933.

Source D

In my opinion the wealth of the country is bound to increase at a very great rate . . . I am firm in my belief that anyone not only can be rich but ought to be rich. Prosperity is in the nature of an endless chain and we can break it only by refusing to see what it is . . . if a man saves $15 a week and invests it in good common stocks, and allows the dividends and rights to accumulate, at the end of twenty years he will have at least $80,000 and an income of around $400 a month. He will be rich.

Adapted from John J. Raskob writing in 1929.
Raskob was Democratic National Committee Chairman.

Source E

Despite the limited purchasing power of most Americans, the big industries continued in the late 1920s to pour out all sorts of items notably goods such as automobiles and luxury home appliances which could only be bought by the middle and upper classes. They could not be easily exported abroad because the high tariffs meant US goods were expensive abroad. Inevitably, the domestic market became overstocked towards the end of the decade – producers were faced with the option of reducing output or selling at a lower price. Both options would result in the laying off of workers.

Adapted from D. Snowman, *America since 1920* (1978).

Questions

1 Study Sources A and B. What do the sources tell you about the stock market boom in the USA in the 1920s?

How to answer this question. To answer this question you should try to do the following:

- Sum up in your own words what the sources suggest about the boom.
- Quote briefly from the sources.

Style. Here is an extract from an answer to this question. Note how the candidate infers from the sources and then uses one of them for evidence.

The sources suggest that the stock market boom was driven by rapidly inflating prices. In Source B the price of shares in Detroit Edison and Co. rises from $151.00 in August 1927 to $350.00 in September 1929. Such a high rate of increase shows that by 1929 the shares were over-priced.

2 Using your own knowledge explain why the Wall Street Crash happened in 1929.

How to answer this question. The key to answering this question is the organisation of your information. The question does not ask you to use the evidence although there might be clues to the answer in the sources, e.g. in Source E it explains the impact of overproduction and tariffs. You need to identify your reasons for the Crash before you start.

Plan. You need to ensure that your answer focuses on the causes of the Crash. Before you start you should write in your plan the key themes which can then become your brief introduction. Here are some examples:

- The Crash was primarily caused by an overheating of the stock market coupled with a downturn in the fortune of America's leading companies.
- The nature of demand, the *laissez-faire* attitude of the government and the collapse in confidence led to the Crash.

3 Study Sources A and D. What is the value of these sources to a historian studying speculation in the USA in the late 1920s and early 1930s?

How to answer this question. To be given a good mark for this question you need to ensure that you explain the value of both sources. You should also try to compare the sources' value.

When you are asked about the value of a source you need to ask the following questions:

- What is the nature of the source?
- Who is the author of the source?
- What is his/her purpose in producing the source?
- Is the source produced as propaganda?
- Has the author deliberately distorted the evidence?
- What is the situation of the author?
- Is the author in a position to know about the subject of the source?
- In your view has the author used the full range of sources available at the time?
- Has the author dealt with the different views from the time?
- How has the author dealt with gaps in his/her evidence? Has he/she simply ignored them?
- How much is the interpretation an example of the kind of attitudes held at the time of writing?

Style. Here is an extract from an answer assessing the value of Source D. Note that the candidate has attempted to use her own information to answer this question. She is also looking at the situation of the author.

The source is most valuable as evidence of the attitudes towards speculation at the time. As chairman of the Democratic National Committee, Raskob shows that the unbounded optimism about the economy's future and the acceptability of speculation was held by Democrats and Republicans. It was only later, after the Crash, that the Democrats sought a new approach.

4 Study Sources C and D. How far does Roosevelt disagree in Source C with Raskob's prioritisation of wealth and prosperity?

How to answer this question. You need to make sure that you do the following when answering this question:

- Briefly plan the areas where disagreement/agreement takes place.
- Refer to, and select information from, the sources.

Plan. Very briefly identify your main line of argument. Below is an example:

- Whilst not rejecting wealth in itself, Roosevelt disagrees with Raskob's prioritisation of wealth. Instead he argues that it should be placed in the context of other factors.

Style. You should try to explain each point you make, quote where necessary and cover as many points as possible. Below is an extract from an answer to this question. The candidate has attempted to deal with this question in this style.

Roosevelt does not criticise the 'mere possession of money' but places it in the context of other factors such as 'the joy of achievement'. In that he is attempting to move attitudes away from those suggested by Raskob, e.g. that the pursuit of wealth is paramount because 'prosperity is in the nature of an endless chain'.

5 Use your own knowledge and the information from Sources B and E. How far do you agree with the view that the United States' economy was weakened by the nature of demand for American goods in the 1920s?

How to answer this question. You are asked to give an analytical answer to this question. The main focus of your answer must be on the nature of demand. To be awarded the top marks you need to do the following:

- Argue using the sources and your own knowledge.
- Link overproduction with other factors, in particular the nature of demand and protectionism.
- Show that you can sustain a judgement throughout the question.

Style. Below is an extract from an answer to this question. The candidate has sustained an argument in a direct style throughout the answer.

Whilst demand for some goods was high for most of the decade, the introduction of protectionist barriers was to have an important impact. A series of measures introducing tariffs was introduced with the aim of protecting American industry and agriculture in the post-war years. In 1922 the Fordney–McCumber Tariff Act was passed. This contained the highest tariff rates in American history. The result was that those countries affected introduced reciprocal tariffs. When in the late 1920s the

American market was saturated, there was no overseas market to soak up the extra production.

Exercise 3 in the style of Edexcel. Using a source as stimulus

Source A

Contemporaries and later critics have blamed the New Deal for not going further, faster; it is always so easy to demand the impossible and tempting to play down the importance of starting something. FDR and his team started a lot, and as he himself said after the 1938 elections: 'It takes a long, long time to bring the past up to the present.' Rather than comparing the New Deal to Utopia it is better to bring out the actual achievements. Of these unquestionably the most important was the preservation of American democracy, the American Constitution and American capitalism. Even if the Supreme Court limited his power he taught it the lesson not to stand in the way of change. He set a new pattern for the relationship between Congress and President. He also made the country used to the intervention of government in order to safeguard the welfare of the people.

From *The History of the United States of America* by Hugh Brogan.

Questions

1 How highly does the author of this source rate the achievements of Roosevelt? Use the source and explain your answer fully.

How to answer this question. The question wants you to focus your answer on Source A.

- In asking you to explain your answer the question is also hoping that you will explain the author's view of Roosevelt's achievements by using your own knowledge.
- You should quote from the source whenever possible. However, you should ensure that your quotes are short and to the point.

Style. You need to answer the question directly. Here is an example of a paragraph showing how you might do that.

The tone of this extract is most positive when describing Roosevelt's achievements. The author rates Roosevelt's achievements highly because he has placed them in the wider context of American political life. So he does not dwell on the mixed economic success of the New Deal but looks at the role Roosevelt's initiatives played in ensuring the 'preservation of American democracy'. Similarly the author praises the modernising influence of the New Deal; its achievement was in modernising the Constitution, e.g.

teaching the Supreme Court 'not to stand in the way of change'.

2 What were the main aims of the New Deal in the period 1933–9?

How to answer this question. Although there is a source at the start of the exercise, the question does not ask you to use it if you do not want to. Instead the source can act as a stimulus; it can give you a clue to at least a part of your answer.

The question here wants you to describe the main features of the New Deal. It would be a good idea for you to organise your description thematically. Themes you might include are:

- Restoring confidence, reducing unemployment, modernising the economic infrastructure, the protection of democracy.

3 Why did the New Deal provoke opposition in the years 1933–9?

How to answer this question. For this question you are to use the source but only as a stimulus. The question asks for an analytical answer. Therefore you need to do the following:

- Answer with a strong line of argument based on a plan of the reasons why there was opposition to the New Deal.
- Show that you understand why various groups opposed the New Deal.
- Use well selected evidence to back up your argument.

Content.
- Source. In the source there are references to those who felt that the New Deal did not go far enough and the Supreme Court which tried to obstruct it as unconstitutional.
- Own knowledge. From your own knowledge you could explain that opposition to the New Deal came from those who felt that the Federal government was becoming too powerful, those who believed in *laissez-faire* and opposed increased taxation and bodies such as the unions who wanted to see further improvements.

Exercise 4 in the style of AQA. Course essay question

Why did the USA economy prosper for much of the 1920s?

How to answer this question. To achieve high marks you need to do the following:

- The key to a successful course essay is a long and detailed plan.
- Your main points of argument need to be clearly thought through.

• You need to link the main factors together in your plan and throughout your essay.

General points on structure. It is important that you think about how you will structure your answer before you try to tackle the question. You will be able to plan before you write your timed essay. To make your plan and answer this type of essay question you need to do the following:

- Read the question carefully and identify what the question is asking you.
- Frame a response to the question which is direct and to the point.
- Include in your plan a list of points which will form the basis of your argument/judgement. You should then briefly map out what you plan to put in each paragraph.
- Start your answer with a brief introduction.
- Keep your paragraphs to the point.
- Choose evidence to back up the points you have made and use it in your answers.
- Conclude in such a way that you clearly state the judgement you have made in response to the question.

Plan. You need to plan your essay to avoid simply running through a narrative account of the 1920s. You need in particular to identify the points of argument which will allow you to do this. Here are some examples:

- Prosperity was a product of a combination of factors. The most important cause was the new technology and production techniques which had been refined by the 1920s.
- However, these new industries were fuelled by demand stimulated by credit and advertising.
- The demand created by war further stimulated the technical improvements.

Content. You must ensure that the content you use covers the 1920s. You should make reference to the following in your essay:

- the impact of the First World War
- the development of mass production techniques
- the impact of the growth of the motor car industry
- the development of radio
- the natural resources of the USA.

A2 SECTION: ANALYSIS AND INTERPRETATION

SECTION 1

What was the impact on America of the First World War?

Since gaining independence in the eighteenth century, the United States had fought only three foreign wars: in 1812 (against Britain), in 1848 (Mexican War) and in 1898 (Spanish–American War). Although these wars were directly the result of US government policies, they were followed by expressions of regret and recrimination that the cherished self-image had been tarnished. This resulted in a reaffirmation of the determination to remain neutral in the face of conflict that was not of America's making. The outbreak of war in Europe in 1914 was, therefore, the first major test of this resolve. Consequently, America's subsequent entry into the war in 1917 was not only traumatic but also controversial.

There are those historians who believe that it could only have been a matter of time before the United States became involved. Great Britain and the United States shared a broadly common culture and partly common history, which would eventually cause the Americans to enter the conflict on the Allied side. Such an interpretation ignores the powerful and pivotal importance of Woodrow Wilson and his attempts to maintain the position of neutrality set for the United States in 1914. This section examines his efforts to keep America out of the conflict. In the light of the failure in 1917 to achieve this, the section goes on to examine the impact of the war on the United States and on the political fortunes of Wilson himself.

HISTORICAL INTERPRETATIONS

From the early 1920s, historians in the USA began to interpret the events leading up to the decision of 1917, focusing particularly on Wilson himself and the factors that influenced him. Initially, such historians based their hypotheses on relatively sparse evidence. They were influenced by the diplomacy of Wilson's closest advisers on the subject – Walter Hines Page (the US ambassador to Britain), Edward House (Wilson's friend and adviser) and the Nye Committee. All of these had supported entry into the war as being not only morally right but also in America's best interests. Later in the decade, however, revisionist historians criticised Wilson's decision as greedy and materialistic, made under the influence of bankers and financiers who stood to gain from American involvement.

Subsequently, as Wilson's diplomacy at Versailles and Wilson himself were rejected, historians focused on the issue of neutrality and the extent to which Wilson, an Anglophile, had applied it fairly. Increasingly, in the 1930s, Wilson came to be blamed for his prejudice against Germany when applying the policy of neutrality. This, it was claimed, forced Germany into the position of having no choice but to use the unrestricted submarine warfare that helped to propel the USA into the war. Americans were receptive to these critical arguments during the thirties because, to them, the rise of fascism in Europe, and its consequent destruction of democracy, made a mockery of the Wilsonian morality that had been used to justify American involvement in 1917. This disillusionment coincided with the period of reaffirmation of neutrality in the face of economic crisis at home and the deteriorating situation in Europe by the mid 1930s. An important factor that influenced perception of the First World War was the harsh treatment meted out to Germany at Versailles. Many liberals came to see it as vindictive (Keynes wrote a diatribe against Versailles, *The Economic Consequences of the Peace*) because of reparations and other conditions. This view was reinforced by French vindictiveness and provocative actions in the 1920s and refusal to disarm or reduce arms in the 1920s and 1930s. Moreover, during the Roosevelt years, and especially as war loomed in Europe, American historians such as **Charles A. Beard**, critically reappraised involvement in the First World War as a justification of the current policies of neutrality. War, they argued, was incompatible with liberal reform and America in the 1930s was more desperately in need of the latter. Historians who developed these hypotheses in the 1930s were clearly influenced by events in their time. There was, therefore, an almost propagandist bias to their work. **Professor Charles Seymour** of Yale University did, however, attempt to look objectively at the evidence. He reached the conclusion that, although Wilson and his advisers were pro-British, there had been an attempt to implement neutrality fairly. It was German submarine activity that forced the issue.

In the 1950s and 1960s, a vast amount of material was available to historians, including Wilson's personal and official papers. These scholars were also writing at a time when the USA had an increasingly significant part to play in world affairs. Wilson was criticised by some for his allegedly moralistic approach to foreign affairs and by others (for example, **George Kennan and Hans J. Morgenthau**, 1951) who argued that

KEY THEME

Realism v. Idealism These two views of foreign policy can be represented by Kennan/ Morgenthau (realists) on the one hand and Wilson (idealist) on the other. They take different stances on how to view foreign policy decision-making. Realism sees international relations in terms of power and security. Foreign policy is to ensure a state's survival.

Wilson's entry into the war and his subsequent ideas for the preservation of peace disturbed the balance of power in Europe. This was not in keeping with American interests at the time. Ultimately, the Versailles Treaty created serious political, social and economic weaknesses that led to the Second World War. If America had remained neutral, Wilson's idea of a negotiated peace ('peace without victory') might have been achieved and future conflict avoided. All of these interpretations assume that Wilson alone had the freedom and autonomy to make crucial decisions. More recent research has emphasised the extent to which Wilson's actions were restricted, as well as the complexity of the causes of America's entry into the First World War.

HOW FAR DID WILSON PURSUE A POLICY OF NEUTRALITY FROM 1914 TO 1917?

Initially, neutrality seemed to be in America's best interests. To many Americans, the events in Europe leading to the First World War must have seemed very remote and distant. Whilst the assassination at Sarajevo, the German invasion of Belgium and the outbreak of hostilities were widely reported throughout the United States, many regarded the war as an entirely European conflict. Above all, it was a war in which the United States should not get involved. Furthermore, it seemed to epitomise the amoral power politics and dynastic squabbling that had led the United States to adopt a policy of isolationism from European affairs right from the birth of the Republic. The view of the realists was that the United States would gain little from involvement, especially when there appeared little threat to US security so long as Great Britain commanded the Atlantic. President Wilson and the government supported this view. On 4 August 1914, they issued a declaration of neutrality, which stated the official American line – the United States would stay out. Whilst this position had wide support, it would be difficult to maintain. A significant percentage of the American population were of German origin, but there was also considerable support for Britain and the Allies. Wilson himself was an Anglophile and felt sympathy for the British position, but he also realised that the war could threaten the unity and social cohesion of his country.

There were certainly great economic advantages to neutrality. The war presented an opportunity for American businesses to sell munitions and foodstuffs to the Allies and for bankers to lend them money. As the fighting disrupted German and Allied industries, American industries could take over their markets, particularly in the British, French and German Empires. Such moves brought great benefits to many Americans and average wage levels rose by 25 per cent during the conflict. Economic advantages were also a challenge to neutrality. When, for instance, Britain began a programme to expand and further equip her army, loans were sought from Wall Street. American financiers approached the government for guidance. Wilson gave permission for loans to be negotiated even though this represented a threat to neutrality. It is also argued that Wilson's agreement to allow an expansion of the trade in munitions with the Allies forced Germany into the position of having to resort to submarine warfare. Refusal to supply additional munitions to Britain would have weakened the position of the Allies to resist German aggression. The pursuit of a rigid policy of neutrality would have meant the refusal to supply arms and loans to either side, but that would have been harmful to America's powerful economic interests upon which Wilson, to some extent, depended. The real significance of these actions lies in the realisation that total neutrality was impossible for a country so strong and powerful as the United States.

Whatever America did was bound to affect the war. Nevertheless, certainly in the early months of the war, Wilson and his officials, whatever their personal sympathies may have been, did adhere quite rigidly to the principles of neutrality even when their actions appeared to be prejudicial to the Allies. In 1914, for example, the government intervened to stop loans to belligerent countries and also the sale of submarine parts to Britain even though this would have advantaged the Germans and denied Britain its right to purchase freely from a neutral America. At the same time, other economic interests had to be considered. American producers and exporters depended on their ability to trade, unfettered by considerations of neutrality, irrespective of the war. In attempting to preserve the rights of American shipping at sea, Wilson was seen, on several occasions, to be pursuing policies that appeared to be anti-British in his attempts to maintain a neutral position. The Royal Navy's blockade of Germany caused friction with the USA over neutral rights to trade. However, it caused less friction than the Germans' U-boat campaign in the Atlantic.

Faced with so many conflicting interests, it is a great tribute to the political skills of Wilson that he managed to keep the United States out of the war for so long. The sinking of the *Lusitania* in May 1915, in which 128 Americans were drowned, led to widespread anti-German feeling and increased the demands for war. Although Wilson ordered the US Navy to increase its preparations for war, he continued to proclaim the idea of peace. Between 1915 and 1916, he supported the diplomatic efforts of his adviser on mission to Britain, Edward House, to negotiate an end to the war. The proposal, which involved a commitment by the USA to join a post-war international peace-keeping organisation, was accepted by Wilson and was put to the Germans. There was an implication, however, that Germany's refusal to comply might result in American involvement. This was not the intention.

The German decision, in early 1916, to suspend its submarine campaign apparently strengthened Wilson's position. In the 1916 presidential election, Wilson was re-elected on the peace ticket, under the slogan, 'He kept us out of the War'. However, the victory over the Republican, Charles Evans Hughes, was narrow, 277 votes to 254, with a substantially reduced vote. Meanwhile, the Germans were considering a peace plan. By the end of 1916, they believed that they had the upper hand in the war and were, therefore, not prepared to consider a compromise peace. They wanted only Wilson's support for a peace plan that would give such substantial territorial gains that even they knew would not be acceptable to Wilson let alone the Allies.

WHY DID WILSON ABANDON NEUTRALITY?

The Germans decided to push for victory by concentrating their naval power on a blockade of Britain. Hence, the declaration in early January 1917 of unrestricted submarine attacks on Allied and neutral shipping in the Atlantic. This was followed on 3 February by the sinking of an American liner. Despite German assurances that this had been an accident, Wilson immediately broke off diplomatic relations. However, he was still hoping to avoid war, although further loss of American lives with the sinking of the British liner, *Laconia*, on 25 February and the loss of three American merchant vessels in March put him under further pressure. Wilson was a peace-loving man and he realised the internal damage that war could do. It could lead to greater social divisions and threaten his programme of reform. But events in 1917 made war inevitable. The proposal, in January 1917, by the German Foreign Minister, Alfred Zimmermann, to enlist Mexican support against the United States angered Wilson and his government. In return for helping Germany, the Mexicans were offered the opportunity of regaining land from America they claimed as theirs. The publication of this proposal in the USA, in March 1917, in the form of a note from Zimmermann to the German ambassador in Mexico left the Americans outraged. This note, together with the German refusal to stop their attacks on neutral shipping, was clear evidence of aggression and in the minds of Wilson and most Americans, made war inevitable. Thus, on 2 April 1917, when Wilson went to Congress demanding a declaration of war, his request was easily granted, both in the Senate and in the House of Representatives.

It was difficult for Wilson to hold the position of neutrality and it was a great achievement to maintain it as long as he did. In the end it was clear that, without American involvement, the Allies were likely to be defeated. As German aggression increased, pressure mounted on him to declare war. British representatives in America, and the American pro-war groups led by Colonel House, stepped up their agitation for US involvement.

Wilson realised that German domination of Europe was not in America's interests. In the end, there was no alternative to war and the vast majority of Americans supported the declaration. His address to Congress, asking for a declaration, was greeted with great cheering, but Wilson could only comment that 'My message today was a message of death for our young men'. Now that America was at war with Germany, war had to be pursued vigorously until victory was achieved.

HOW WAS THE UNITED STATES AFFECTED BY INVOLVEMENT IN THE FIRST WORLD WAR?

All countries involved in war experience social and economic change and the United States during the First World War was no exception. Income tax was raised to 6 per cent and a surtax of up to 77 per cent was placed on incomes of over $1 million per year. The railroads were placed under the control of a Railroad Administration chaired by William Gibbs McAdoo and the use of fuel strictly regulated. Employer–worker relations were controlled by the government. The Espionage Act of 1917, which became the Sedition Act of 1918, made it a crime to criticise the government for its conduct of the war. It is a good example of government taking powers it would not be able to enjoy in time of peace. Wilson was able to appoint outsiders to important government positions. Bernard Baruch, the Wall Street financier, became Head of the War Industries Board, and Herbert Hoover was placed in charge of food administration. German music, literature and philosophy were denounced

US soldiers setting off to fight in Europe.

and often banned. All immigration from Europe was stopped. Many black people began to leave the South and to seek work in northern factories, where wages were higher. Increased racial tension often resulted. In July 1917, in race riots in East St Louis, Illinois, 39 blacks and 9 whites were killed. Two months later at Houston in Texas, in further riots, 17 whites and 13 blacks were killed.

But it was in the conduct of the war itself that most changes could be seen. Shortly after the declaration of war, the US fleet joined with the British navy to clear the Atlantic of German submarines. Army Commander, General John Pershing, set out to raise and train an army for Europe. The task was not as easy as he thought. Only 75,000 volunteers answered the call to arms and conscription had to be introduced in the Selective Service Act. By September 1918, there were over 1 million American soldiers in Europe and they were an important factor in the eventual Allied victory. In the Meuse–Argonne Offensive which began in late September 1918, the presence of fresh and well-equipped American troops proved an important turning point and led to the eventual German surrender. Perhaps the greatest impact of the war, however, was on the families of the 112,432 American soldiers who had been killed in Europe. Together with millions of other Americans, these families were beginning to ask why their sons and fathers had died and to wonder whether their sacrifices had been in vain. They were also unlikely to forget that it was Woodrow Wilson who had taken the American nation into such a destructive war.

SECTION 2

Why did the Americans reject Wilson and the Treaty of Versailles?

This section considers the way in which, after the First World War, the Americans rejected Woodrow Wilson and the Versailles Treaty, and the extent to which US foreign policy after the First World War may be labelled 'isolationist'. Some historians believe that the US position after the end of the European war represented a radical change from the internationalist stance taken previously. Others take the view that the change was not radical, but merely represented a return to a long-held isolationist position. We also need to consider whether, in fact, it was isolationist or whether it was merely an attempt to preserve US sovereignty and freedom of action. The answers to these questions form an essential basis to understanding US foreign policy throughout the period.

WHAT DID WILSON WANT TO ACHIEVE AT THE TREATY OF VERSAILLES?

Soon after the United States entered the First World War, Wilson began to think about the peace that would follow it. He set up a 'think tank' of academics and foreign policy experts to work on ideas for a peace settlement. Wilson was aiming for treaties that would settle the grievances that had caused conflict and would ensure that another European war would not occur. Wilson was an idealist and was looking for ways to settle disputes between nations without war. He believed that plans for future European peace would give the world new hope, but realised that such ideals would be difficult to implement in the face of the self-interest of nation states. He is sometimes criticised for his ideals of collective security on the basis that they aimed at destroying the concept of balance of power that some historians argue was necessary to maintain stability in Europe. Nevertheless, he remained convinced that his ideas occupied the high moral ground and that eventually they would be accepted.

Wilson's Fourteen Points, published in January 1918, reflected much of his idealism. It was certainly idealistic to think, for instance, in the first five clauses that a code of conduct could be established between nations. It would also be difficult to implement his principle of 'self-determination' amongst those peoples living in the old defeated empires of Eastern Europe. The idea of 'freedom of the seas' contained in the

The Paris Peace Conference, January 1918. Wilson is sitting on the right.

second of Wilson's proposals was strongly opposed by Britain, whilst the French, preoccupied by thoughts of revenge against Germany, were not really interested in any of his ideas. It was, however, great testimony to Wilson's obstinacy and negotiating skills that many of his Fourteen Points were implemented, particularly his ideas for independence for many millions in Eastern Europe. Although some European powers at the Paris Peace Conference may not have agreed with Wilson's plans for peace, they could not ignore them. The Americans had influenced the outcome of the war so much that any ideas they had for future peace had to be listened to and Wilson made sure they were.

Wilson could, therefore, claim considerable success at Versailles but perhaps his greatest achievement was the inclusion in the Treaty of his idea to establish a League of Nations. The original concept of an international organisation to keep world peace belonged to English liberal thinkers of the nineteenth century. Wilson adopted their ideas and developed them into his brainchild. In particular, he stressed the importance of member states signing up to a Covenant. They agreed that they would attempt to settle disputes between each other peacefully. Economic sanctions would be followed, if necessary, by military action against those countries which were aggressive. Wilson was sufficiently realistic to understand that the success of the League would depend on the goodwill of its members and that such a quality might not always be forthcoming. That it may have failed later to keep world peace in no way calls into question the motives of those who helped to form the League.

Wilson was certainly one of those and it represents possibly his most important achievement.

WHY WERE WILSON AND THE TREATY OF VERSAILLES REJECTED IN THE USA?

Perhaps one of the greatest of ironies was that whilst many of Wilson's ideas for a peace settlement were widely accepted in Europe, they were virtually completely rejected back home in America. During the course of the Paris Peace Conference, Wilson was absent from the United States for six months. The negotiations were difficult and wrecked his health. His preoccupations in Paris inevitably led to some neglect of domestic issues but it is difficult to see how this could have been otherwise. Wilson had to be present in Paris. They were his ideas and the success of the negotiations depended on him – no one else could have conducted them. But even before the Peace Conference began, support for the President appeared to be waning. The Democrats were defeated in the Congressional elections in the summer of 1918 and the public mood in America was perhaps beginning to change. By the time of his return at the end of June 1919, Wilson was surprised and disappointed to find that the change was complete. The American public had now reached the point of rejecting not only Versailles and the idea of further US involvement in Europe, but also Woodrow Wilson himself.

What were the reasons for this rejection? Strongest opposition to Wilson and his plans for a peace settlement and the creation of the League of Nations came understandably from the Republicans. They campaigned against his support for free trade and attacked the treaty to improve their own chances of victory in the 1920 presidential elections. But for many, there were wider issues. The impact of the war had had its effects and many Americans did not want to see any further European involvement. After all, over 112,000 young Americans had been killed and no more blood should be spilt. The failure of the Europeans to solve their own problems was no reason why the United States should get dragged in. Thousands of Americans did not want a repeat of their experiences in Europe after 1917 and wanted to turn their backs on that possibility.

As well as these factors, there were other issues. The United States was basically isolationist in its outlook and its involvement in the First World War was a break with that tradition. It now wished to return to its normal outlook as a nation. Further European involvement would have continued the break. That is one interpretation of the rejection of Wilson and Versailles. Henry Cabot Lodge, the Republican chairman of the Senate Foreign Relations Committee, who led the opposition to the President, was neither an isolationist nor against the League. He thought that Wilson had not thought his ideas through properly and that they represented a threat to the nation's freedom of action.

Refusing to compromise, Wilson embarked on a gruelling nation-wide tour to persuade the American people to support his peace plans. He failed, suffered a series of strokes and remained an invalid until his death in 1924. The Senate decided in March 1920 that the United States would neither sign the Versailles Treaty nor join the League. The Republican presidential victory in late 1920 was the final death blow to Wilson's dreams. Certainly, the United States now wanted nothing to do with the Versailles Treaty or European involvement through the League. The Democratic candidate, James Cox, who, in the Wilson tradition, supported such involvement, was heavily defeated. Wilson's great ideals and plans for European peace with America at the head were now at an end.

SECTION 3

The 1920s: the prosperous years?

INTRODUCTION

The 1920s are often regarded as a unique decade in American history. The overwhelming impression is of unequalled prosperity shared by the whole social spectrum. The decade is also characterised by frantic financial speculation, rebellion against authority and uncontrolled crime. In many respects this is a stereotypical view that is potentially oversimplistic. This section builds on previous knowledge of the period and explores the extent to which these were years of prosperity for all Americans.

KEY POINTS

The points to be considered are:

- the extent of prosperity and the developments that underpinned it
- the extent of the problem of poverty, the reasons for it and the inadequacy of attempts to deal with it
- contemporary attitudes towards the poor
- the extent to which the prosperity of the twenties was secure.

HISTORICAL INTERPRETATIONS

Historical interpretations of the 1920s have depended greatly on the perspective from which the period has been viewed. Historians writing in the period of the Depression, for example, were clearly informed by a larger source of evidence and influenced by the mood of the time which laid the blame for the Depression on the Crash and the speculation and economic expansion that preceded it. By this time, business as the creator of wealth and prosperity was in disrepute and businessmen were perceived as the villains of the piece.

From the more enlightened position of the era of the New Deal, the decade is judged to be reactionary, dominated by selfish and greedy businessmen. During the 1930s, historians of the period were in possession of evidence that highlighted the corrupting influence of the materialism that prosperity engendered. Marxist historians such as **Lewis**

Corey and **John Chamberlain** condemned the twenties as the triumph of 'monopolistic capitalism'. It was also seen as a reactionary period, a time of prejudice and bigotry characterised by the racist activities of the Ku Klux Klan, discrimination against immigrants that destroyed the 'American Dream' for thousands.

On the other hand, in the late 1940s, in the aftermath of the Second World War, the decade was seen more positively as the period when the wealth that enabled the USA to support the Allied cause was created. Historian **Bernard De Voto** contradicted earlier interpretations by claiming that the twenties were not negative or irresponsible, but were made to look that way by the literary figures of the day. **George Soule**, an economic historian, claimed in 1947 that in the twenties the rich were getting richer and that the poor also were getting richer, but at a much slower rate.

Few historians in the 1920s, however, would disagree with the view that the United States enjoyed unrivalled economic prosperity in the 1920s and they praised the businessmen whom they considered had created it. Amongst Americans living at the time, there was a widely held belief that economic progress was unstoppable. **Charles and Mary Beard**, for example, in *The Rise of American Civilization* (1927) attributed prosperity to the rapid growth of industry and mechanisation. This, in the context of *laissez-faire* politics, produced the spirit of optimism and confidence that made investment and even greater prosperity possible. Following the end of the First World War, America was being transformed into an increasingly industrial and urban society.

Lewis Mumford saw the development of the modern American city as a symbol of the material success enjoyed by the nation. But he also recognised that it represented the spiritual poverty of its inhabitants. This was the theme of the work of **Harold Stearns** in his book *Civilization in the United States* (1922). He complained bitterly about the superficial quality of modern American life as it became increasingly materialistic. Whilst these two writers, in particular, were powerful critics of American society at this time, they were a small minority confined to the literary classes. Their views were certainly not typical of the vast majority of Americans, who were more than happy to share the benefits of levels of prosperity previously unheard of. New techniques of industrial production, like those introduced by Henry Ford, would lead, they believed, to the final elimination of poverty.

Americans, who had lived through the idealism of the Progressive Era and the First World War, saw the 1920s, not as an aberration, but as a return to 'normalcy'. They were overwhelmingly confident in the idea of unlimited progress and prosperity, so much so that they became dismissive of the persistence of poverty amongst significant sections of the population. This has been recognised and considered in the work of recent historians of this period, such as **Hugh Brogan**, **Paul Johnson** and **Maldwyn Jones**, who recognise the prosperity and vibrancy of the time but also its inherent weaknesses. These include the stance of the Republican administrations that encouraged unfettered economic development, protected it with short-sighted fiscal policies and followed reactionary or naively insensitive policies that failed to respond to the needs of all Americans.

Evidence of prosperity. A mass of statistical information supports the view that the USA entered a period of unrivalled prosperity in the 1920s. Gross National Product, which in 1919 stood at $72.4 billion, had risen to $104 billion by 1929. Throughout American industry, real wages rose by 26 per cent in the 1920s and unemployment fell from 11.9 per cent to

Increasing prosperity led to mass consumerism in 1920s America. This is a Thor washing machine, fitted with a General Electric motor, on sale in 1929.

3.2 per cent. Hours of work declined as new production techniques were introduced. Output per worker in manufacturing increased by 43 per cent between 1919 and 1929, whilst wages, salaries and prices did not rise at anything like the same rate. With labour costs falling, profits increased and business continued to expand. Millions of Americans enjoyed the benefits of new levels of consumerism. The production of refrigerators, which stood at 5,000 in 1921, rose to 1 million by 1930. Washing machine and vacuum cleaner sales rose at a similar rate. In 1912, 16 per cent of Americans lived in electrically-lit dwellings; by 1927, the figure had reached 63 per cent. Buying on credit enabled a large percentage of working-class families to own a car. The relative prosperity of the working classes can also be measured in terms of increased leisure time. For example, an estimated 80 to 100 million Americans went to the movies every week by the end of the decade. They also listened to their own radios, read magazines and shopped in mail order catalogues from their increasingly comfortable homes.

The level of prosperity is also indicated by evidence of improvement in health and life expectancy. In 1900, average life expectancy was 47 years; by 1930, this had risen to 60 years. And whereas in 1900 there were 7 million Americans aged 55 years and over, by 1930 there were 15 million in the same age range. In 1928, most Americans would have agreed with Herbert Hoover, their newly elected President, that in the United States, poverty was about to be eliminated forever.

HOW WAS THIS WEALTH CREATED?

Undoubtedly, the American economic boom of the 1920s was, to some extent, the legacy of the growth and development of 'big business' in the early decades of the century. It was created and led by imaginative and enterprising businessmen such as Henry Ford who, at the time, were admired as heroes, but later vilified as 'robber barons'. The development of mechanisation and modern methods of mass production were undoubtedly a new and crucial factor. Moreover, business enterprise was encouraged and supported by government. The Republicans introduced measures to protect American industries from foreign competition and then largely withdrew from introducing further legislation that might hinder their success. They only returned to law-making if business required them to do so. Wages, working hours and conditions were to be negotiated at the workplace with the employers holding the upper hand. This is one reason why trade union membership declined over the period and business profits boomed.

Perhaps the economic boom of the twenties is best characterised by stock market speculation. Such activity depends not on the easy availability of cheap finance but, as **John K. Galbraith** argues, on confidence and an accompanying optimism that everybody can become rich. In the 1920s, most Americans had exactly that feeling of trust and confidence. They were prepared to speculate, not just on the stock market but also by buying cars and a whole range of consumer goods, often on credit. Many must have wondered how long the period of boom and prosperity would last. After all, did it not always end in collapse and slump? This was the generally accepted view of the economic cycle. The Harvard Economic Society stated in 1929 that it believed that the slump was overdue. The 'seven years of plenty' had run their course and a period of economic depression was about to begin. Later on in the year, they would be proved right.

WHY DID POVERTY PERSIST?

For a sizeable percentage of the population there had never been 'years of plenty'. In many respects, the growing prosperity of the 1920s lulled people and politicians into a false sense of reality. As lifestyles changed, it seemed impossible to imagine that, even if poverty existed in the early years of the decade, it would remain. Nevertheless, research carried out by the Brookings Institution for the period from 1900 to 1930 revealed that 16 million families (i.e. 60 per cent of the total number) received less than $2,000 a year, the figure that was regarded as required 'to supply only basic necessities'. This represented approximately 70 million people who were living below the poverty line. Who were these people and why were they poor in this apparent age of affluence?

Farmers. Farmers were amongst the poorest. These were the people whom the consumer boom passed by. Their 'golden age' had been in the war years when American crops had been in demand in Europe. They had borrowed heavily to increase production; consequently the collapse of the agricultural market after 1919 was particularly devastating as they were unable to repay loans and mortgages. By the early 1920s, farm incomes ranged from $1,240 to $460 a year, less than the average national income. Of America's 5.8 million farming families, 54 per cent (around 17 million people) survived on an income of less that $1,000 a year. Their distress was acute.

African-Americans. In the southern states incomes fell below $200, a reflection of poverty amongst the African-American population. George Schuyler, an African-American intellectual, commented during the Depression years that:

> 'the reason why the Depression didn't have the impact on the Negro that it had on the whites was that the Negroes had been in the Depression all the time.'

During the war years, the massive drift of the African-American population into the cities had transformed what had been fashionable areas into poverty-stricken ghettos. They had been initially lured there by lucrative wartime jobs, but this was short-lived. The jobs went, and the soldiers returned, bringing with them hate and violence, but the African-Americans remained. Poverty was especially acute in the Harlem and Manhattan (New York) ghettos and those of Chicago and Philadelphia. In Harlem, death rates were 42 per cent higher than in other parts of New York due to high incidences of childbirth and infant mortality, tuberculosis, pneumonia and heart disease aggravated by the lack of medical care. Life was also made worse by the racist activities of the Ku Klux Klan after its re-emergence in 1924.

Other groups in poverty. Other groups who endured poverty included the old, families headed by women, the disabled and infirm. Thousands of immigrants also found it difficult to establish themselves in their new homeland, particularly where they faced discrimination. Textile towns in New England and coal-mining areas in Kentucky and Illinois were in more or less permanent slump with high levels of unemployment.

WHAT WAS DONE TO HELP THE POOR?

In an age of such obvious national prosperity, it may appear surprising that poverty could be tolerated. It might also be reasonable to expect that some of the wealth that was being created would be used for poor relief in some form. This did not happen. In the early twenties, the agrarian and reforming lobby of both parties in Congress combined in an effort to relieve the suffering of the farmers. It secured passage of the Capper–Volstead Act (1922), which allowed farmers to form co-operatives by exempting them from the laws against trusts, and the Intermediate Credit Act (1923), which set up banks to make loans to groups of farmers. If anything, however, government action only aggravated the situation. The Fordney–McCumber Act (1922), for example, which protected industry by imposing high tariffs, was a disaster for farmers. Their distress was aggravated in 1927 and again in 1928 when President Coolidge vetoed the McNary–Haugen Bill that would have cushioned farmers against plunging prices. The failure of the federal government to help farmers out of poverty deepened the divisions between the rural and urban areas of the USA in the 1920s.

KEY THEME

Republicans and 'laissez-faire'
Republican business self-interest did not want regulation that would affect unit cost of production and lower profits, but they supported market regulation – high tariffs – which helped sustain prices and profits.

Moreover, *laissez-faire* politics prevented any government intervention to help industrial workers on inadequately low wages. Miners' strikes, for example, in support of demands for higher wages in 1921 were generally dealt with repressively. When violence broke out in West Virginia during a strike, Harding responded by sending in troops. He ignored the recommendations of a federal commission of enquiry even though it clearly indicated the severity of the miners' situation. When Congress did attempt to pass reforming legislation, its legality was questioned in the Supreme Court. Trade unions, handicapped by legislation, were helpless, nor did they have the funds to provide any kind of relief for their workers. Some firms did develop 'welfare capital' to help their employees, but these were largely skilled workers. Some states established departments of public or social welfare and increased their spending on welfare to the benefit of the elderly and young mothers. The impact of these actions was limited. By 1931, 93,280 families were receiving benefits paid to mothers, but 3.8 million families headed by females received nothing. Where grants were paid by state authorities, they varied immensely. In Arkansas, for example, the monthly grant was a mere $4.33 compared to the $69.31 paid out in Massachusetts.

The poor in some areas were helped by private charity. This amounted to $750 million in 1929, compared to $500 million of public spending on welfare provision. Unlike their counterparts in Britain, the poor were unable to help themselves. They were such a diverse group ethnically, and confined to slum areas of towns and cities, that they were incapable of organising themselves to form self-help groups. They were entirely dependent on social workers or others to bring them relief.

WHY WAS SO LITTLE DONE TO HELP THE POOR?

The answer to this question says much about the values and attitudes of American society in the 1920s. Firstly, the Republican administrations believed that social responsibility was not the job of the state except in the fields of law and order and national defence. Whilst there were clearly progressives within Congress who had reform on their agendas, intervention to provide relief from poverty was beyond the commonly-held concept of the role of government. Nor was it prepared to direct others to reform practices or make provision, hence its reluctance to interfere with the direction and operation of business. Intervention was also perceived as a contravention of the freedom of individuals to provide for themselves. In any case, poverty was regarded as cyclical and therefore short-term. As the prosperity of the twenties increased, there was a confident optimism, from the President downwards, that the USA was on the verge of permanently solving the problem of poverty. Consequently, there was no need for intervention.

By the twenties, there was a deeper understanding of the causes and effects of poverty, largely as a result of investigative journalism. Social workers and activists were pressing for reform. However, they aspired to changes that would put an end to poverty. They were not interested in

KEY THEME

Social Darwinism The Social Darwinism of William Graham Sumner was widely subscribed to in the nineteenth and early twentieth centuries. It was an 'intellectual' sociological version of rugged individualism.

short-term palliatives that might actually minimise the effectiveness of their case. Nevertheless, some entrenched prejudices remained. Amongst these was the view, commonly held earlier in the century, that the poor were feckless and idle – the Victorian concept in Britain of the 'undeserving' poor. In America, however, this became further tainted by fundamentally racist attitudes. Poverty kept the poor in their place and where the poor were African–Americans, Catholic and Jewish immigrants, this was regarded as entirely desirable. Sadly, the failure of poor people to join together to form self-help groups was not exclusively a result of practical and organisational difficulties. It is clear from contemporary comments that there was a resigned acceptance amongst many poor people that poverty was inevitable and their own poverty was their lot in life:

> 'Always going to be more poor folks than them that ain't poor . . . I guess I always will be. I ain't saying that's the government's fault. It's just down right truth, that's all.'

HOW SECURE WAS THE PROSPERITY OF THE 1920S?

Was the Crash inevitable? There can be no doubt that a significant proportion of the American population was enjoying unprecedented prosperity, feeling secure in the belief that it was there to stay. Galbraith's argument that it is this mood of confidence and optimism that really explains the willingness of people, even ordinary people, to speculate with their savings by buying shares is supported by a contemporary intellectual:

> 'The commonfolk believe in their leaders. We no longer look upon the captains of industry as magnified crooks. Have we not heard their voices over the radio? Are we not familiar with their thoughts, ambitions and ideals as they have expressed them to us as a man talks to his friend?'

Galbraith also poured scorn on the idea of the 'seven years of plenty', the view that good things will come to an end in the natural scheme of things. Galbraith and other historians have, however, identified features of this prosperity that suggest it rested on very insecure foundations and that the economic infrastructure could not support such rapid expansion.

The crucial importance of investment and the unequal distribution of wealth. In 1929, the 5 per cent of the population with the highest incomes received about one third of all personal income. The unequal distribution of income meant that a small percentage of the population was very rich. These were the investors who received huge profits from industry because, while output was increasing, wages and prices remained fixed at a fairly low level. This 5 per cent spent their profit on luxury goods and invested it. When they failed to do both of these things, the economy was in trouble.

The high percentage of poverty, particularly amongst farmers, also weakened the economy since it placed limitations on the spending power of significantly large sections of the population.

Speculation is frequently cited as a factor in destabilising the economy. It is claimed that the ease of obtaining credit, together with the rapid increase in the value of shares, led to frenzied gambling on Wall Street. Whilst Galbraith minimises the importance of investment on credit, the fact that, when prices began to destabilise, so many ordinary people had their savings tied up in investment ensured the panic selling that characterised the Crash.

Banking. Galbraith identifies this as the weakness that was particularly significant in helping to ensure that the Crash precipitated the Depression. The banking structure in the USA was inherently weak because the banks were relatively small-scale, independent ventures. In the event of one bank failing, its assets were frozen and depositors were denied access to their savings. This precipitated panic amongst the customers of others and a subsequent run on the banks. Hence, a domino effect was produced. If one fell, the others soon followed. Since the banks were deprived of customer savings, industry and business were denied the investment capital to cushion them from the adverse effects of the slump and avoid bankruptcy.

Lack of government control of industry. In the long term, high tariffs imposed by government to protect industry made it relatively difficult to sell goods abroad. For most of the period, this was not a serious factor. Galbraith claims that order books from department stores as late as 1929 suggest that domestic demand for goods kept up. But the lack of control facilitated the growth of a large number of new companies during the boom years of the 1920s, many of them with the intention of making quick profits through speculation. Some of those involved were swindlers and frauds. Perhaps too many companies were formed, many of which ran into difficulties and quickly cut back on investment when economic troubles began.

Consequently, it took only a short-term misjudgement of the demands of the market to trigger disaster. Overproduction led to unemployment and a fall in prices causing a reduction in profits that hit the crucial 5 per cent of luxury buyers and investors. It took only a relatively small downward turn in market values to precipitate the panic selling of shares that brought America's golden age of prosperity to a close.

CONCLUSION

The 1920s were undoubtedly an age of prosperity for a much wider social spectrum than had ever happened before. Mass production of consumer goods and the more affluent lifestyle of so many people are evidence of this. However, the continuing existence of poverty experienced by so many different groups of Americans, and the failure of anyone to deal with it, limits the extent to which the period can be judged to be an age of prosperity. Depression was ever present in the lives of many Americans. In any case, it was a fragile prosperity as the Crash of 1929 clearly demonstrated. It is difficult to see how this could have been avoided given the *laissez-faire* Republican policy that provided neither controls nor secure structures that would facilitate healthy economic growth.

SECTION 4

Prohibition: a 'noble experiment' that failed?

INTRODUCTION

It has been argued that, if any single factor was responsible for the social and moral 'revolution' of the 1920s in America, it would have to be Prohibition. Evasion of the Volstead Act was imaginative and varied. It was also blatant, violent and corrupt. The clandestine meetings of bootleggers, offshore rendezvous of smugglers, illegal speakeasies and even the gangland battles in Chicago can lend a dubious sparkle to this quite unique period of American history. This commonly-held interpretation of the impact of Prohibition is detailed in Chapter 4 of this book. Such colourful images can, however, also distort and mislead. This section aims to encourage a more balanced view by examining the wider aspects of the causes and consequences of the introduction of Prohibition. Closer examination of what appears on the surface to be an outrageous imposition of federal legislation that fundamentally attacked individual liberty and freedom, can suggest that it was, in fact, a response to a huge groundswell of public opinion. It was the only piece of reform legislation in the Republican era although, in this respect, the federal government followed rather than led. Moreover, for everyone who evaded the law, there were at least the same number, if not more, who actually supported it throughout the period that it remained on the statute books. For it is important to remember that the USA is a vast country with significant regional differences. Its society is cosmopolitan, divergent in culture, attitudes and values. The USA was and still is a highly religious society, i.e. Christian. This was important for support of Prohibition especially among the Baptists and Methodists. It is, therefore, possible to argue that the failure of Prohibition was largely due to the fact that it was over-ambitious rather than fundamentally unjust or ill advised. In addition, people's priorities changed over the period in question.

KEY POINTS

To reach a balanced assessment, it is necessary to consider critically the following issues:

- the origins and purpose of Prohibition and how it came to be federal policy
- the extent of its support and where this support came from

- the reasons for its failure
- the reasons for its repeal in 1933.

THE ORIGINS AND PROGRESS OF THE PROHIBITION MOVEMENT

The Prohibition movement was not peculiar to the USA. At the turn of the century, other countries were experimenting with limiting or totally banning the production and consumption of alcoholic drinks. At the same time as America was going through the process, Canada had also enacted Prohibition laws. To find the origins of the Prohibition movement in the USA, it is necessary to look back into the nineteenth century. It is true to say that Prohibition emerged from a moral crusade against the devastating effects of excessive drinking. This was a common response to the impact of industrialisation shared by many countries that went through this process of social as well as economic change. It was convincingly argued by reformers that money spent on alcohol deprived families of food and clothing. Drunkenness caused violence in the home and crime on the streets. Its debilitating effects reduced efficiency in the workplace. This was the cause taken up by the founders and members of the **American Society for the Promotion of Temperance**, formed in 1826 in Boston. The cause appears to have been well supported. The Society claimed to have 5,000 branches by 1834, whilst the **Washington Temperance Society**, formed in 1840 to rehabilitate alcoholics, became a national organisation. Support came mainly from religious organisations

Women conducting a campaign against Prohibition, in Birmingham, Michigan, 1930.

and reformed alcoholics whose campaign was bolstered by the publication of temperance literature. By 1855, a number of eastern states had already passed legislation either controlling or prohibiting the consumption of alcoholic drink.

In the second half of the nineteenth century, pressure increased for Prohibition legislation. By this time, employers who formed the American Anti-Saloon League joined religious pressure groups such as the Methodist and Episcopal churches, in the campaign. Add to this the distinctive female action of the **Women's Christian Temperance Union**, founded by Frances Willard in 1874, and it is not surprising that, by the beginning of the twentieth century, there was mounting pressure for Prohibition particularly from rural states. By this time, the number of saloons had reached 100,000 nationally and in addition to drunkenness and violence, they were the focus of gambling and prostitution.

The impact of the First World War. When the First World War broke out in 1914, 19 states had passed Prohibition legislation. The war provided the Prohibitionists with further ammunition to support their cause. They emphasised the need to conserve grain supplies especially those used in the production of beer and spirits. Moreover the fact that the majority of brewers were of German origin – Pabst, Schiltz, Anheuser-Busch – meant that the Prohibition lobby could harness anti-German wartime hostility. This was strong amongst some politicians who were dubious about the potential political power that the wealth created by the breweries could give to their owners. Meanwhile, more and more state legislatures were passing Prohibition laws. This reforming trend was a reflection of the 'progressivism' of the closing years of the nineteenth and the first decade of the twentieth centuries – the belief that government had a responsibility to resolve social problems. This had expressed itself in a variety of social reforms regulating child labour, working hours of women and safety in the workplace. The reforming zeal of the progressives led them into efforts to control morality in the cities. In this connection, Prohibition must be seen in the context of a plethora of other legislation that sought to control behaviour and establish a common code of moral values. This included prostitution as well as restrictions on gambling, use of birth control, observance of the Sabbath and censorship of books and films. Its fundamental purpose, therefore, was reform to improve society. Leading progressives were Republican and this belies the claim that Republicans were against government intervention. On these kinds of social issues, and on high tariffs, the Republicans were in the vanguard calling for government action.

HOW DID PROHIBITION COME TO BE FEDERAL LAW IN 1920 AND WHO SUPPORTED IT?

By 1920, Prohibition laws had already been passed by 33 of the 48 states. Approximately 63 per cent of the total population was 'dry'. Undoubtedly, the pressure for action came from the rural areas and small towns. The support was predominantly middle class, Protestant and white. It arose partially as a crusade against perceived moral decadence. Industrialists also gave powerful support on the basis that temperance would bolster efficient productivity. The movement also attracted some support from powerful and wealthy individuals such as John D. Rockefeller.

There were also elements in favour of Prohibition that were inherently racist. The southern states embraced Prohibition because they wanted to deprive their still significant African-American population of alcoholic drink. The South was also the Baptist Bible Belt. Rural and small-town America viewed with distaste the violence and immorality of the eastern cities where they associated the production and consumption of alcohol with the culture of the European Catholic, immigrant population. In this context, Prohibition can be interpreted not only as prejudice and discrimination but also as an attempt to control and enforce the conformity of minorities to a set of moral values determined by the majority.

The influence of the female and family lobby cannot be underestimated, particularly as this was especially strong in the western states. Here, women were empowered by the fact that they had the vote much sooner than women in other parts of America. Since the days of the 'Women's War' of the 1870s when women marched en masse to close down saloons, women's organisations had continued to push for Prohibition. By 1919, they lent the weight of their support to the Anti-Saloon League. This organisation now had a great deal of political influence, and put up its own candidates for official positions. In those states where women already had the vote, they could ensure that it was used to put those who would support their cause into state legislatures. Hence, by the time that the 18th Amendment was presented to the states by Congress, two-thirds of the states whose representatives made up its membership were already 'dry'.

WAS THE IMPOSITION OF PROHIBITION A FAILURE?

Reactions to the law. To some extent, the answer to this must be that it was not a complete failure. There certainly were those, all over the USA, who devised imaginative ways to evade the law on a small scale by making their own 'moonshine' or with bogus medical prescriptions for alcohol. Others risked their health by obtaining and consuming inadequately refined industrial alcohol. 'Bootlegging' became a lucrative business for some and the rapid increase in the number of 'speakeasies' is testimony to the defiance of the cities in the east. Nevertheless, there were large sections of the population who welcomed Prohibition. It is often claimed that the consumption of alcoholic beverages increased dramatically. Whilst this may be true of cities such as Chicago, the statistics do not support this claim nationally. On the contrary, figures show an overall drop from 9.8 litres (2.6 gallons) of alcohol per person per year in the period before the introduction of state Prohibition laws (i.e. 1906–10) to 3.7 litres (0.97 gallons) by 1934. Moreover, whilst the crime rate did increase, it was not as dramatic during the 1920s as is sometimes claimed. Concentration on the cities distorts the national picture. Generally, there was a fall in drink-related crime. After the Prohibition laws were repealed, the figures show that alcohol consumption never again reached the pre-Prohibition levels, suggesting that, in one sense, the laws did have a long-term reforming effect on the drinking habits of a significant proportion of Americans.

Prohibition and organised crime. The fact that the Prohibition, or Volstead, Act was fairly rapidly repealed following the Democratic Party victory in the 1932 presidential elections is often interpreted as indicative of its disastrous effects. This judgement arises largely from the established link between the illegal sale of alcoholic drink made necessary by Prohibition and organised crime. In Chicago, for example, the wealth that gangsters such as Al Capone obtained by smuggling liquor and setting up illegal drinking clubs provided the capital for the other rackets – protection, drugs and prostitution. The Mafia also established itself in the USA through trafficking in illegal liquor. It cannot be categorically stated, however, that organised crime on this scale, the political corruption and the gangland warfare that went with it all, would not have grown up anyway without the stimulus of Prohibition. All of this kind of corruption existed in Chicago and New York during the preceding 20 years or so, albeit on a smaller scale. The economic boom of the twenties and the affluence it created would almost certainly have provided alternative opportunities for organised crime.

Problems of enforcing the law. Certainly, the imposition of Prohibition was ambitious. As in the case of any reforming legislation, the extent of its success was in direct proportion to the money that government was prepared to spend on its enforcement. The federal government set up the Prohibition Bureau and appointed commissioners and officers to inspect and remove stores of alcohol and the means of producing it. The mechanisms were in place to bring to justice those who broke the law to whatever degree. However, enforcement officers were far too few to police the whole of the USA effectively, even though the numbers were increased from 1,520 in 1920 to 2,836 by 1930. They were also very poorly paid and consequently were an easy prey to bribery. Vulnerability to bribery did not just apply to poorly paid commissioners. High-ranking police officers and key local politicians in the cities were in the pockets of racketeers such as Al Capone and John Torrio. Even when officers were honest and did their jobs efficiently, it soon became evident that the system was unable to cope with the implications of law enforcement. Recognising this inadequacy, more and more people were prepared to risk breaking the law. Rebellious young people were attracted by the illegality of alcohol. Drinking was another form of protest. Jail sentences for violation of the Volstead Act had reached 44,678 by 1932. Federal prisons were inadequate to deal with this volume of convictions.

Whilst it is possible to argue that the 'noble experiment' was doomed to failure, the time of its final demise was fixed more by events beyond it rather than by its own intrinsic weakness.

WHY WERE THE PROHIBITION LAWS FINALLY REPEALED?

The inability of the government effectively to enforce the law was a factor in encouraging opposition and demands for its repeal. It is often argued that it was over-ambitious to expect a successful ban on alcohol. Part of the reason for this was cultural. For sections of America's immigrant population, the drinking of beer and wine was an intrinsic part of their cultural heritage. Immorality and decadence were not implicit in this. For them, abstinence from alcoholic beverages was completely alien, whereas for those of puritanical Protestant origins, temperance was more of a way of life.

The 1928 presidential election campaign. During the mid to late twenties, there was some rethinking of the things that really mattered to the majority of Americans. Gradually, the concept of individual freedom came to be regarded as of greater importance than individual morality. Within this context, Prohibition came to be seen increasingly as an infringement of this vital principle, particularly in the cities. Hence, the repeal of the 18th Amendment became a key issue in the 1928 presidential elections. The Democratic Party candidate, Alfred Smith, four times Governor of New York, pledged to end Prohibition and was overwhelmingly defeated by the Republican candidate, Herbert Hoover. This alone cannot be interpreted as indicative of the strength of support for Prohibition. There were clearly other more important issues. Smith, an unashamedly flamboyant New Yorker, was a 'wet' and certainly had appeal to some city voters – notably the immigrant communities. This, together with the fact that he was a Catholic and a city dweller, did not sit well with small-town mentality which was critical of the decadence of city life and opposed to immigration. These factors, together with the obviously overwhelming desire to preserve the prosperity of the 1920s, contributed to his defeat. It does indicate that Prohibition was not such an overwhelming failure by 1928 that people were so desperate for its end and these other factors could be rendered insignificant by it. Smith did, however, regain the support for the Democrats of all the 12 cities that had voted Republican in the 1924 elections. This was a reflection of the divisions that Prohibition was at least reinforcing. Even in 1931, when it seemed to be clear that the experiment had failed, the Wickersham Commission set up to report to the government recommended that Prohibition should continue.

Internal Revenue collections: the loss of revenue from alcohol during Prohibition compared with the years which preceded and followed it.

Revenue from taxation on alcohol 1919–37 ($000s)

1919	$483,051
1920	$139,871
1921	$82,623
1922	$45,609
1923	$30,358
1924	$27,586
1925	$25,905
1926	$26,452
1927	$21,196
1928	$15,308
1929	$12,777
1930	$11,695
1931	$10,432
1932	$8,704
1933	$43,174
1934	$258,911
1935	$411,022
1936	$505,464
1937	$594,245

(From *Historical Statistics of the United States. Statistical Abstract*)

The end of Prohibition. The catalyst that spurred on the repeal movement was, however, the Depression that followed the Wall Street Crash of 1929. The return of the brewing industry held out the hope of more jobs and the creation of some wealth for the nation. Some industrialists and businessmen also supported repeal because they believed that the sale of alcohol would boost taxation and remove some of the burden from themselves. Certainly, Prohibition had resulted in a significant reduction in government revenue from the production and sale of alcoholic beverages (see the table). This presumably had been anticipated and can thus be cited as evidence of the perceived necessity of such legislation. By the early 1930s, however, it was also a strong argument supporting repeal.

During the Depression there was also a movement of the population to the cities. This potentially reduced the 'dry' vote in rural areas but was not sufficiently significant to overwhelm the city 'wets'. When Franklin D. Roosevelt stood as the Democratic candidate in the presidential elections, repeal of Prohibition was promised and possibly contributed to his huge victory. By this time, the Anti-Saloon League had a rival organisation – the **Association Against the Prohibition Amendment (AAPA)**. This was an organisation of wealthy people who used their influence (as the ASL had done previously) to ensure that they would get supporters of the repeal of Prohibition into Congress and other key government positions. Congress did propose a 21st Amendment to the Constitution to repeal the 18th Amendment that had imposed Prohibition.

Even at the end, it is clear that Prohibition still had significant support. To ensure that the 21st Amendment was ratified by the states and to counter any opposition that might occur amongst representatives in rural states, Congress requested the election of special conventions to vote solely on the ratification of the 21st Amendment. Only in this way could its passage be almost guaranteed. In 1933, 73 per cent of the specially convened delegates voted for the repeal of Prohibition. In spite of this, states still had the authority to introduce their own controls on the production and consumption of alcoholic drinks and many continued to do so, but it was no longer a federal issue. Inevitably, repeal led to an increase in per capita consumption but this never reached the levels of the late nineteenth century that had precipitated the 'noble experiment'.

CONCLUSIONS

Prohibition is most frequently interpreted by historians as a social and moral experiment that was a total disaster. It led to mass evasion, especially in urban areas, and gave rise to a lucrative business in smuggling and illegal manufacture. It stimulated organised crime and gangland warfare. Nevertheless, it was also well supported, especially in rural America. It is tempting to speculate that, without the Depression, it might even have survived on the statute books for much longer. And it may have contributed to a long-term reduction in American alcohol consumption.

SECTION 5

The role of women in America 1919–41: continuity or change?

BACKGROUND

In July 1848, **Lucretia Mott** and **Elizabeth Cady Stanton** organised a women's convention at Seneca Falls, New York. The meeting itself was intended as a protest. Lucretia Mott, a Quaker, had campaigned enthusiastically for the abolition of slavery. However, she was denied a leadership role and was particularly angry when she attended a World Anti-Slavery Conference in London in 1840 and was not allowed to take up a place on the platform because she was a woman. For her, this humiliating experience was a turning point. When the convention at Seneca Falls finally took place, it produced a declaration of women's rights that could be interpreted as the birth of feminism in the USA.

This assertion of rights received little female support. American women had different priorities and different perceptions of their role in society. There were also significant cultural differences that determined attitudes and aspirations amongst different groups of women. From the late nineteenth century onwards, women were involved in a number of key issues and campaigns, some political, some social and some economic. The extent to which the position of women changed significantly is, however, a matter of debate.

HOW FAR HAD THE POSITION OF WOMEN CHANGED BY 1920?

Education. Education had been a significant factor in the second half of the nineteenth century in bringing about a change that some women had in their self-awareness. A number of institutions of higher education were admitting women by this time and allowing them to qualify for entry to the professions. In 1849, **Elizabeth Blackwell** became the first woman to gain a medical degree. She then provided opportunities for women to receive training in medicine in the New York Infirmary for Women and Children, which she opened with her sister, Dr Emily Blackwell. In 1853, America had the first female ordained minister and by the 1870s, women were slowly entering the legal profession. Women were also making their mark in the world of journalism and literature.

Towards the end of the century, there was some expansion of opportunities for higher education. Radcliffe, a women's college attached to Harvard, was founded by Charles William Eliot and in 1880, Bryn Mawr College near Philadelphia was training women for entry into most of the professions. Opportunities continued to expand. By 1890, 4 million women were in higher education. By 1910, there were 7.8 million studying in a variety of academic disciplines.

Social issues. Women activists in the late nineteenth and early twentieth centuries are illustrative of the 'new' American woman of the day. These were particularly active in the cause of social reform. **Harriet Beecher Stowe**, author of *Uncle Tom's Cabin*, did much through her books to gain support for the anti-slavery cause. Mott and Stanton became involved in the anti-slavery movement through their husbands. Stanton also worked with her husband in the anti-slavery movement but, after the Seneca Falls Convention, she became more actively involved in campaigns for women's rights, not just promoting them amongst male politicians but also educating and raising awareness amongst women themselves.

Large numbers of working-class women were already in the workplace. Many of these were young immigrant workers who worked long hours in 'sweatshop' conditions for very low wages. In the early 1900s, those who were prepared to stand up for themselves had joined trade unions and resorted to strike action to improve their conditions. Increasingly, it became clear that only intervention by the government with appropriate legislation could improve their situation permanently. But how could Congress be persuaded to pass this kind of legislation?

Politics. Politics were of little interest to women even though Elizabeth Stanton had founded the National Woman Suffrage Association in 1869 along with Susan B. Anthony. Whilst many middle-class women provided strong support for the anti-slavery and temperance movements and others were active in seeking a ban on child labour, the possibility that success in these ventures might have been better assured if they had a political voice seems to have eluded the rank and file of female reform activists. It was the suggestion by abolitionists, after the end of the Civil War in 1865, that a new amendment to the Constitution should give all men the vote, irrespective of race, colour or creed, that stirred some women to perceive a fundamental injustice in the proposal. Their efforts had done much to bring about the end of slavery, yet they were not considered worthy of inclusion in the extension of the franchise. This sense of injustice was aggravated further as immigration accelerated. Immigrant males were given the vote almost immediately whilst it continued to be denied to women born in the USA.

KEY THEME

The 14th Amendment This established the right of all citizens to equal protection in the eyes of the law. It defined a citizen as one 'born or naturalised in the United States'. This, therefore, included African-Americans.

Nevertheless, activists had little success on the national scene either in stirring up women to assert their rights or in persuading politicians that they should give women the vote. There were, however, notable successes at state level, particularly in the West and Midwest. By the time of America's entry into the First World War, women had the vote in 12 states and **Jeannette Rankin** of Montana became the first woman to enter the House of Representatives in 1917. Nevertheless, the National American Woman Suffrage Association, under the presidency of **Carrie Chapman Catt**, continued to campaign for the vote for all women. The cause was not particularly helped by the more aggressive campaigning activity of **Alice Paul** and the National Woman's Party in 1917, who used the tactics of the English suffragettes with similar disapproving social reaction among the majority and the political establishment. In 1920, Woman Suffrage Associations were successful in achieving equal voting rights with the passage of the 19th Amendment to the Constitution. This was undoubtedly partly the result of the efforts of women on the home front during the war. However, the question that remained to be answered was whether this newly acquired political power would significantly change the position of women.

THE 'ROARING TWENTIES': A DECADE OF OPPORTUNITY?

On the surface, the freedom and affluence that characterise this period would seem to make it potentially a golden age of opportunity for women. Methods of mass production both increased job opportunities for women and provided the labour-saving devices that promised liberation from time-consuming domestic work. The media boom of the twenties provided images of affluent young women – the flappers – who had apparently broken the traditional mould and who were enthusiastically setting new trends in fashion and behaviour. These images are misleading. The true picture is difficult to define because it is clear that American women in the inter-war period continued to hold different and often conflicting views of their role in society and of their ambitions. This undoubtedly limited the extent of change. Men had definite expectations of women, although these also varied.

The male perception. In spite of what seemed like a social revolution in the twenties, the traditional view of the American woman, inextricably bound up with home and family, continued to be pervasive. Nor did the close association of 'manliness' with the ability to provide for wife and family diminish. To some extent, women were revered and respected by men for their strength of character and endurance. This was especially true in the West where women had shown courage and perseverance during the period of settlement in the mid to late nineteenth century. The legacy was further enhanced by the fact that, there, men significantly

Two flappers dancing the Charleston on the roof of Chicago's Sherman Hotel.

outnumbered women. This certainly gave women the upper hand. As a sociologist of the day, Edward A. Ross commented:

> 'In the inter-mountain states where there are two suitors for every woman, the sex becomes an upper caste to which nothing will be denied from streetcar seats to ballots and public offices.'

This helps to explain why women in the West were given the vote before those in any other part of America. Apart from the fact that this was sometimes used to attract families to go west, it also created opportunities for women who were interested in politics or public office that they might not have enjoyed elsewhere at that time. It cannot be entirely coincidental that the first women to achieve positions of public influence were in the West and Midwest. In addition to Jeannette Rankin of Montana, **Mary McDowell** became Commissioner of Public Welfare in Chicago in 1923. **Mary Howard** of Utah became the first female mayor in the USA and **Bertha Knight Landes** became the first female mayor of a large city when she won the elections in Seattle in 1924. **Mary Margaret Bartelme** of Illinois was the first female judge, whilst **Miriam Ferguson** (Texas) and **Nellie Taylor Ross** (Wyoming) became the first female state governors when they were elected in 1925. At the time, these women were quite exceptional. The traditional male view was that politics was not for women, not always because they considered them intellectually inadequate, but often because they considered that politics was too dishonest and disreputable for women.

Generally, however, men's admiration for women took the form of an expressed need and desire to protect and cherish them. There was also a recognised belief that women's boundless talents and abilities were best used in the home. This was, frankly, a view that the vast majority of women supported. During America's involvement in the First World War, for example, women flooded into the workplace to sustain the home front whilst the men were away fighting. It is clear in this statement from the New York Labor Federation that, when the war ended, it was the duty of women to resume their domestic role in order to make jobs available for the returning soldiers:

> 'The same patriotism, which induced women to enter industry during the war, should induce them to vacate their positions after the war.'

Similar sentiments were expressed when women entered the workforce during the Second World War, with similar results.

The female perspective. Returning to the home was a duty that the majority of women readily accepted. Moreover, when the franchise was extended to women in 1920, the attempts of Carrie Chapman Catt and the National League of Women Voters to educate women were largely ineffective. If women failed to shake off the domestic role, it could be argued that it was largely as a result of their lack of unity and clarity of purpose. Indeed, many women saw their traditional feminine role as a satisfying and empowering one. As Paul Johnson puts it:

> 'The historian is driven to the conclusion that, for the great majority of American women, voting came low in their order of priorities. American wives in particular preferred to exert evident and satisfying

control over their husbands to the infinitesimal chance of determining the selection of a president.'

Hence, the vast majority of women were unaffected by the achievement of suffrage for women. For African-American women in the South, it was an empty victory since they continued to be denied their voting rights. For large sections of the urban and rural population, women were forced by poverty to concentrate on the daily struggle to survive, rather than on their rights. Even those women who appreciated that the extension of the franchise potentially empowered them were divided on how this power should be used. Feminists chose to pursue the cause of **equal rights** and began as early as 1923 to campaign for an **Equal Rights Amendment**, a campaign which ultimately failed 50 years on. Others concentrated on narrower aspects of reform such as equal pay for equal work or equality of opportunity in employment. Women's leaders such as **Jane Addams** advocated the use of the vote to secure wider **social reform**. Addams, therefore, opposed the pursuit of equal rights because she believed that this put the success of more important social legislation in danger. This included legislation to regulate working hours and create special conditions for women, to abolish child labour and to set a minimum wage. Educated African-Americans, such as Mary Talbert, campaigned for legislation to prevent lynching, incidences of which increased in the 1920s with the re-emergence of the Ku Klux Klan. Even within the ranks of those who supported some social reform, there were philosophical differences, particularly over the issue of the meaning of equality. For example, some women argued that to campaign for legislation that created special conditions to safeguard women in the workplace placed the emphasis on the differences (and implicit weaknesses) of women and contradicted concepts of equality. It was the difference between those who argued that women and men were equal and those who rejoiced in the differences.

Success in the sphere of **social legislation** was limited. A Women's Bureau was created within the Department of Labor in 1920 and, in 1921, the Shepherd Towner Bill made funds available for maternity and infant health education. But this success was short-lived. Opposition from the medical profession limited the effectiveness of the Shepherd Towner initiative and progress towards regulating child labour and working hours was slow and generally ineffective.

Even where female pressure groups were effective in bringing about reforming legislation, most notably in the case of the introduction of Prohibition, there were divisions. Right-wing women's organisations opposed Prohibition on the grounds that it limited freedom. In Denver, Colorado, some became part of an auxiliary branch of the Ku Klux Klan and actively campaigned against the feminist movement by using propaganda that portrayed women who campaigned for equal rights as spinsters and lesbians.

The thoroughly 'modern woman'. What did this mean? That was the burning question in the 1920s. No one really knew the answer. Certainly, a different lifestyle separated the young and perhaps more affluent women from the rest. The girls, who have come to characterise the jazz age, were only united in their determination to rebel and to reject the accepted norms of the day when it came to dress, hair, correct behaviour and sex. But the world of Zelda Fitzgerald and *The Great Gatsby*, which some of the flappers inhabited and others aspired to, was generally transitory. Ideas about what the future held were even more confused. This confusion was described in 1924 by Freda Kirchwey, a left-wing feminist, in *Our Changing Morality*:

> 'The old rules fail to work . . . Slowly, clumsily, she is trying to construct a way out to a new sort of certainty in life.'

It was an experience that affected young Mexican-American women. They also bobbed their hair and adopted the flapper fashion. Educated African-American women, however, tended to be more conservative. They needed to avoid controversy in order to win the struggle for respect and equality in a fundamentally racist society. It is probably true to say that the younger and more rebellious female was more certain about what she was not, rather than what she aspired to be. She rejected the moral values and expectations of her mother and grandmothers. She was not interested in the social reform issues that were providing a platform for the older female generation.

Education, however, continued to be important to women and opportunities expanded especially for middle-class women. They increasingly undertook higher degrees, including doctorates, even though these tended to lead to traditionally female occupations, such as teaching and library work. The legal and medical professions continued to discriminate and to limit the opportunities that were available for women. Consequently, middle-class educated women came to focus increasingly on campaigning for the accessibility of the professions to their own kind as opposed to working for greater freedom and equality of opportunity for all women.

The decade saw the expansion of educational opportunities for African-Americans who considered education as essential to furthering the cause of social and economic equality and the recognition of their rights. In 1921, Carey Thomas founded the Bryn Mawr Summer School for Women Workers in an attempt to make education available to working-class women. Voluntary religious groups such as the Young Women's

Christian Association created opportunities for young women from different cultural heritages to come together to discuss issues that were of common concern.

Women and work. The consumer boom of the 1920s and especially the availability on credit of labour-saving devices created not only jobs but also the opportunity for all women and especially for married women. By 1928, sales of vacuum cleaners, irons, refrigerators and washing machines had risen phenomenally. Married women entering the workforce rose in the period from 22.8 per cent of working women to 28.8 per cent. But jobs, like the goods that they were producing, were not accessible to all women and, in the workplace, women faced discrimination in wages. They also faced the hostility of male trade unionists who argued that if women needed special legislation to protect them in the workplace, perhaps they should not be there. They particularly saw women as a threat not only to the availability of jobs for men, but also to securing favourable wage rates for their male members. When the Great Depression hit the USA after 1929, and unemployment escalated, women were, once again, expected to give up their jobs to men. This was particularly hard in poor families where the woman was the only breadwinner and for female heads of households who were condemned to extreme poverty at a time when there were no welfare benefits.

Some working-class women did turn to trade union activity to defend their rights. In 1929, this resulted in a violent strike in North Carolina in which six women were killed. Such unions as existed for women, however, only spoke up for the cause of white women. African-American women were condemned, by racial discrimination, to very low paid, menial work, as were Mexican-American women. Japanese-Americans usually found their way into domestic service or small family businesses.

The significance of the Great Depression. The impact of the Depression is significant in an assessment of the extent to which the position of women in American society had really changed by the early 1930s. The trend towards an increase in the number of women in the workplace, especially married women, might be taken as indicative of change both in perceptions and attitudes to women as wage earners. However, unemployment exposed the reality. Undoubtedly, the increase in job opportunities was created by methods of mass production which provided opportunities for women workers. Increased demand during the consumer boom of the twenties may also have made female employment a necessary expedient. Moreover, the opportunities offered by credit buying for working-class families to possess luxuries, such as radios, refrigerators and cars, made it acceptable for wives and mothers to go out to work. It is tempting to speculate on how the role of women might have changed had the boom continued. The wave of condemnation and criticism of women workers that followed the Crash suggests that the position of women in the workplace had been generally tolerated rather than accepted during the years of prosperity.

The 1930s: a 'new deal' for women? To a large extent, the changes introduced by Roosevelt merely continued the trends that had been visible during the 1920s and reinforced by the Depression. New Deal policies to regenerate the economy were discriminatory since they were strongly biased towards the male breadwinner. Legislation set minimum wages (Fair Standards Act 1938) but retained differentials. Welfare provision aided young mothers in low income families, but humiliated them in the process. Married women who were still in work by the late 1930s tended to be from very low income families. By this time also, some states still retained legal restrictions on married women working. Educated single women continued to find it difficult to obtain work commensurate with their abilities. They had been forced out of work as teachers, librarians, social workers and book-keepers and were predominantly employed in lower status clerical jobs by the end of the thirties. The New Deal did stimulate the growth of a service economy which offered employment to women as beauticians, hairdressers and waitresses. African-Americans and other minority groups struggled on unsupported. The only positive trend that emerged from the New Deal for them was that the failure of the government to act on their behalf strengthened their will to organise themselves into pressure groups such as the Association of Southern Women for the Prevention of Lynching. In the process, they developed a new and assertive self-awareness.

If any women benefited from the Roosevelt years it was really only the small number of highly educated women whose talents and abilities he recognised and used. The outstanding example was **Frances Perkins**, who became the first woman to serve in the Cabinet when Roosevelt appointed her Secretary of Labor in 1933. Reactions to her appointment are interesting in that they indicate the entrenched views of many people towards women. Businessmen, politicians and trade unionists were all critical of her appointment particularly because they knew her as a social reformer standing for causes of which they disapproved. She certainly used her position to push through much of the social reform that she had previously supported in the early days when she worked with Jane Addams – minimum wages, maximum hours, limitation of child labour. She did not overtly pursue the cause of women other than by her own example.

CONCLUSIONS

How far had the position of women really changed by 1941? The answer to this question lies in the criteria that may be used to evaluate change.

Perceptions of equality. This was evident amongst educated middle-class women. Certainly, there was a recognition that women's talents were not confined to the domestic sphere. Nevertheless, interpretations amongst women themselves as to the meaning of equality and how it could be achieved were varied and conflicting. There is, therefore, little evidence of a women's 'movement' as such, united in its aims. On the contrary, women were divided throughout the period either by aspirations, class or racial origin. This inevitably restricted achievement of goals. Nor is there evidence, except in just a few parts of the USA, that the perceptions of men had changed. For the majority, a woman's place remained securely in the home. Moreover, there is little doubt that this was a view shared by the majority of women. The family and family life remained the most important social institutions that could only survive if women maintained their traditional role.

Admission of women in the professions. The expansion of educational opportunities, at least for middle-class women, is a feature of the period. There are outstanding examples of women who established themselves in the professions and in public life. They remained a minority, however. Generally, those who were successful did not attempt to mix a career with marriage, home and family. Moreover, opportunities for advancement, especially in the professions, remained limited.

Women in the workplace. There was an increase over the period of married women entering the workforce. However, they were restricted and forced into limited occupations. There was inequality in pay and conditions. There was little job security. Both world wars gave women brief glimpses of another kind of life, but there was an expectation and an acceptance that these experiences were temporary. By the end of the 1930s, married women in the workplace were forced there by poverty.

Women, legislation and politics. The extension of the franchise is perhaps the one significant recognition of the changing role of women. However, the fact that its potential was not recognised by women themselves limited its potential for further change. Support for an Equal Rights Amendment was lukewarm. Perceptions of equality were muddled. Nor was change likely to happen until women became sufficiently ambitious to enter politics in greater numbers and men were prepared to encourage them to do so. There is evidence that women could exert pressure for change when they combined together. The imposition of Prohibition is an example of this. In other respects, government did not intervene in any other way to bring about change in the position of women.

SECTION 6

What were the main features of US foreign policy 1921–41?

HISTORICAL INTERPRETATIONS

Some historians hold the view that, in the 1920s, successive Republican governments, supported by the American public, followed an isolationist foreign policy. The United States rejected the Treaty of Versailles and the League of Nations and turned its back on involvement in European and security affairs. It raised barriers around itself to keep out immigrants and foreign goods. According to this view, this isolationism continued in the 1930s. Roosevelt was too preoccupied with domestic economic revival to become involved in foreign affairs. When war did break out in 1939, he was determined to keep America out and only joined in reluctantly in 1941 after the Japanese attack on Pearl Harbor. Roosevelt did not want war, but the general consensus is that he thought the United States would have to become involved sooner or later and moved cautiously as public opinion permitted to facilitate US entry into the war. There is evidence of this in

KEY THEME

Isolationism The USA was clearly not isolationist in economic affairs, e.g. the Dawes and Young Plans.

- the increasingly harsh economic sanctions towards Japan
- military talks with the British
- the destroyers-for-bases deal
- convoying help for the British
- Lend-Lease
- the August 1941 summit with Churchill.

As a result of the First World War, the United States had become a leading world power and could not keep out of world affairs even if it wished to do so. It had too many vital interests to ignore what was happening in the world and would become directly involved if those interests were threatened. This section examines the main features of US foreign policy over the period and considers the validity of these differing interpretations.

THE ISSUE OF ISOLATIONISM IN THE 1920S

A considerable amount of evidence can be assembled in support of the view that after the First World War the United States entered a period of isolation in its foreign policy. The electors rejected Woodrow Wilson and with him the Treaty of Versailles and membership of the League of Nations. Certainly, Harding, in his inaugural speech as President in 1921, seemed to support this position. From now on, he proclaimed, the United States would not become involved in the affairs of other countries or in alliances limiting its freedom of action – unless its vital interests were threatened. Would America now enter what Wilson called 'sullen and selfish isolation'? Within the Republican Party, there were those like Secretary of State Charles Evans Hughes, and Commerce Secretary Herbert Hoover, who argued that such a foreign policy position was no longer tenable. The First World War had changed the United States into a leading world power. Even if it wanted to, it could not turn its back on what was happening in the rest of the world. It had to be involved if only to maintain world peace. Such involvement was also in America's economic interests. The United States was the world's most prosperous economy and needed increasing access to overseas markets. One of the purposes of its foreign policy was to help to make this possible.

For Hughes and Hoover, therefore, the question was not whether or not the United States should be involved in world affairs or be isolated – the real issue was the extent and nature of its involvement. Thus, whilst membership of the League was out of the question, American observers attended Assembly meetings in Geneva. By 1930, US delegates had attended over 40 League conferences dealing with such issues as public health, drugs and counterfeiting and been involved in the General Disarmament Conference at Geneva, whilst in 1934 the country joined the International Labour Organisation. In similar vein, whilst America never joined the International Court of Justice, which it was instrumental in establishing, there was always an American jurist on the bench. So, whilst the United States may officially have been uninvolved, it was not isolationist if that was what its interests demanded.

The Washington Conference. In many respects, the Washington Conference is a good example of the United States becoming directly involved in world affairs because its interests demanded it. The events of the conference contradict the notion of an isolationist foreign policy. It began in late 1921 and lasted into 1922. It was called by the United States and was the first international conference to be held in America. The Americans called it because they wanted to see a limit to naval armaments and an easing of tension in the Far East. Opinion in Congress and amongst the American public favoured arms reduction. A naval arms race involving the United States, Japan and Great Britain could prove very costly and make it impossible for the Harding government to cut taxes. More importantly, the Washington Conference offered the opportunity for the United States to pursue its own foreign policy interests without joining the League which, many argued, would limit US freedom of action.

The main American concern at this time and the chief reason for the naval arms race was the growing power of Japan. Following the end of the First World War, it had acquired former German colonies in the Pacific and, therefore, posed a potential threat to routes and communication links between Hawaii and US possessions in Guam and the Philippines. The Americans were also worried that the Japanese would take advantage of civil war in Russia to seize land in the south of that country. The Anglo–Japanese Alliance (1902) had been modified in 1911, but still meant that Britain could go to war against the United States on behalf of Japan. Thus, the United States took the initiative and called the Washington Conference because it was clearly in its foreign policy interests to do so.

When the Conference opened on 12 November 1921, the American Secretary of State, Charles Evans Hughes, announced a detailed plan to limit naval arms. For the next ten years, no battleships were to be built. The existing ratio of American, British and Japanese naval strength, 5:5:3, was to be maintained and to do so, 66 battleships would have to be scrapped. The plan also provided a ratio of 1.75:1.75 for France and Italy. For a variety of reasons, not least the cost, the powers accepted Hughes's proposals and signed a Five-Power Naval Treaty on 6 February 1922. A Four-Power Treaty in which the United States, Great Britain, France and Japan guaranteed each other's possessions in the Pacific had already been agreed. It was added to by a Nine-Power Treaty respecting the independence of China. The Senate approved all the treaties which were welcomed as beginning a new era of peace. The end of the Anglo–Japanese Alliance was significant for US influence in the Pacific.

The Washington Agreements had many weaknesses. They imposed no limits at all on the size of armies or air forces and those on the size of navies applied only to battleships and aircraft carriers. Above all, there was no method of enforcing any of the limits agreed. There were no sanctions to apply to those who broke the agreements and the Soviet Union was excluded from the conference. Nevertheless, it was the first general agreement on arms limitation and enabled many countries to reduce arms spending. For a period, it helped to make the Pacific a more peaceful and stable place. This stability was to be threatened later by the growth of a militaristic Japan, which had been isolated by the ending of the Anglo–Japanese Alliance and 'humiliated' by not being treated as an equal in naval terms.

American leaders continued to press for the Five-Power Treaty to be extended to all types of warship. To achieve this, Coolidge initiated a disarmament conference at Geneva in 1927. France and Italy refused to attend and those countries which did take part could not agree on the size of cruiser fleets. The negotiations were a failure but were followed in 1930 by the London Naval Conference. The United States, Great Britain and Japan adopted a 10:10:6.5 ratio in cruiser strengths and a 10:10:7 ratio in destroyers, with Japan granted parity in submarines. Certainly, in negotiating naval strengths, the United States had taken the lead throughout the decade with some apparent satisfaction at the outcome. This was largely because at the time the United States saw the naval power of others as *the* major security threat to itself.

The Kellogg–Briand Pact, 1928. The idea of an international agreement outlawing war had grown in the United States since the end of the First World War. It had powerful support, including William Borah, chairman of the Senate Foreign Relations Committee, the philosopher John Dewey and James Shotwell, a Columbia history professor. Shotwell persuaded the French Foreign Minister, Aristide Briand, to announce the wish of the French government to sign a pact with the United States outlawing war between the two countries. The Americans saw this as a French attempt to enlist US support against Germany. The problem was that the plan had massive backing amongst the American public. The US government saw the danger of being drawn into European alliances supporting the French, but could not ignore public opinion. In a piece of masterly diplomacy, the new US Secretary of State, Frank Kellogg, suggested that the agreement should be extended to include other powers. On 27 August 1928, the Kellogg–Briand Pact was signed by the United States and 14 other nations, eventually to be supported by 62. Whilst all those who signed it agreed to renounce war, the pact did not state how it was to be enforced. This was exactly what the American government wanted. The Senate approved the pact by 85 votes to 1; public opinion had been satisfied but the pact was meaningless. Most important of all, it meant that the United States could not be dragged into any conflict against its wishes.

War debts and financial considerations. Because the First World War changed the United States from a debtor into a creditor country, there was clearly a sense in which it could not turn its back on world affairs and retreat into isolation. Financial and business considerations often exerted strong influence over foreign policy and this is well illustrated in relations with Europe in the 1920s. During the First World War, the Americans had lent Great Britain, France and Italy a total of $10.35 billion, most of it spent in the United States. After the war, the Allies argued that the debt should be seen as the American contribution to victory and should be cancelled, in return for which the French and British would cancel debts owed to them. To the Americans, the loan was a business transaction and should be paid back. The only hope of repayment was for the Allies to take reparations from Germany. When, in 1923, the French invaded the Ruhr after Germany defaulted on its repayments, the United States was inevitably dragged in. A plan, put together by Charles Dawes in 1924, proposed a reduction in reparations payments to $250 million with an immediate US loan to Germany of $200 million. Although Dawes was a private banker, the proposals were clearly influenced by the US government. It was very much in America's interests to see the growth of a politically and economically strong Germany. Such a country would provide good opportunities for American business investment and be less vulnerable to communist revolution.

The Dawes Plan was only envisaged as a temporary measure to help Weimar Germany through the immediate problems of 1923 and 1924. It was replaced in 1929 by the Young Plan which reduced the German reparations bill from $37 billion to $8 billion. In all, between 1923 and 1930, American investors lent Germany about $2.5 billion. The Germans paid about the same amount as reparations to the Allies who, in turn, repaid a similar sum to the Americans to help clear war debts. Thus, in the economic and political recovery of Weimar Germany, the United States was deeply involved. So great was this involvement that most European economies became reliant, directly or indirectly, on American capital and investment. Such heavy reliance was to have disastrous consequences following the collapse of the US economy in 1929.

Latin America and the 'Good Neighbor' policy. Traditionally, Latin America and the Caribbean were regarded as areas of American influence and control. From the 1820s the United States saw itself as the regional superpower in the Americas. The Monroe Doctrine (1823) summarised this viewpoint. By the end of the First World War, Cuba, Haiti, the Dominican Republic and Nicaragua were under American military occupation. Most Latin American republics were subject to strong US economic influence. This influence increased in the 1920s and investment more than doubled. Officially, US policy was to reduce the level of political intervention and American troops were withdrawn from Cuba in 1922 and from Santo Domingo in 1924. In 1925, they left Nicaragua, but Coolidge sent US marines back a year later when rebels threatened American lives and property. Although Hoover sent arms into Mexico in 1929 in support of President Callas, he was a great advocate of reducing intervention. The Clark Memorandum, which Hoover published in 1930, did not specifically give up intervention, but it did accept that the United States no longer had a policing role in the Western hemisphere. Thus, when revolutions broke out in Brazil, Panama and Cuba in 1930–1, the USA did not intervene. American troops left Nicaragua in 1933 and Haiti in 1934. The term 'Good Neighbor' was first used by Franklin Roosevelt, but the policy was taking shape some years before.

America still retained a massive financial interest in the region, but would be much less directly involved politically – this new approach represents a significant change in foreign policy direction.

The Far East. Despite the Washington Agreements, tension between America and Japan was increasing. An Asian exclusion clause in the 1924 American Immigration Law created great bitterness and led to anti-American riots in many Japanese cities. What really concerned the Americans, however, was the growth of Japanese militarism and the threat it represented to US interests in the Far East. When the Japanese invaded Manchuria in 1931, China appealed to the League of Nations and to the United States under the Nine-Power Treaty and the Kellogg–Briand Pact. Secretary of State Henry Stimson may have been prepared to act in support of the League, but Hoover would have none of it. Stimson was reduced to sending notes to China and Japan stating that the United States would not recognise any changes to territory brought about by force. This Hoover–Stimson Doctrine of non-recognition did nothing to stop Japan and, in 1932, Manchuria became the Japanese puppet state of Manchukuo. Stimson may have wanted to intervene against Japanese aggression, but it is difficult to imagine what action could actually have been taken. America's armed forces were not in a state of readiness to fight and there was no support amongst the public for military action.

FRANKLIN ROOSEVELT AND NEW DEAL DIPLOMACY

Franklin Roosevelt became US President at a time of increasing international tension. Shortly before his inauguration, Japan had left the League of Nations and its aggression in the Far East was increasing. Hitler had come to power in Germany and was announcing his intention to rearm.

In his early political career, Roosevelt, in the Wilson tradition, was an internationalist. He supported the Versailles Treaty and US membership of the League. By the time he stood for election as President, he was a moderate isolationist. Had he not changed his position, he would not have gained the Democratic nomination for the presidency in 1932. Although Roosevelt would again embrace internationalism, once elected President he maintained his isolationist position. His main priority was to improve the desperate economic plight of the country and he would countenance nothing which might threaten this. In particular, his New Deal policies needed the support of his own Democratic Party with its very strong isolationist wing.

The 'Good Neighbor' policy. Building on foundations laid by Hoover, Roosevelt pledged non-intervention in the affairs of Latin American states at the Montevideo Pan-American Conference in 1933. He entered into agreements with many states, significantly reducing but not completely removing American influence. His decision to withdraw US troops from Haiti and the Dominican Republic made him very popular in Latin America. The treaty signed with Cuba in May 1934 cancelled the **Platt Amendment** which had existed since 1901. It led to a reduction, but not to the end, of American influence on the island, rights to the naval base at Guantanamo Bay being ceded to the United States. A similar treaty was signed with Panama in 1936. The Americans mediated a truce in the Chaco War between Bolivia and Paraguay in 1934, leading to a peace treaty in 1938, and negotiated commercial treaties with Latin American states. The 'Good Neighbor' policy may have led to the United States moving away from armed intervention in Latin America, but this was not the same as withdrawal. There were strong American economic interests in the region which the United States had no intention of abandoning, nor its position as predominant power. Reciprocal trade agreements and the establishment of an Export-Import Bank in 1934 were intended to strengthen American economic interests not weaken them. Nevertheless, the 'Good Neighbor' policy did represent a significant change in US foreign policy in the region and resulted in considerable support throughout Latin America for the United States when war did eventually break out. An important architect of the policy was Under-Secretary of State Sumner Welles.

KEY TERM

The **Platt Amendment** was incorporated into the Cuban constitution in 1901. By it the Americans left Cuba but retained certain military rights.

What was the role of Cordell Hull? In 1933, Roosevelt sent Secretary of State, Cordell Hull, to the World Economic Conference in London, called to agree measures to stabilise world currencies and reach agreements on tariffs. In contrast to the many who advocated protectionist policies, Hull was a firm believer in free trade and was convinced that it was the way to revive world trade and help those countries hit by economic depression. He also believed that the USA had an important part to play in these developments. These ideas belonged very much to Hull himself and not to Roosevelt and his government. At a key point in the talks, Roosevelt sent one of his advisers, Raymond Moley, to London, who told Hull that Roosevelt would not support any measures which might adversely affect the success of his New Deal policies, i.e. he was not prepared to set the value of the dollar and keep it stable at that point. Hull had no choice but to leave the talks. In 1934, however, when the dollar value was at a more competitive level, Roosevelt supported Hull in Congress to secure the passage of the Reciprocal Trade Agreements Act. This allowed the Roosevelt administration to lower tariffs by 50 per cent with those countries who agreed to do the same. Between 1934 and 1938, Hull negotiated reciprocal treaties with 18 other countries, mainly in Latin America but also with Great Britain in 1938. Generally, these treaties favoured the Americans, who grasped the opportunity to increase exports whilst imports into the United States remained at a low level. All these trade negotiations were driven by the pursuit of American economic interests. If those interests could be advanced by co-operation, then the United States would co-operate. If not, it would remain isolated.

How did the USA attempt to maintain its neutrality? There is some degree of disagreement amongst historians as to Roosevelt's position on neutrality as the situation in Europe deteriorated. By 1935, it was becoming increasingly clear that Europe was moving towards the brink of war. A civil war raged in Spain, Mussolini invaded Abyssinia and Hitler was threatening Austria and Czechoslovakia. Roosevelt is portrayed by historians such as Hugh Brogan as a statesman whose natural inclination towards internationalism made him anxious to play a role in stemming the fascist tide in Europe, but who was seriously hampered by political forces at home. Paul Johnson sees these arguments as an excuse for his lack of commitment to world peace and his preoccupation with problems at home.

Nevertheless, in the face of such violent aggression, the overwhelming mood amongst the American public was isolationist. They did not want to see the United States dragged into a European war as had happened in 1917. In fact, a report by a special Senate investigating committee chaired by Senator Nye of North Dakota seemed to suggest that America had entered the First World War following pressure from armaments manufacturers. Within Congress, politicians from opposing parties united to carry a number of bills designed to make sure that the United States remained neutral. Some of these were clearly designed to avoid some of the dilemmas that led Wilson's actions during the First World War to be deemed unneutral. The Johnson Act of 1934 forbade American citizens lending money to foreign countries that had not paid past war debts. Beginning in 1935, Congress passed a series of Neutrality Acts that apparently made it virtually impossible for Roosevelt to give aid of any kind to warring states. It is suggested, however, that he could have used the wide powers that he had been given to intervene in the passage of this legislation if he had wanted to do so. The first Act (1935) gave the President power to place an embargo on arms shipments from America to the belligerents. Under this Act, both sides were equally regarded as 'belligerents'. It removed the distinction between aggressor and victim. The following year, a second Act stopped loans to countries engaged in war and, in 1937, the terms were extended to include raw materials.

How did Roosevelt respond to the coming of war? Roosevelt repeatedly sought to modify and later repeal the Neutrality Acts. But he did little that might have helped reduce the risk of war. Roosevelt appeared unsympathetic to the plight of German Jews as news of their persecution was relayed to Washington by the American ambassador in Berlin. A great deal of suffering had been inflicted before he agreed to relax the immigration laws to enable more Jews to enter America. What really worried Roosevelt was Japanese aggression towards China. Despite following a partly isolationist policy, the United States did take a particular interest in Asia, largely because many Americans worked there, often as teachers, missionaries, technicians and advisers to governments. When, in 1937, Japan went to war with China, the Americans responded by placing a gradual embargo on goods. Realising that war was drawing closer, in January 1938 Roosevelt called for naval rearmament. Congress responded with the Naval Expansion Act of May 1938, which authorised expenditure of over $1 billion over the next decade to create a navy equal to the size of the combined fleets of Germany, Italy and Japan. Early in 1939, Roosevelt obtained a further $525 million to strengthen air bases.

In many ways, the position taken up by the United States towards increasing European tension in the 1930s is understandable. As in the First World War, events in Europe must have seemed distant to many Americans struggling to find work as the economy came out of the Great Depression. The isolationist approach followed by Roosevelt was entirely in tune with the thinking of most Americans. If public opinion in Britain and France was slow to wake up to threats to world peace, it can hardly be surprising if the Americans reacted in a broadly similar and equally reluctant way.

War in Europe. When war finally broke out in Europe in September 1939, Roosevelt realised that the United States would not be able to remain completely neutral for long. Hitler's rearmament programmes meant that Germany was well placed to fight a full-scale war. Britain and France, on the other hand, who had followed a policy of appeasement, were much less well prepared for war when it came. US neutrality, therefore, affected Britain and France much more than Germany. Roosevelt realised that Hitler had to be stopped. A new Neutrality Act passed through Congress in November 1939 repealed the arms embargo and allowed belligerents to buy arms on a **'cash and carry'** basis. It did, however, retain the ban on American loans to nations at war. Later in the year, extra money was voted by Congress to expand the army and navy and to boost aircraft production to 50,000 a year.

KEY TERM

'Cash and carry' The Atlantic 'cash and carry' clearly advantaged Great Britain which had naval supremacy there (in spite of the activities of U-boats).

Lend-Lease. By 1940, Roosevelt knew that it was only a matter of time before America would be at war. He clearly supported Britain and did not hide the fact that he was an enemy of Hitler. A Selective Service Act was passed allowing young men to be conscripted, but despite the news from Europe, by 1940 less than 10 per cent of Americans favoured voluntary entry into the war. In late 1940, Roosevelt was re-elected President still promising to keep America out of the war. The Lend-Lease Act of 1941 gave Roosevelt the power to send material aid to countries whose defence was vital to the United States. By 1945, Britain had received $28.94

billion of aid in the form of arms and military equipment. Lend-lease was extended to China in April 1941 and to the Soviet Union in September. By the end of the war, the main recipients were the countries of the British Commonwealth (63 per cent) and the Soviet Union (about 22 per cent) although the total number of countries receiving aid was 40. The Lend-Lease Act allowed Roosevelt to take payment from those countries in whatever form he wished, but not cash repayments. The America First Committee was an influential pressure group that opposed aid to the Allies because it feared direct US military involvement. It claimed a membership of 800,000 but failed to stop Lend-Lease and the repeal of the Neutrality Acts. Nevertheless, as late as May 1941, 79 per cent of Americans still opposed voluntary entry into the war.

Pearl Harbor. On 7 December 1941, Japanese planes carried out a surprise attack on the American naval base at Pearl Harbor, Hawaii. The bulk of the US Pacific fleet was destroyed. At the same time, Japanese forces attacked Siam, the Philippines, Malaya and the Dutch East Indies. The next day, Congress declared war on Japan. On 11 December, Germany and Italy declared war on the United States. In reality, the United States had been gearing up for war throughout 1941. In March 1941, Roosevelt had given permission for damaged British warships to be repaired in American dockyards and, in April, American naval patrols began seeking out German submarines and reporting their positions to the British. In June, the President ordered the freezing of all German and Italian assets in the United States and, in July, American marines landed in Iceland to prevent a German occupation. In the spring, negotiations had begun to forge an Anglo–American alliance (see below), leading to a meeting

US Army Infantry units march up Fifth Avenue, New York, June 1942.

between Roosevelt and Churchill at Newfoundland in August. Although he was still stating in public his wish to keep America out of war, by this time Roosevelt had accepted the inevitability of US involvement.

The 'Special Relationship': Churchill, Roosevelt and the Anglo–American Alliance. Shortly after the outbreak of the Second World War in September 1939, Franklin Roosevelt sent a brief but important note to Winston Churchill, Britain's First Lord of the Admiralty. Roosevelt wrote to Churchill seeking information about the war. He was also anxious to make contact with the man tipped to take over as Prime Minister should Neville Chamberlain be forced out of office. Roosevelt was right to establish this early contact for, on 10 May 1940, Churchill became British Prime Minister.

Thus began a friendship between Roosevelt and Churchill that grew into the Anglo–American Alliance and was a key factor in the Allied victory in the Second World War. Both leaders had much in common. They shared a considerable experience in naval matters and an interest in history. During the course of the war, the two leaders exchanged many messages, letters and telephone calls. They met in person nine times, including the meetings at Teheran and Yalta with the Soviet leader, Joseph Stalin. Together, they were responsible for beginning what later became known as 'summit diplomacy' – regular meetings between world leaders to discuss international problems.

The first of these summits took place off the Newfoundland coast in August 1941 and resulted in the Atlantic Charter, a set of principles aimed at governing relations among states when peace was eventually achieved. The last summit involving Roosevelt took place at Yalta in February 1945 and attempted to consider the future of Europe after what now appeared to be the certain German defeat. The last actual meeting between the two leaders took place at Cairo on their return home from Teheran when they discussed the atom bomb.

The friendship between Churchill and Roosevelt was not without difficulties and tensions. There were important differences over the question of when and where to open a second front in Europe and over how Britain would make payments for materials sent from America under lend-lease. Furthermore, as the war continued with Allied victory more certain, Churchill became increasingly concerned about the developing relations between Roosevelt and Stalin which seemed increasingly to exclude Britain. Churchill was concerned about how these relations might develop in the post-war world to the detriment of Britain and its Empire.

Nevertheless, there remained a remarkable degree of co-operation between the two leaders which reached its height with the signing of the

Atlantic Charter in August 1941. Perhaps of more immediate importance was the creation of the Combined Chiefs of Staff – a joint British and American military command with authority over all Anglo–American operations. It continued until the end of the war and led to the invasion of Normandy, the development of the atom bomb and the final defeat of Germany and Japan. Most important of all for Churchill, the Alliance locked the United States into accepting the idea that victory over Germany and Italy in Europe must come before the defeat of Japan.

Roosevelt died on 12 April 1945 and did not live to see the Allied victory. Nevertheless, he personally and through his relationship with Churchill had made an important contribution to that victory. In a message to Roosevelt's wife, Eleanor, Churchill wrote:

> 'I have lost a dear and cherished friendship which was forged in the fire of war. I trust you may find consolation in the magnitude of his work and the glory of his name.'

An assessment. By conviction and political upbringing, Roosevelt was an internationalist in the Wilsonian tradition. He at least superficially embraced isolationism to secure the Democratic nomination for the presidency in 1932. In the years leading up to the Second World War, Roosevelt followed policies which, he considered, would further American interests. Sometimes they were isolationist but there are plenty of examples of US involvement, for example in Latin America and the Far East. It is sometimes suggested that Roosevelt was a passionate defender of freedom and democracy throughout the world and would have actively defended it much earlier had it not been for the isolationists at home. There is little evidence to support this view. Perhaps the historian Paul Johnson offers a more realistic although somewhat controversial assessment:

> 'It is a myth that FDR was anxious to bring America into the war and was prevented from doing so by the overwhelming isolationist spirit of the American people. The evidence shows that FDR was primarily concerned with his domestic policies and had no wish to join in a crusade against Nazism.'

KEY THEME

Munich Agreement 1938
The Nazi invasion of Czechoslovakia in defiance of what was agreed at Munich gave clear evidence to the democratic world of the expansionist tendencies of Hitler.

Few would argue with the opinion that the revival of the US economy through the New Deal was Roosevelt's main preoccupation, often to the exclusion of foreign policy issues. Nevertheless, it can also be argued that possibly after the Munich Agreement in 1938 and the destruction of Czechoslovakia, Roosevelt came to realise that war was increasingly likely and that the United States should prepare for that possibility. Certainly, by 1941, he realised that Germany represented as great a threat to the United States as did Japan and was clearly worried that, following the invasion of Russia, America would have to face Germany alone.

SECTION 7

Franklin Roosevelt and the New Deal

Franklin Roosevelt was the most important American political figure of the twentieth century. He occupied the White House as President for 12 years, being re-elected on three occasions. During his years as President, America was transformed from a country of small towns governed by *laissez-faire* economics into a modern, industrial, world power that would dominate the second half of the twentieth century. Roosevelt made an enormous contribution to this transformation, yet the nature and extent of his achievements are the subject of great controversy. His policies aroused strong passions and few were neutral towards him. Many Americans who lived through his years as President regarded him as a saint, someone with whom they were able to identify personally. Others saw him as evil, a traitor to his class.

HISTORICAL INTERPRETATIONS

Historians have dealt with Roosevelt in different ways. Many of those writing in the 1950s and 1960s, within memory of his death, treated him sympathetically, although some criticised him for not doing more to restructure the Democratic Party. However, Roosevelt is normally attributed with having forged a dominant coalition – the South, organised labour, ethnic minorities, and the liberal professions – which lasted until the Nixon period, when the South was exploited by Republican conservatism and drawn away from the Democratic Party at the level of presidential elections. Some from the political left have seen the New Deal as being essentially conservative, preserving both capitalism and class-based elitism. Some writing in the 1980s criticised him for increasing the power of the president and the federal government.

Generally, progressive historians such as **Henry Steele Commager** (1945) and **Arthur Schlesinger** (1948) have seen the Roosevelt years as part of the progressive movement within American political life, as part of the struggle of the people against vested interests. Roosevelt was therefore viewed as part of a liberal tradition that went back to Wilson and beyond and reappeared under Kennedy and Johnson.

Conservative historians, such as **Flynn** (1956) and **Hofstadter** (1955) have been more critical. They view the New Deal as a radical departure from traditional American values, an attack on liberty and the free enterprise system, which, according to Flynn, was replaced by policies based on 'permanent crises and an armaments economy'. Hofstadter went further and suggested that the New Deal was founded on the mistaken Democratic belief that America under the Republicans was a sick society and that to improve it the federal government had to become involved in social security, in helping the unemployed and in controlling wages and hours.

Rexford Tugwell (1957), a former economic adviser to Roosevelt and a firm believer in government control of economic affairs, criticised him for his lack of planning and for 'playing it by ear', without any long-term strategy. **William Leuchtenberg** (1963) believed that the very pragmatism, criticised by Tugwell, was the essential strength of the New Deal and was a welcome change from the rigid economic thinking of both Hoover and the political left.

Clearly, there is a whole range of different interpretations of Roosevelt and the New Deal. Nevertheless, in a poll of American historians taken in 1983, he was voted the second greatest US president after Lincoln. This section attempts a balanced assessment of his achievements and legacy.

WHAT WAS ROOSEVELT'S POLITICAL PHILOSOPHY AND THINKING?

Much of the debate that surrounds Roosevelt and his New Deal programme involves the nature of the philosophy that underpinned it, rather than the detail of the programme itself. Was it, on the one hand, an extension of progressivism, another stage of the battle to control and reduce the power of business monopolies and vested interests? Alternatively, was Roosevelt a pragmatist, unaffected by potentially dogmatic ideologies? Or was he, as his political opponents such as Herbert Hoover believed, a **Keynesian**, whose actions were a fundamental attack on the liberties of the individual embodied in and protected by, the US Constitution?

Roosevelt was on the broad progressive wing of American politics in that he believed that government had a responsibility to govern in the interests of its citizens. Beyond this, he had no deeply thought-out political philosophy. His approach to political questions when he was elected in 1932 was essentially practical and pragmatic. He responded to the problems and challenges as they occurred. Problems, such as the banking crisis and high unemployment, could only be solved by direct action. Practical measures were needed to create jobs. Roosevelt's belief in direct action, experimentation and an open-minded, flexible approach to problems is one of the reasons for his appeal to the American public. It also helps to explain why the political speeches he made during the 1932 election campaign were full of inconsistencies. He promised welfare and job creation programmes without any indication about how they were to be paid for. At the same time, he pledged to cut federal spending and balance the budget. Despite these confusions, the American voters elected Roosevelt because, compared to Hoover, he promised action and conveyed a sense of optimism that the problems facing the country could be solved. He was elected in 1932 with 57 per cent of the popular vote. In the end, many voted for him because they had little or nothing to lose. Roosevelt believed strongly in ideals not dissimilar to Woodrow Wilson's. The Atlantic Charter and the United Nations embodied many of the humane liberal values for which Roosevelt stood. He also attacked imperialism and colonialism. However, because he was a realist he often compromised on issues.

Nevertheless, his pragmatism frustrated some of those who had the task of implementing and developing his strategies. Rexford Tugwell, for example, criticised him for failing to grasp the opportunities that the crisis of the thirties offered to introduce fundamental and lasting social reform that would have permanently benefited previously disadvantaged groups. Whatever his shortcomings might have been in this respect, Roosevelt did establish the principle that, in an advanced industrial society, government responses to deal with economic and social issues were not only desirable but essential. Hence, democratic government emerged strengthened in the USA from the kind of economic catastrophe that helped to destroy it elsewhere, e.g. in Germany.

WHERE DID SUPPORT FOR THE DEMOCRATS COME FROM?

It is not difficult to account for the landslide victory of 1932. The complete failure of Hoover and the Republicans even to begin to address the economic and social distress of the Depression meant that they stood condemned in the eyes of the electorate. This is not to diminish in any way, however, the personal appeal of Roosevelt. He brought to his presidential election campaign his record as a reforming governor of New York State who had attempted to rescue his people from the devastating effects of the Depression. His humanitarianism coupled with his supreme confidence that he could make a difference were undoubtedly infectious, whilst his imaginative use of the media to reach the people was invaluable. Throughout his three terms in the White House, he retained the support of a broad spectrum of American society. Hence he drew support from such diverse groups as African-Americans in the northern cities and southern white conservatives, along with farmers, organised labour and all those groups who, by 1936, may not have benefited enormously from reform but were still hopeful and confident in Roosevelt's determination to deliver his promises. In the process, however, he made individual enemies amongst his own supporters and caused a rift amongst Democrats as some of his actions became more controversial. By 1938, it was clear that his popularity was beginning to wane.

In the meantime, however, his cause may also have been helped by the failure of the opposition to attract mass support. Increasingly, during the thirties, the Republicans represented the forces of class and reaction – big business, financiers, critics of federal intervention in social and economic reform. The reduction in taxation and government spending, accompanied by a return to state administration of relief and reform, that they advocated in their electoral programmes was not a promising proposition. It could not have been less appealing to the mass of the people. As Roosevelt himself put it:

> 'Never before in all our history have these forces been so united against one candidate as they stand to-day. They are unanimous in their hate for me – and I welcome their hatred.'

HOW 'NEW' WAS THE NEW DEAL?

KEY THEME

The New Deal and federalism The New Deal created a 'national economy' and broke the back of federalism in the process. Indeed, federalism over the years has been dealt other heavy blows, such as during the Civil War.

The New Deal programme, described in detail in Chapters 9–11 of this book, has been described by some historians as revolutionary and by others as evolutionary. The reasons for the former view are not difficult to find. The extensive powers given to Roosevelt by Congress in 1933 for the Hundred Days were unprecedented, as was the level of intervention that he subsequently endeavoured to maintain. Moreover, it is true to say that the position of the President and the role of the federal government were permanently changed. In this respect, the Roosevelt years were a significant turning point in the political development of the USA. This is not to say that his exercise of power was unfettered. By 1935, he was experiencing increasing difficulty in moving forward his reforms. Some established customs and practices may well have been weakened by the New Deal policies (*laissez-faire* economics, for example), but essential elements of the Constitution remained intact to challenge him, most notably the Supreme Court and on occasions, Congress. Big business concerns such as Ford Motors were still forces to be reckoned with. This hardly constitutes a revolution.

Schlesinger argues that the New Deal was a natural progression from the reforming tendencies of earlier administrations, for example Wilson's New Freedom Program before 1917. Reforms along the lines of the New Deal would almost certainly have been introduced at some time, he claims, albeit in a different way. Hence the basis for the assertion that Roosevelt's programme was, in fact, evolutionary. It is reasonable to respect the claims of those historians who go on to suggest that the revolutionary ethos of the New Deal arises from the timing, speed and short-term intensity of its introduction and implementation. The Depression is, therefore, crucial to the argument. It dictated both the speed, the extent and the degree of necessary government intervention that accompanied the earlier New Deal legislation. In the larger scheme of things, it could be argued that the attempts to introduce more fundamental reforms, such as those that characterise the second New Deal, are indicative of the political evolution of an industrial state.

TO WHAT EXTENT WAS ROOSEVELT PERSONALLY RESPONSIBLE FOR THE NEW DEAL?

It can be argued that Roosevelt's main contribution to the New Deal lay in his humanitarian concern for the well-being of the more vulnerable sections of American society, his vision of the necessary course of action to rescue the USA from the Depression and his unique ability to reassure the American people and inspire them with confident hope. In this respect, he was the architect of the New Deal. He provided the framework. He gathered together intellectuals who could advise him on the feasibility of his schemes, although, as they frequently disagreed with each other, their influence should not be exaggerated. He showed ability and purpose in his careful selection of individuals, who had a clear view of what needed to be done, to carry out his broader plan. Of these,

Camp F-24 of the Civilian Conservation Corps clearing rocks from a truck trail in Snoqualmie National Forest.

Frances Perkins, **Harry Hopkins**, **Harold Ickes** and **Robert Wagner** are the most notable.

Roosevelt was, personally, most closely associated with the Civilian Conservation Corps (CCC) although, having conceived the idea, he still left others to resolve the fine detail, as Frances Perkins later described in her biography of Roosevelt:

> 'In one of my conversations with the President in March 1933, he brought up the idea that became the Civilian Conservation Corps. Roosevelt loved trees and hated to see them cut and not replaced. It was natural for him to wish to put large numbers of the unemployed to repairing such devastation. His enthusiasm for this project, which was really all his own, led him to some exaggeration of what could be accomplished. He saw it big. He thought any man or boy would rejoice to leave the city and work in the woods.
>
> It was characteristic of him that he conceived the project, boldly rushed it through and happily left it to others to worry about the details. And there were some difficult details. The attitude of the trade unions had to be considered. They were disturbed about this program, which they feared would put all workers under a "dollar a day" regimentation merely because they were unemployed.'

(Frances Perkins, *The Roosevelt I Knew*, 1946)

It must not be assumed, however, that Roosevelt passively allowed others to carry out the work of giving shape to his ideas. Ultimately, he held the power and there are notable examples of his intervention: his withdrawal of US involvement in the London International Economic Conference, for example, in 1933, when he pulled the rug from under the feet of Cordell Hull. His timely exercise of power secured the passage of the Wagner Act in 1937 even though he had been dubious about its close links with organised labour. This was done to anticipate and block any negative actions of the Supreme Court. Nevertheless, he did place a great deal of faith and trust in those whom he chose to implement the New Deal.

The appointment of **Frances Perkins** as Secretary of Labor was probably one of Roosevelt's most confidently daring acts. She was the first female Secretary of Labor, and he was warned that she would lack credibility with male industrial administrators with whom she would have to deal. However, he not only appointed her but accepted her most ambitious proposals to lift the USA out of the Depression. By the time of her appointment in 1933, Perkins had long been interested in radical social reform causes as a social worker. She had been involved in the work of Jane Addams at Hull House in Chicago, providing a home mainly for immigrant girls, and was politically active in the movement to introduce labour reform, particularly the regulation and ultimately the abolition of child labour. She had served on the Industrial Board of New York State during the administration of Alfred Smith (1919) and as an Industrial Commissioner when Roosevelt became State Governor in 1929.

It was Perkins who, in 1933, presented Roosevelt with a package that partially underpinned the National Recovery Administration that he readily accepted:

> 'I proposed immediate federal aid to the states for direct unemployment relief, an extensive program of public works, a study and an approach to the established federal law of minimum wages, maximum hours, true unemployment and old-age insurance, abolition of child labour, and the creation of a federal employment service.'
>
> (Frances Perkins, *The Roosevelt I Knew*, 1946)

Subsequently, it was Frances Perkins who supported Robert Wagner in promoting the National Labor Relations Act that created the National Labor Relations Board. According to her biography, this legislation was prepared without Roosevelt's involvement:

> 'It ought to be put on the record that the President did not take part in developing the National Labor Relations Act and, in fact, was hardly consulted about it. It was not a part of the President's program. It did not particularly appeal to him when it was described to him. All the credit for it belongs to Wagner.'
>
> (Frances Perkins, *The Roosevelt I Knew*, 1946)

From comments in her biography, she clearly believed that this was a particularly significant piece of legislation since it led to a dramatic increase in trade union membership (2,225,000 in 1933; 14,000,000 by 1945) although she admits that some unions misused the power that the Act had given them. This had not been anticipated.

During the attempts by the Second New Deal to implement more fundamental reform, Perkins was responsible for the Fair Standards Act. This embodied many of the reforms for which she had long been campaigning – maximum working hours, minimum wages, the abolition of child labour and a minimum age for employment of young people in dangerous occupations.

Like Frances Perkins, **Harold Hopkins** had also served under Roosevelt when he was Governor of New York State. He was also interested, like Perkins, in social welfare and had been active in implementing relief through the New York State Temporary Emergency Relief Administration set up by Roosevelt in 1931. He was a man of strong convictions and clearly critical of a *laissez-faire* system that accepted the inevitability of poverty:

> 'I believe the days of letting people live in misery, of being rock-bottom destitute, of children being hungry, of moralizing about rugged individualism in the light of modern facts – I believe those days are over in America . . . we are going forward in full belief that our economic system does not have to force people to live in miserable squalor in dirty houses, half fed, half clothed, and lacking decent medical care.'
>
> (Harold L. Hopkins, *Spending to Save*, 1936)

KEY THEME

Roosevelt and Hopkins It is often said that a person should be judged by the company they keep. If this is true, then Roosevelt should be seen in an idealistic light. Hopkins was very close to Roosevelt and, although that created political difficulties for him, he continued to use Hopkins in a key role right through to the end of his life.

He worked closely with Roosevelt in implementing the President's job creation schemes. In particular, he masterminded the Works Projects Administration, employing 3 million people in his public works programmes building highways, bridges, parks and public buildings. Although he was subsequently criticised for the short-term nature of these jobs, they did provide spending power and restore self-esteem, both important in a nation struggling to survive economic depression.

Harold Ickes, too, had been impressed by Roosevelt's record as Governor of New York State. In the 1932 election, he worked hard to draw those Republicans who had become disillusioned with their party's failure to confront the Depression into the Democratic fold. Having been put in charge of the Public Works Administration, he set about the job to spend money wisely and to implement programmes that would make a lasting difference.

> 'Many billions of dollars could properly be spent in the United States on permanent improvements. Such spending would not only help us out of the depression, it would do much for the health, well-being and prosperity of the people. I refuse to believe that providing an adequate water supply for a municipality or putting in a sewage system is a wasteful expenditure of money.'
>
> (Harold Ickes, *Back to Work*, 1935)

In March 1934, the *New York Times* observed that Roosevelt had placed the PWA in efficient hands. This extract gives some indication of Ickes's

The First New Deal: the National Recovery Administration (NRA) – a case study

A detailed description of the first tranche of New Deal measures appears earlier in this book. The intention here is to examine the NRA in order to gain insight into many of the issues surrounding the New Deal programme generally and the NRA in particular.

In many respects, the NRA, and the NIRA that set it up, illustrate some of the fundamental aims and principles of the New Deal in its first phase. This was an aspect of the 15 proposals put forward by Roosevelt to deal with an emergency situation. The NRA, working alongside the job creation schemes of the Public Works Administration (PWA), must be regarded as central to his plans to tackle unemployment and industrial recovery. The intention of the NRA was to work with employers, great and small, to produce agreements that would provide jobs which, in turn, would reduce unemployment, increase spending power and consequently create the kind of renewed confidence in industry that would stimulate investment and economic growth. Fundamentally, the NRA was biased towards supporting industry. It sought to agree viable prices, avoid overproduction and so avoid firms becoming bankrupt by limiting competition.

In theory, this sounded reasonable. It involved the agreement of businesses to produce a code of practice that involved agreeing prices, wages, working hours and the conditions for fair competition. Under its director, General Hugh Johnson, there was an enthusiastic, optimistic but naive beginning. There were notable successes in the process of negotiating codes. These were principally in the cotton and coal industries where child labour was abolished. Generally, however, the weaknesses of the hurriedly composed legislation became apparent in spite of the razzamatazz of big parades and blue eagle signs that proliferated in businesses great and small.

Success depended on businesses being prepared to accept that there was a cost to regulating wages and working hours – a reduction of profits. Many obviously did, as is evidenced by the fact that the NRA successfully created 2 million jobs. However, disagreements soon developed. Small businesses felt dominated and intimidated by big organisations. Few employers really accepted the principle of making concessions to their workers and especially objected to Section 7a that tried to introduce the principle of collective bargaining. Henry Ford actually refused to agree to the codes although he introduced wage and working hours agreements in his works on his own initiative.

Whilst there was some success in bringing a degree of stability, there was no visible sign of industrial recovery. Johnson increasingly found difficulty in ensuring that businesses were keeping to the codes that had been agreed and was reluctant to use the sanctions that had been established by the NIRA to deal with such situations. Even before the Supreme Court began the process of declaring the NRA unconstitutional in 1935, Roosevelt was being accused of exceeding his constitutional powers. Brogan suggests that the action of the Supreme Court was of benefit to Roosevelt in establishing the fact that he was still bound by the limits of the Constitution. The real problem was whether the federal government had the constitutional right to regulate aspects of the US economy on a national basis. New Deal legislation (e.g. NIRA) used the interstate commerce clause of the Constitution, which empowered the federal government to regulate interstate trade, in attempts to reach inside the states and regulate commerce and industry. The Schechter case claimed that the interstate commerce clause could not be construed in this way and therefore sections of the NIRA were struck down as unconstitutional. Thus the challenge for Roosevelt was to find some way of acceptance for laws which sought to regulate the national economy and which 'reached inside the states', and he tried to pack the Supreme Court but failed. However, the political pressure that developed in the course of that failure was brought to bear on the Supreme Court for blocking what many saw as essential reform. That forced the 'switch in time that saved the nine', i.e. one of the Supreme Court judges switched to voting for economic regulation.

methods and attention to detail as well as of his commitment to the project:

> 'Mr. Ickes knows all the rackets that infest the construction industry. He is a terror to collective bidders and skimping contractors. He warns that the PWA fund is a sacred trust fund and that only traitors would graft on a project undertaken to save people from hunger. He insists on fidelity to specifications; cancels violated contracts mercilessly, sends inspectors to see that men in their eagerness to work are not robbed of pay by the kickback swindle.'

Reference has already been made to the significant and individual contribution made by **Robert Wagner**. Wagner had been appointed in 1933 as the first chairman of the National Recovery Administration. As a lawyer and in his early political career, industrial working conditions and practices had been his particular interest. Hence his important contribution to the development of the National Labor Relations Act of

1935 and the Board that was subsequently established. Roosevelt was very nervous of this move to empower organised labour. There were political implications for giving more power to the unions but also there was the implicit reduction in the control of industrialists over their workforce. Wagner's intention, however, was to regulate and reduce labour disputes by providing a structure for collective bargaining, thus removing picket line violence and avoiding the disruption to production that was caused by strikes. Consequently, organised labour would facilitate a healthy economy. His earlier efforts through the NRA had largely been sabotaged by the big and powerful industrial concerns. Only legislation such as the NLRA was likely to weaken these influential forces. The subsequent rise in trade union membership was a tribute to Wagner's success in the long term. There was also a decline in the number of workers injured in industrial disputes. Wagner's pivotal role in bringing about this reform is confirmed by Rexford Tugwell in his book *The Democratic Roosevelt* (1957):

> 'Senator Wagner had been chairman of the National Labor Board during the first half of the NRA. During that service he had seen how little could be accomplished without powers to enforce the principles that were supposed to be those of all New Dealers. Such intractable employer corporations as Weirton Steel, Budd Manufacturing and Ford Motor were either refusing compliance or were making use of company unions to avoid collective bargaining.
>
> In February 1934, Senator Wagner induced Franklin to issue two executive orders authorizing the Board to hold elections for determining bargaining agents and to present violations to the Department of Justice for prosecution. But Wagner was convinced that more was necessary and on 1st March he introduced a Labor Disputes Bill.'

Wagner was also personally interested in the concept of government housing support. He was able to persuade Roosevelt to give his support to the provision of money to finance low cost housing. This was embodied in the Wagner–Steagall Act, the passage of which Roosevelt supported in 1937. This Act set up the United States Housing Authority that administered spending on housing schemes.

In conclusion, then, whilst Roosevelt was clearly the architect of the New Deal in broad terms, much of the detail was placed in the hands of capable administrators who themselves had a vision of social justice, economic stability and of the appropriate pathways to achieving their goals. Roosevelt was obviously closely associated with most of these developments although apparently not all of them. The success of all the New Deal schemes, even though some were short term, was to a large degree the achievement of his 'New Dealers' of whom Frances Perkins must be one of the most outstanding. However, Roosevelt's consummate political skills and leadership qualities must not be ignored.

IN WHAT WAYS WAS THE SECOND NEW DEAL DIFFERENT FROM THE FIRST?

The detail of the Second New Deal is described in Chapter 11 of this book. The fundamental differences between the first and second New Deal are a matter of debate and argument between historians. To some extent, this discussion rests on the extent to which Roosevelt's policies moved further to the left in that the legislation of 1935 and afterwards had a preoccupation with social reform and an anti-capitalist stance. This is clearly suggested by the movement away from working directly with business interests and towards an apparent alliance with organised labour. It was almost certainly not the case that Roosevelt wished to alienate the capitalists but it is not difficult to see why it must have appeared so. Legislation such as the National Labor Relations Act was bound to be perceived as an attack on the independence of employers, especially after the federal government refused army support to remove 'sit in' strikers at the General Motor Corporation during the strike of 1936–7. The ultimate capitulation of General Motors and United Steel to the strikers and their union demands did not help to allay these fears. Moreover, the potential power and status that the legislation gave to workers via their union membership had the effect of creating an increasing political awareness amongst organised labour. Inevitably, this manifested itself in support for the Democratic Party generally and Roosevelt in particular. Given his desire to balance the budget, Roosevelt's Second New Deal reforms put huge pressure on taxation and especially on corporate taxation. This also upset industrialists and persuaded them that his policy was anti-capitalist. Ultimately, their concerns were ill-founded. It was never Roosevelt's intention to alienate capitalists, only to bring them under some form of control.

Arguably, the essential difference lies in the fact that the actions of the first New Deal were predominantly emergency measures intended to kick-start the economy, set it on the path out of the Depression and, at the same time, relieve the distress that it had caused. By 1935, people such as Perkins and Hopkins were considering longer-term reforming measures that would create a fairer society, a cause that they had both espoused for many years. Roosevelt was undoubtedly part of this thinking, if not entirely convinced about all its aspects. He was certainly concerned, by this stage, to balance the budget, which increased taxation, especially for companies.

The Second New Deal was an interesting mixture of much needed economic reform, if the mistakes of the 1920s were not going to be repeated, and the laying of the foundations of a modern welfare system. In the case of the former, the Banking Act of 1935 established a central banking system under some degree of federal control through the Board of Governors of the Federal Reserve System. This reduced the danger of a collapse of the system as had happened in 1929. The help given to farmers by the Soil Conservation and Domestic Allotment Act was a recognition of the long-term problems of farmers and an attempt to replace the support that had been sabotaged by the Supreme Court when it declared the AAA to be unconstitutional in January 1936. The impact of Wagner's National Labor Relations Act has been referred to above but, in addition to its implications for labour relations, its clauses dealing with child labour were reforms that women's groups, in particular, had been campaigning for since the second half of the nineteenth century. To some degree, these reforms were the consummation of the programmes of the progressive politics of sections of the Democratic Party in the days before the Republican ascendancy of the 1920s.

The Social Security Act of 1935, though limited and sometimes discriminatory, especially towards some groups of women, was nevertheless a starting point. Roosevelt, himself, realised this when he described it as just the 'cornerstone' of a future welfare system for the USA. Much of this reform grew out of the first New Deal, but was intended to be more fundamental and permanent. It did, however, increase criticism and opposition to Roosevelt in many quarters. These seemed to form an uneasy coalition in 1937 when he launched his plans to reform the Supreme Court.

THE SUPREME COURT 'CRISIS'

The opposition to many of Roosevelt's New Deal programmes has been described earlier. It is appropriate here to consider the reaction to the policy that he adopted towards this opposition. Under the terms of the Constitution, the President could nominate members of the Supreme Court as vacancies occurred, usually through death or retirement. As a long-serving president, Roosevelt was in the unusual position of having never appointed a justice to the Supreme Court. The majority of its members were 70 or over and all were Republicans. This was partly because the conservatives on the Supreme Court hung on, hoping to survive longer than Roosevelt's reign in the White House so that they could prevent legislation like AAA and NIRA being accepted as constitutional. By 1937, the Republican Party had formulated its own response to the troubles of the Depression and were fiercely critical of Roosevelt, apart from a minority on the left of the party who had some

KEY THEME

The Supreme Court and Roosevelt The question was, should federalism and state rights in the economic sphere be upheld? The judges thought yes (legally and constitutionally they were probably right in the strict letter of the law; politically and in terms of the broad principles that underpin the Constitution they were probably wrong). Roosevelt thought no.

sympathy for the New Deal. It is, therefore, not surprising that a Republican Supreme Court would block Roosevelt at every suitable opportunity. This started in January 1935, when it began the process of declaring the NIRA invalid, a process that it completed in May of that year. By the beginning of 1937, Roosevelt had clearly decided that the time had come to act. So important was this to him that all other reform programmes appear to have been put on hold during this period. In any case, he recognised that he could not make any further progress when his efforts were likely to be negated by the Supreme Court.

Following his re-election in 1936, he obviously believed that his position was inviolate and he announced his intention to reform the Supreme Court. The purpose of this did not need to be spelt out. The perceived obstacles had to be removed. On 5 February 1937, he asked Congress for permission to appoint additional Supreme Court judges for every one of the current membership that was over the age of 70 years. These amounted to six of the nine judges. For all of those critics, including the disillusioned wing of the Democrats that existed by this time, alarm bells sounded. His 'Court-packing' plans would have increased the membership of the Supreme Court to 15. Rumours and hints of authoritarianism now seemed to have some credence since Roosevelt, the champion of democracy, appeared to be developing more dictatorial tendencies. What next? These considerations did not sit well with many people, only too aware at the time of events in Spain, Italy and Germany.

In fact a potential 'crisis' was averted as one judge resigned and one switched sides. Subsequently, Roosevelt was able to replace through retirement, almost all of the nine judges. In one sense, his move had succeeded because from this point the Supreme Court adopted a different approach. Hence, potentially controversial legislation such as the National Labor Relations Act and the Social Security Act was declared constitutional by the Court in 1937. Yet, to some extent, the damage to Roosevelt's reputation had been done and the party became more deeply divided. He lost the support of many Democrats who had never really been 'New Dealers' but had appreciated that they could be assured of election if they ran in the Roosevelt camp. Particularly as the Second New Deal seemed to suggest a re-alignment of the Democrats with organised, urban labour, many representatives found themselves under pressure in their constituencies to oppose Roosevelt's plans. This was especially true of rural areas which resented the apparent preference given to urban workers. The southern states, particularly, disliked the minimum pay regulations established by the National Labor Relations Act since they benefited African-American workers. This perhaps gives rise to some cynicism about the number of Democrats who ever believed in Roosevelt's New Deal packages but, certainly, the formation of the American Liberty League and the defection to it of some leading

Democrats, such as Alfred Smith who had once supported Roosevelt, is some indication of increasing disillusionment.

That this disillusionment was justified must have been confirmed for some by the slump that hit the USA in 1938. Just at the point when Roosevelt needed to convince so many people that his policies were right and that they were working, recession reared its ugly head again. Unemployment escalated and any gains that might have been made by New Deal programmes disappeared. It is difficult to predict what might have happened without the outbreak of the Second World War in Europe which rescued America's finances and quickly put people back to work.

CONCLUSIONS

How successful was the New Deal Programme by 1941? There is no disagreement among historians with the view that the New Deal brought about only a partial recovery of the American economy. By 1939, 9.5 million Americans were still unemployed. It was not until 1941 that full employment and prosperity returned, a result of rearmament following the outbreak of the Second World War. They also agree that in March 1933, Roosevelt had no properly thought-out programme to tackle American unemployment and that certainly in its early stages the New Deal consisted of a set of schemes hastily put together, often without much consideration. In some ways, this feature persisted in the years that followed. There was sometimes a great amount of frenzied activity without much clarity about what was intended. Perhaps, this was entirely in tune with Roosevelt's own approach, which was essentially practical and pragmatic. This also probably explains why Roosevelt himself appeared vague and evasive about the direction in which New Deal policies were heading. These features of Roosevelt's presidency do not seem to have been apparent to the mass of American electors. At least, if they had, they did not prevent him becoming possibly the most popular president of all time.

What does rouse considerable debate among historians about the New Deal is whether it was a radical answer to America's economic problems or whether it was largely conservative, shoring up the existing capitalist structure. There are some aspects of the New Deal that were radical. The work of the Agricultural Adjustment Administration, for instance, whether it was successful or not, was different from previous practice. The idea of paying farmers to leave land uncultivated attracted much criticism but was an attempt to solve a long-standing farming problem. The Social Security Act, with all its imperfections, was a first attempt to create a welfare state, whilst the National Labor Act tried to set up a legal framework for industrial relations. Conversely, New Deal labour reforms can be interpreted as an attempt to make workers happier with the existing capitalist system. They created more stable conditions and actually helped to stop the spread of radicalism. Equally, because the New Deal did not fundamentally redistribute income between rich and poor, it left capitalism in control, at the same time making it more acceptable to those who had to work within it.

What were the achievements and legacy of the New Deal? The New Deal helped to give birth to the idea within America of the 'semi-welfare' state, that the government had a responsibility to look after the welfare of its citizens. It extended the rights of workers and began for many of them social security payments. It introduced much needed controls on the banking system and stock exchange and set up a central banking system. It began the idea of government having a responsibility for regulating the economy, in contrast to the *laissez-faire* economic thinking of many in the 1920s. Thousands of miles of roads, many bridges and the TVA dams are part of the still visible legacy of the New Deal era. Washington became much more important as a centre of political power and the Supreme Court slowly abandoned the stance it had adopted in its challenges to New Deal policies. At a time of economic depression, the New Deal helped to restore national morale. It offered hope to groups who had felt excluded from the mainstream of American life – Catholics, Jews, blacks and women – and there was a greater representation of these groups at various levels in the Roosevelt administration.

What were the criticisms of the New Deal? Specific criticisms of the New Deal are often centred on the achievements of particular agencies. The Agricultural Adjustment Administration, for instance, did nothing to help the worst-off farmers, whilst the NRA, set up by the National Industry Recovery Act, often interfered in relations between workers and employers to the detriment of both. Issues of race were largely ignored and there was a failure to tackle the long-term housing problems facing the nation. The federal government built only 180,000 new houses during the New Deal years. Criticism of Roosevelt and the New Deal centres also on the way in which it led to an increase in the power of the presidency and an unbalancing of the Constitution. There is no doubt that Roosevelt gave the US presidency a much higher profile than it had enjoyed during the period of the Republican ascendancy. The 'fireside chats' and media press conferences were innovations that made millions of Americans more aware of the role and power of the President. The large amount of legislation needed to introduce New Deal policies put Roosevelt at the very centre of the political process, laying the foundations for further growth in presidential power in the years following. Some historians and experts on the Constitution regard this trend as undesirable because it upset the system of checks and balances that had always been the foundation of the US Constitution, because too much power became vested in the President. This concern may help to explain why, in 1951, the 22nd Amendment to the US Constitution confined a President to ten years in office.

What legacy did Roosevelt leave for the Democratic Party? Largely as a result of the New Deal, the Democratic Party became very popular with the American electors. Except for a relatively short period in the 1950s, they were the congressional majority party until the late 1960s. Roosevelt set out for the party a broad agenda that it still maintains. It placed the party firmly on the liberal wing of American politics and saw government as having a duty to look after and care for its people. The modern Democratic Party believes in a mixed economy and in a modest welfare state. Lyndon Johnson, who became US president after the assassination of John Kennedy in 1963, said of Roosevelt:

> 'He was like a daddy to me.'

This tribute sums up well the affection and reverence with which modern Democrats viewed Roosevelt.

Roosevelt's death, on 12 April 1945, came as a great shock to the American people. It was followed by a great outpouring of unprecedented popular grief and public mourning. Millions of Americans, for the first time, had been able to identify with their President and his New Deal policies. Not all of them were successful but that did not seem to matter because at least some attempts were being made to improve their lives. They also recognised his outstanding contribution to the Allied victory in the Second World War.

According to Alistair Cooke, the best epitaph to Roosevelt was provided by a journalist, Westbrook Pegler:

> 'As a social and political liver-shaker he has had no equal in our time in this country. Ornery, tricky, stubborn, wayward and strong as a bull . . . He looked nice and dressy back there in 1932 . . . there was nothing in his past record to indicate what a cantankerous hide he would turn out to be . . . Anyone who gentles Mr. Roosevelt is simply imposing a handicap on himself, for he won't gentle you back . . . But never in our time have people been so conscious of the meannesss which a complacent upper class will practise on the help, and of the government's duty to do something real and personal for the assistance of those who are so far down that they can't help themselves. He needs to be fought all the time, for he has an enormous appreciation of himself and of any idea which he happens to approve, but if the country doesn't go absolutely broke in his time, it will be a more intelligent and better country for him.'

A2 ASSESSMENT: ROOSEVELT AND THE NEW DEAL

Exercise in the style of OCR

Source A

Through four years of experience, this New Deal attack upon free institutions has emerged as the most important issue in America. All the men who are seeking mastery in the world are using the same weapons. Their philosophy is founded on the coercion and compulsory organisation of men. Their ideas are not new. Most of them had been urged on me.

I rejected the notion of 'economic planning' to regiment and coerce the farmer. That was born of a Roman despot 1,400 years ago and grew into the AAA. I refused national plans to put the business of government in competition with its citizens. That was born of Karl Marx. I vetoed the idea of recovery through stupendous spending to prime the pump. That was born of a British professor [Keynes].

From a speech by Herbert Hoover who was the Republican President between 1929–33. In the speech Hoover is criticising the New Deal.

Source B

Conservative critics of Roosevelt condemned his radicalism, and during his lifetime and shortly thereafter one frequently read of the 'Roosevelt Revolution'. With the lengthening of perspective historians began to label him more commonly as a progressive rather than a radical. In possibly saving America by a mild injection of socialism, he may have averted a violent overdose thus saving the capitalist system. He may have headed off collectivism by a major dose of reformism.

Writers of the radical New Left have downgraded the extent of Rooseveltian reform. In particular they have stressed the opportunities for socialistic change that were not pushed, and have written off the New Deal as a holding operation for American capitalism. More specifically, critics charge that Roosevelt short-changed the 'forgotten men', especially labourers, unemployed blacks, unskilled workers and slum dwellers.

The historian T.A. Bailey explains the debate about the success of the New Deal in *Probing America's Past, Volume II* (1973).

Source C

When the reform energies of the New Deal began to wane around 1939 and the Depression was over, the nation was back to its normal state: a permanent army of unemployed and twenty or thirty million poverty-stricken people effectively blocked from public view by a high, prosperous and fervently consuming middle class.

What the New Deal did was to refurbish middle class America, which had taken a dizzying fall in the depression, to restore jobs to half the jobless, and to give just enough to the lower class (a layer of public housing, a minimum of social security) to create an aura of goodwill.

The historian H. Zinn argues that the New Deal did not lead to fundamental change, in *New Deal Thought* (1966).

Source D

Despite its failure to end the Depression, the New Deal stands as one of the most creative periods in American political history. The United States survived the worst extended economic downturn in its history with its political system intact, indeed strengthened, at a time when democracy was under siege throughout the world. The federal government accepted the responsibility for intervening in economic life when private initiatives faltered and for protecting and promoting key elements of the welfare of its citizens. America's welfare state was born during the great depression of the 1930s.

The New Deal's accomplishments, while substantial, went only so far. Federal programmes remained small, benefits limited and temporary. Not everyone benefited equally from the New Deal programmes but the majority of Americans in the 1930s were simply too grateful for federal aid to complain that it did not go further. Such federal assistance, coming at a time when many citizens had few, if any, personal resources to fall back on to deal with unemployment, illness and old age, was often the difference between survival and going under.

The historian D. Nasaw gives a positive interpretation of the New Deal. The source is taken from *The Course of the United States History, Volume II: From 1865*, published 1987.

Questions

1a Analyse the differences between the judgements in Sources C and D about the achievements of the New Deal.

How to answer this question. The question is centred round a comparison of the two sources. To answer the question well you need to do the following:

- Make use of both sources and ensure that you draw real comparisons between the two.
- Point out the differences between the sources.
- Use your own knowledge to back up your conclusions.
- Evaluate the sources by commenting where appropriate on their value, utility and reliability.

A top mark will be awarded to the answers which evaluate and explain the differences.

Content. Before you start writing you should try to identify the differences between the sources. Source C stresses the continuity in American life despite the New Deal. However, Source D stresses the social and political changes brought about by the New Deal.

- The sources differ because of the different criteria by which they judge the New Deal. The author of Source C judges the New Deal's impact on the American society and economy. The author of Source D tries to look at the New Deal in the context of the effect the New Deal had on the political system.
- When the sources look at the economic impact of the New Deal they judge it against different criteria. Source C criticises the New Deal for failing to tackle deep-seated weaknesses in the American economy. Source D takes a different stance and suggests that the immediate impact of the New Deal was positive.

Style. You should try to be as direct as possible when answering the question. Below is a paragraph from an answer to this question. The candidate is pointing out the differences between the sources' attitudes to the impact of the New Deal on the American economic system. Notice that the candidate has attempted to focus directly on the question set.

The sources take a very different view of the impact of the New Deal. The author of Source C is dismissive in claiming that for six years the New Deal did nothing more than return the economy to 'its normal state'. However it is clear that the author of the source believes that the New Deal was not sufficiently radical and is attacking it from a political standpoint. This contrasts with the attempts of the author of Source D to take a more objective and measured view. In highlighting the innovation of state intervention he is clear in his conclusion that the change brought about by the New Deal was both radical and permanent.

1b Using Sources A to D, explain why the New Deal has continued to be an issue of debate among historians.

How to answer this question. To be marked at the higher levels of the mark scheme you need to do the following:

- Refer to all four sources. With each source you must interpret the source, i.e. what it says that will help you deal with the question, evaluate it and compare it against your own knowledge.
- Try to show that you understand the issues surrounding the New Deal.
- Plan your answer. Try to avoid dealing with the sources in alphabetical order. In your plan you should be able to look at the answer thematically. In the case of this question that means looking at the different features of the New Deal debated by historians.

Style. Below is an extract from an answer to this question. Note how the candidate has taken the sources as a set and is looking at the wider context of the New Deal and politics.

Another reason why the New Deal has continued to be such an issue of contention is the fact that many historians are conditioned in their views by their political viewpoints. An alliance of the New Left and right-wing politicians and historians has attacked the New Deal for its ineffectiveness. Their arguments are reflected in those put forward in Source A and Source C. The former source is deeply flawed as it is part of an election campaign and yet its claim of the ineffectiveness of 'economic planning' is one shared by many historians. Similarly, there are many on the left who share the view of the author of Source C that the New Deal was superficially creating little more than 'an aura of goodwill'. However, those who have attempted to tackle the issue of the New Deal from a more objective standpoint, e.g. the author of Source C, are more willing to give it credit for its achievements as well as point out its pitfalls.

Essays in the style of OCR

Introduction. To be awarded top marks in essays of the type given below, you will be expected to do the following:

- **Analyse throughout the essay.** This can be done by making sure that you plan a line of argument before you start writing. At the start of each paragraph you must make the next point of your argument, explain it and then use evidence to back up your point (see next point). There is a clear difference between narrative (telling the story) and analysis (putting forward a reasoned argument in response to a question).

You need to start each paragraph with words that will lead on to analysis. These might include:

The most important reason.........
Another key point is that.........
One should argue that.........
Essentially.........

If you use the following words at the start of a paragraph you are more likely to fall into a narrative style of writing:

In (followed by a date).........
This was followed by.........

- **Back up your argument by using well selected evidence.** The evidence you select must be accurate and relevant to the point you are trying to make.
- **Make a clear and consistent attempt to reach a judgement.** In your essay you must argue throughout. You must reflect on the evidence you have given and make points which answer the question directly.
- **Show evidence of independent thought.** You do not have to be original. Independent thought means that you have reflected on what you have read in this and other books and that you can explain the ideas that you have picked up in your own words.
- **Language skills.** It is essential that you write in paragraphs, that you are grammatically accurate. There are two tips to ensure this takes place:
  - Always read your work through after you have finished and correct any errors.
  - Get into the habit of structuring your essays in such a way that a new point of your argument means a new paragraph.

Questions

1 Consider the arguments for and against the claim that the causes of the Great Depression were long term.

How to answer this question. Before you start writing you should study the question carefully. There are two important points to note:

- The question asks you to balance the arguments for and against but by asking you to consider them it will hope that you come to a clear conclusion.
- The focus of the question is the debate about the origins of the Great Depression.

Content. In answering the question you might deal with the following areas:

- The problems of the agricultural sector throughout the 1920s.
- The impact of the stagnation of the 'old industries' such as textiles and coal.
- The uneven nature of demand in the American economy and the over-extension of credit.
- The decline in the construction industry from 1926.
- Protectionism and the issue of overproduction in American industry.
- The fall-off in demand for cars and the issue of the Ford Model A.

2 To what extent was isolationism between the wars the result of economic factors?

How to answer this question. The answer to a question of this type is most commonly 'up to a point but'. You need to argue the extent to which foreign policy was the result of economic problems but then go on to explain the other factors that caused the policy of isolationism to be adopted.

Plan. In your plan you should look to isolate your main points of argument. In this case you might well wish to challenge the question as its stands. Below are examples of the line of argument you might use to answer this question.

- To a certain extent there are connections between isolationism and economic problems, an example being the link between the Neutrality Acts and the Great Depression.
- However, isolationism developed in a time of relative prosperity, i.e. the 1920s.
- It can be questioned whether the United States was as isolationist as the question suggests.

Style. In answering the question you need to adopt as direct a style as possible. Below is an extract from a candidate's response to this question.

However, the extent of the United States' isolationism should not be exaggerated. When its interests were perceived to be at stake then governments were prepared to involve themselves fully in diplomacy. The Naval Arms Conference of 1921–2 and the Washington Treaty of 1924 saw the United States take a leading role in negotiating the balance of power in the Pacific. The concern over Japanese naval expansion led to action by Secretary of State Charles Hughes.

BIBLIOGRAPHY

P. Boyer et al, *The Enduring Vision: A History of the American People* (D.C. Heath and Company 1995)

H. Brogan, *Penguin History of the United States of America* (Penguin 1990)

A. Cooke, *America* (Pavilion 1973)

P. Fearon, *The Origins and Nature of the Great Slump 1929-32* (Macmillan 1979)

J.K. Galbraith, *The Great Crash* (London Deutch 1973)

M.J. Heale, *Franklin D Roosevelt, The New Deal and War* (Routledge 1999)

P. Johnson, *A History of the American People* (Phoenix Giant 1997)

M. A. Jones, *The Limits of Liberty* (Oxford University Press 1995)

A. Kessler-Harris, *Out of Work: A History of Wage-Earning Women in the United States* (Oxford University Press 1982)

S. Rowbotham, *A Century of Women* (Penguin 1999)

F. Scott Fitzgerald, *The Great Gatsby* (Penguin 1994)

F. Scott Fitzgerald, *The Jazz Age* (New Directions 1996)

J. Steinbeck, *The Grapes of Wrath* (Warner/Chapell Plays 1991)

There is a wide range of US websites containing information on topics within this period. Searching by topic will produce a fairly extensive list. Many of these are US university sites containing student studies. The following open up a range of additional weblinks including those to the White House archives and the Library of Congress:

http:// www.cspresidency.org
http:// www.americanpresidents.org

INDEX